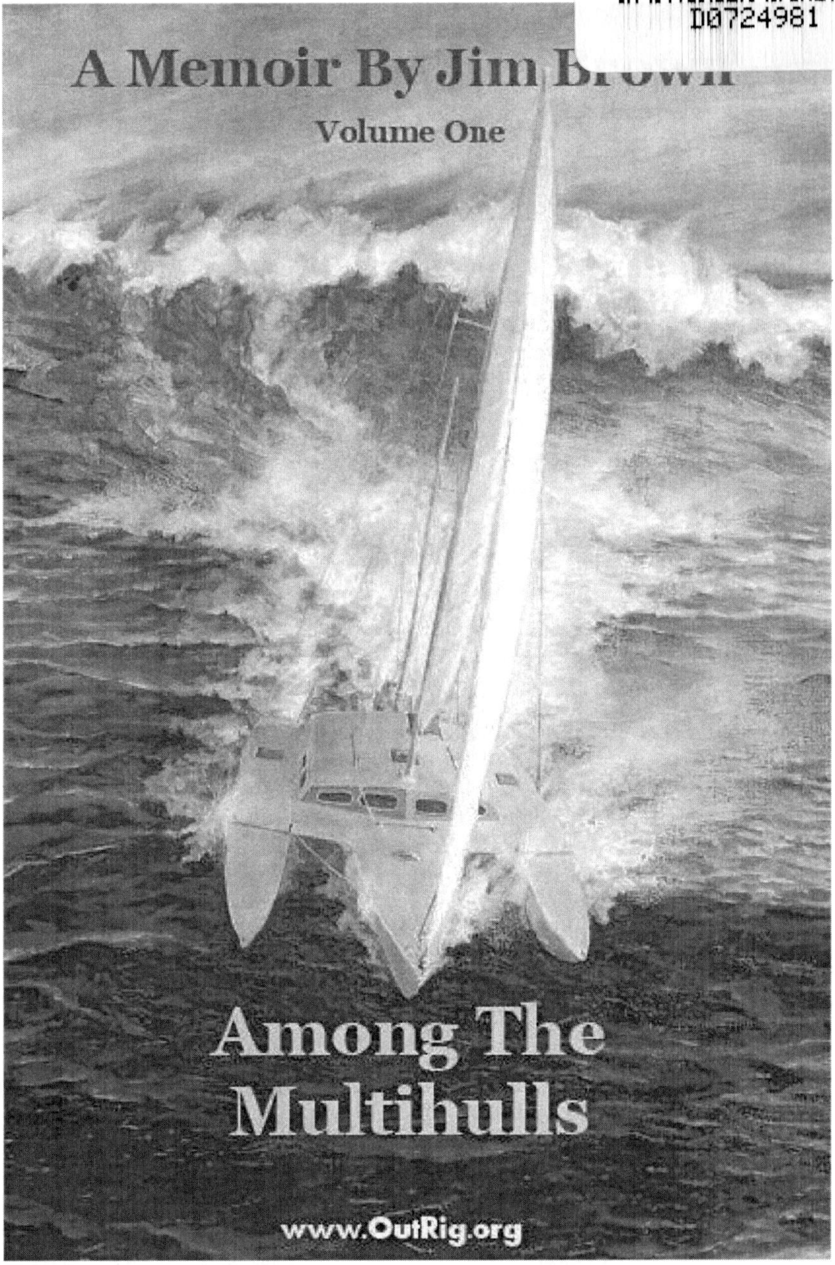

BookSpecs Publishing
Pennsville, NJ

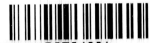

Among the Multihulls

Published by BookSpecs Publishing
BookSpecs is a trademark of BookSpecs Publishing, and is registered in the U.S. Patent and Trademark Office.

BookSpecs Publishing, 16 Sunset Ave., Pennsville, NJ 08070
http://www.OutRigMedia.com

ISBN 978-0-9721461-5-9
LCCN 2010911686

ABOUT THE COVER:
"The Thousand Mile Wave" - Painting by Bruce Alderson

Arthur Piver, "father of the modern trimaran," postulated in 1967 that it was possible for a multihull to achieve a run of 1,000 miles in 24 hours (the usual racing day's run of that period was about 200 miles). According to Piver, setting such a record would require sailing into the Roaring Forties of the Great Southern Ocean at the bottom of the world and catching one of the giant waves that often sweep that area. Piver's trimarans, he contended, could surf such a wave and therefore travel at the wave's own speed, said to be about forty knots. By surfing continually at the wave's reputed speed, the thousand-mile record could be achieved. Despite the fact that waves are intermittent, not running continuously as a single crest, this kind of postulation illustrated the multihull bravado and the can-do cultural tone of the sixties, yet Piver was roundly criticized at the time for his bombast. Forty years later in 2007, a "day's run" record of 796 miles in 24 hours was set by the French trimaran GROUPAMA 3. This run was achieved without surfing, but by straight sailing speed through the water. This suggests that it is probably only a matter of time before the thousand-mile barrier is broken by a modern sailing multihull. Such performance illustrates the multihull's unprecedented energy efficiency even when running under wind power alone, and it is this energy factor that now assures the future usefulness to humankind of modern multiple-hulled watercraft, power and sail. This book tells of their modern origins.

BACK COVER PHOTO:
Picture taken by Terry Messer

ABOUT THE AUTHOR:

James W. Brown, marine architect, multihull pioneer, builder, sailor, teacher, author.

In the 1950s—
Helped build the first large molded fiberglass boats in the U.S. Built the first modern cruising trimaran and sailed it on a 2,000-mile ocean voyage with bride Jo Anna.

In the 1960s—
Designed the SEARUNNER Series of ocean cruising trimaran sailboats for amateur building. These designs attracted some 1,600 builders worldwide; several have completed world cruises.

In the 1970s—
Sailed the coasts of Central and South America with family. Wrote The Case for the Cruising Trimaran published by International Marine, which sold 11,000 copies. Developed and patented the "Constant Camber" method of producing compound-curved plywood modular boat components.

In the 1980s—
Transferred Constant Camber technology to peasant fishermen in several remote locations in Africa, The Philippines, and the Central Pacific Islands where it is now used to produce sophisticated working watercraft for fishing and transportation. Wrote often for the yachting press. Personal trimaran SCRIMSHAW selected by the editors of Sail as among "The 100 Greatest Sailing Yachts in North America." Taught wood-epoxy technology at the WoodenBoat School.

In the 1990s—
Inducted into the Cruising World Hall of Fame. Guest lecturer at Mystic Seaport on yachting history and at University of North Carolina for architectural seminars. Designed small multihulls for mass production in rotomolded polyethylene, thousands sold for rental and expedition service. Voyaged to Cuba. Designed several large catamaran excursion craft built with Constant Camber and certified by U.S. Coast Guard for carrying passengers on offshore routes.

In the 2000s—
Recipient, award for outstanding achievement, New England Multihull Association. Co-founder, the OUTRIG! Project, "to collect, preserve and

disseminate the history and lore of modern seafaring." Seventy-five years old (2008), two grown sons (both boat designers and builders). Writes, sails, kayaks, and resides with Jo Anna, wife of forty-nine years, in rural Tidewater Virginia.

DISCLAIMER

A lot of crazy stuff transpired in the early days of modern multihulls, probably because of the chaotic global context from which these aberrant boats emerged. In today's litigious world (especially the US, by far the most litigious country), apparently something needs to be said to disabuse the reader that these pages should be construed to constitute negligence, deviance, conspiracy or terrorism or other crimes too fierce to mention. Just because you read about it here doesn't mean that the author, publisher, down loader, printer or mailman is endorsing, condoning or espousing that anyone in possession of his or her faculties undertake to replicate, mimic or surpass any of the harebrained exploits, foibles and achievements that comprised the early-modern multihull mania. Just because you read about it here in no way implies that it was cool, commendable or smart. In fact, some shellbacks will assert that one good way to waste and/or ruin – even lose – your life is to get strung out on multihulls. So, just by proceeding beyond this paragraph the reader agrees to hold harmless the whole wide world and a pig from any consequences expressed or implied resulting from partaking of the content of this ramble. Period!

Read on?

For Mary

Illustrations

What? There ain't none! Oh yes, there are, lots of them *online*.

To minimize the cost of making available in print, on paper, the text for this buoyant blather about boats, no pictures are included with the words. Instead the author's considerable collection of graphics – everything from snapshots and cartoons to design drawings and videos – is available at the URL address listed below. Furthermore, these comprehensive graphics come complete with Jim Brown's running commentary, his audio narration, far more informative than printed captions alone. These remarks can tell a story that runs parallel to, but does not duplicate, the written narrative, and can be viewed alone, before, after or intermittently during the reading of the text. In this way the images, both moving and still and unlimited by printing cost, can augment the story line in ways not found in books with few (if any) photos, and these can be added to with time.

The following Internet link appears at the end of each chapter in Volume One and will take the reader to the illustrated audio narrative relating to that chapter, or all the "audio graphics" .... **www.outrigmedia.com/books/atm-volume-one.html**

Contents

FOREWORD

The ancient outrigger canoes of Pacific Oceania can seem almost like Jurassic creatures to us today, yet they still survive in great numbers, largely unchanged for two or three millennia. However, in the mid 1900s the old outriggers began to spawn bizarre mutations, creatures that resembled their Stone Age forbears only vaguely and so were thought to be "freaks," incapable of reproduction. Surprisingly, they contracted DNA from stuff like plywood and plastics, and the fittest ones among them survived to prove viable – even invasive -- in such diverse environments as lakes, bays sounds and seas. Occurring now as three distinct species, catamaran, trimaran and proa, they are classified in the genus multihulus, and their rapid emergence – even dominance in some ecosystems – indicates a sea change in the age old phylum of surfus watercraftus.

No, your author is no biologist and no multihull progenitor, although I am sometimes charged with having sired certain of these aberrant sailing critters. In defense I contend to being just another deviant progeny of the true multihull forbears. One of the youngest devotees at the time these boats were whelping, I am now apparently one of the last whelpers, at least one of the last to be afflicted with probably-a terminal case of acute storytelling. Furthermore, I profess to know a little something of the Darwinian vitality that drove these mutant vessels into being. Because this momentous, maritime event is largely ignored by the nautical naturalists of today, it is something of that vitality, that drive, which this ramble now endeavors to disclose.

I think we early multihullers were not unlike the early aviators who abandoned normal lives to go barnstorming around the country giving aerobatic demonstrations of their flying machines. They were sometimes called aerobats. We, however, were known by other names, like "yachting's underdogs," and "the hell's angels of the sea." As with the early aircraft, sometimes our boats looked like back yard-built contraptions. They were even called "sailing reptiles" and "anti-yachts," but in these often cantankerous craft we went slashing through the harbors and across the oceans, at times behaving like The Magnificent Men in Their Sailing Machines. It was like running away with the circus, and often performing without a safety net. All right, we took some bad falls, and as "aquabats" we did not endear ourselves to the Corinthian establishment. But we surely did put on a show. Still do!

What follows, then, is my account of how modern multihulls happened. If you ask any shellback how it all happened, they answer by telling how it all happened to them. So this is the story of how modern multihulls happened to me, of how they shaped my life and the lives of my colleagues and clients, my family and friends.

It is told as a memoir, and we all know how it is with memories. They invade our thinking without regard for time, and it's often hard to figure where they fit in, where their story really starts. Sometimes they can be hard to describe because they seem to have happened to someone else or in another life, yet with some of them we can almost feel that old soaring sensation, and we can remember clearly what the scene looked like, as if it's going on right now!

Surely I'm not alone among septuagenarians to see things. Maybe it's just the senior's long-term memory trip, the sudden yesterday, and the blue hair's increased presence of the past. But for me it's stronger than that, it's like spying on my ships and shipmates and myself, especially my self! But I have an excuse, an explanation for why such mind's-eye recollections are abnormally intense for me. They're what I get to, see, for slowly going blind. There is a big blank blotch in my central vision that looks like I've put both index fingers in the butter and then pressed them to my glasses. The periphery around the smears looks like I'm peering through a driving rain. This is a common affliction called macular degeneration. It is age related, epidemic in America, and largely untreatable so far. It leads to what's called legal blindness, you can't read, can't drive, and can't quite tell what's on your fork until it's in your mouth. It's both adventurous and frustrating but it doesn't hurt, it doesn't kill, and it seldom deprives one of "walk around" vision at least when there's plenty of light.

Of course there's nothing bright about a slowly growing darkness, but believe me; you do get something for it: Failing eyesight can make memory strikingly visual. Such images are nothing new to those who suffer vision loss. They are said to be neurologically akin to the "phantom limb" sensations felt by amputees, so I call them "Phantom Visions." They are not like seeing, but being seen. For example, if I close my eyes and contemplate my time among the aquabats, often the "sights" that appear are... Well, I'll try to describe them as the chapters go along. The doctors call them "formed hallucinations," and they happen in print just as in memory – in the present tense.

Foreword

Of course my memories of multihulls are but a snippet of the whole story, for there are thousands of relatively unknown multihull designers, builders and sailors – pioneers all – whose stories are pleading to be shared. What's more, those now-obscure episodes are vital to understanding the context from which modern multihulls are now emerging big time. To collect those stories we invite submissions to our Website from anyone with a true, multihull-related story to tell. Yes, I love to tell my own stories, but half the reason for my telling them here is to entice others into telling theirs.

The OutRig! Website is a place for us all to do the telling, and its listings are chronological, a "time line" of multihull history. We must accept, however, that our mind's-eye recollections do not play chronologically. They can embark from anywhere in time, even in mid passage, and the only way to "watch" them is to jump aboard.

Casting off!

Jim Brown
Hick Neck, Virginia
June 21, 2010

OutRig!

Jim Brown's Online Multihull History Project

The Ancient, Modern and Ongoing History of Trimarans, Catamarans and Proas on Display ...

- The Origins of Modern Multihulls
- Personal Accounts of Modern Multihull Pioneers
- Design, Construction & Operation of Modern Multihull Vessels
- Essays & Featured Stories by Jim Brown & Others
- Outrig News & Events
- Seafaring Literature & Multimedia
- Timeline of Multihull History & Lore
- Rare Video, Audio & Print Materials
- A Place to Share *Your* Multihull Story

Visit www.OutRig.org and catch the wave to this unique multihull sailing community!

1

TO BUILD A BABY

1968 > 72

There we are, both of us ducking the smoke. A thick slab of chuck is broiling beside the fire. Walt throws another redwood knot into the blaze, ashes fly, and he is covering his suspended wine glass with the same hand that clutches it. We are talking boats, and I am challenged to explain why I am building one. Walter says, "A man doesn't build a boat just to stay out of the bars, you know. He builds a boat to make up for the fact that he can't build a baby."

After my laughter and guffaws, in which Walt does not participate, he adds, "Not funny. A boat is the most life-like thing a man can produce, the most responsive to the environment and to his vane attempts at control. What else can a guy produce with his own body that so closely simulates a living thing?"

In the bottom of Big Creek Canyon where Walt and I are talking, there is a small alluvial flat. It is only a hundred feet wide and about four hundred feet long, with the creek running on the north side against the steeper cleft side of the canyon. This makes room for our two little houses and a tool shed. The buildings remain from a former Forest Service fire camp, which Jo Anna and I rent from the beneficent McCrary brothers who own the canyon and the local lumber mill. The only vehicular access to our home, unless one chooses to ford the creek at low water, is a logging road. It descends through thick forest on the rubble side of the canyon, and makes for all low gear both coming and going. It is the dry season, so Walt Glaser has forded the creek.

He is a little known but artful trimaran designer, a sharp-featured and sharp-minded cynic who often makes his self-deprecating points with humor. He calls his design series "SALLY LIGHTFOOT, the only trimarans that stumble through the water." Actually, I have always thought his boats are salty and seamanlike. They will surely climb to windward, for they have nice big centerboards.

I had met Walt in the early sixties, and knew of his pioneering voyage to Hawaii and back in his somewhat-modified Piver 35-foot trimaran. It was now 1968, and I was preparing to go voyaging with my family in our own trimaran, one that I had designed myself and was slowly building in this canyon.

Walt Glaser's real gift to "the "multihull movement" was his grasp of the manner in which a boat, and especially boat building, fulfills the human male. He helped me realize that these crazy multihulls were not just vehicles; they were serving other, more cerebral human needs.

As I realize he is serious, my grin subsides. He continues, "You know how a woman is fulfilled by identifying herself as a mother? You know, sons or daughters, how many, how old, doing what? Well in the same way, a man seeks to identify himself as a..... Something! A father? That's not creative enough. As a... What else? He has to fill in the blank."

"Boats can do that?" I ask skeptically.

"Absolutely," he replies. "We're like the voice crying in the wilderness. We plead, 'Here I am, please notice me.' 'I am a boating man.' And the wilderness answers. That's nice, but so what? There are lots of boating men.' But If you fill in the blank with something like, 'I am a multihull man,' that puts a handle on you boy! The wilderness mumbles grudgingly, 'Okay, multihulls are cool so you're different. You realize of course that you'll have to pay the price of being cool and different, but we of the wilderness do hereby notice you.' Now! All at once you've got a straight pipeline to the most crucial facet of human development, your very own identity."

Except for the growling noise of an occasional vehicle, there was constant music from the creek in this place. The creek-organist, according to her seasonal whims, varied the repertoire between trilling in summer and blaring in winter. The logging road continued up the canyon along the creek for a mile. It passed shallow pools with lurking rainbows in summer and spawning steelhead in spring. In winter one hiked past knee-high leafy mushrooms crawling with salamanders in their mating séance, rare albino redwood saplings sprouting from stumps, and little tributary creeks gurgling from deep beds of giant ferns.

A mile upstream the canyon terminated in a steep granite wall. On that wall a sinewy sixty-foot waterfall hissed into its pool below.

Swimming there with my wife and kids, I could almost sense our mammalian heat being dispersed into bracing water which trees would drink, fish would breath and spiders would dance upon all the way to the Pacific coast about four miles downstream. And from there? Yes, I imagined something of our human taste would mingle into all the seas upon which we hoped one day to sail. But we were starting at the headwaters and had a long way to go to embarkation.

The sides of this canyon had been logged the first time in the late 1800's, its prime redwood timber utilized to fire the boiler of the steam generator that first brought electrification to the Santa Cruz area. The stumps of those electrifying trees had rotted away leaving what looked like bomb craters. Around these voids grew offspring, each of a size that one could reach only half way around their trunks. These rings of redwoods had sprung from the root systems of their long-since assassinated forbears. These tight circles of trunks formed occasional atria throughout the forest.

However, these were but satellites, for in the center of the alluvial flat, right beside our home, stood two of the original monarchs that the loggers had saved, and these two made all other redwoods and firs now growing in the canyon look like houseplants. The pair stood so close together that a human could stand between them with outstretched arms, hands grasping the ridges and ruts of their hoary fireproof bark, and gaze straight up to see that no branches grew between the boles until their crowns. It was like gazing from the bottom of a 200-foot well. Furthermore, the lower branches of this pair, themselves of saw log size, sprang outward from the twin columns to arch downward and form a grand boreal grotto. About thirty feet high and seventy feet wide, this vault was open at all sides, and on the ground a few fir logs lay as peripheral pews. The fire pit, a rough circle of rocks, comprised the central alter for this cathedral-in-the-round. It was in this monument that we regularly worshiped – in our own way – the sacrament of family and friends in Eden.

It is autumn, so the creek is well down into its banks. Lacking floods in recent years, the watercourse has become choked with weedy alders, which further muffle its gurgling. While pondering the insight that Walt has shared, I notice that except for the occasional squeals from our kids and yelps from our dogs, who are all busy damming a swimming hole, there is little activity in the canyon. The campfire snaps occasionally, and the thick chuck roast, smeared with mustard and herbs, roasts beside the flames sizzling invitingly. Walter goes on:

"And talk about identity! How about being a pioneer? We've always known we are sailing virgin water with these boats. Building a multihull is like having a kid that you know is going to grow up to be president. The potential of these boats is enormous. They are definitely going to affect the future of seafaring, and we know it. Not everybody does, but we do."

"How do we know?" I ask.

"Because we've been to sea in them. We've seen for ourselves how inherently right they are. How they let you make mistakes and get away with it, how they can slash to windward and surf downwind and ride at anchor like a duck and slide in onto the beach just for the fun of it. And how they thrill the sailor right down at the pit of the pituitary. And most of all, how they tell us who we are. We're pioneers in something that's wide open, that's unregulated, and that is so free and off-the-wall that you can see directly the results of your own efforts and decisions, good or bad! And what you see is something never seen before. That's rare these days. It's exciting. It's irresistible."

"How do you mean 'irresistible,'" I ask.

"Well, you see it every time someone buys a set of plans. You are offering them a means to enter the fraternity where anything is possible. You offer them the speed to show their heels to the establishment, the power to escape normality, to go anywhere, to see the world. What red-blooded identity seeker can resist that?"

Thinking back today I must have found Walt's insights a revelation, for I never again doubted that I was offering something worthwhile to my clients. No longer did I feel like a phony, capitalizing on the feats of others and the hysteria of the times. In our brochures and slide shows, I began to shape my message in terms of escape, survival, freedom and identity.

SCRIMSHAW...

It worked, for my wife Jo Anna and I soon found ourselves to be, for the first time in our married lives, some seven hundred dollars in the black. With this exceptional asset, we began to build our own boat. I fixed up the little tool shed on the place as a shop, finished the plans for the 31-foot Searunner trimaran, and started cutting its frames. It was the most gratifying work I had ever undertaken, but I had no idea it would be three and a half long years before SCRIMSHAW would be borne upon the water.

Anyone who says a boat project will break up a happy home should consider the overall fragility of that marriage and find another factor on which to place the blame. No doubt a boat will test a good marriage, as it has ours for the last thirty-seven years (yes, at this writing in 2009 we still have SCRIMSHAW), but she also has been a prime ingredient in the adhesive that has held us together as a family. What is that ingredient? It was blind luck, providence. Fifty years ago I happened on a woman who was looking for authentic adventure, and who was willing to buy into my trip. Jo Anna's unflagging support of my boating binge has allowed the boat to make an essential difference in our family lives, and after a half century of marriage we still sail in the same crew.

And the kids? Our two sons Steven and Russell (then sub teens but now in their late forties) were camping overnight in the upside-down hull before it was even planked. They were too small to help much in the construction, but watching me work drew them into the shop where they insisted on using the tools in their own projects. Allowing this seems now to be the only vocational thing I ever gave them, for today they are both professional multihull designers, builders and sailors in their own rights.

But finishing the boat was a serious challenge. The multihull anatomy is complex, and despite the simplicity of the tools and skills required to build such a structure out of plywood, lumber and glue, the task seems at times interminable. There are three hulls to build, you have to join them all together somehow (and building that platform is like building yet another hull!), and then there's the hardware, mast, rigging, sails, plumbing, wiring, controls and – most daunting – all the sanding, fiberglassing, painting and finishing inside and out. It really takes time, money and commitment.

During the years I was learning of this commitment, action on the multihull scene was becoming increasingly frantic. It was the late 1960's, so the anti-war movement was getting nasty, as were the government scandals and the body bags. Catamarans, trimarans and ferro-concrete monohulls were popping up and popping out of back yards and boat builder's communes all over the country but especially in California. Many were built in the hinterland and trucked to the sea or to rivers for journeys to the coasts. Jo Anna and I were selling plans enough to support ourselves and our SCRIMSHAW habit.

Building her was an addiction. I kept drawing plans and giving talks to the multihull clubs in Seattle, San Francisco, Los Angeles and New York, but the boat tantalized me at the same time. It was my respite from swimming non-stop in the multihull maelstrom. With the phone ringing constantly, the mail pouring in with questions to be answered, and uninvited drop-ins continually finding their way down our logging road just to listen to the horse's mouth, I was not able to spend much time on our boat for the first two years or so, but her skeleton slowly took shape in the canyon.

We had lots of client/friends; many of them were building our boats under similar circumstances; make a living and make a boat at the same time. We developed a system of "planking parties," like the old barn raisings wherein one builder would get as much done as possible by himself, like cutting and fitting all the plywood planking for his hulls, and then call in the cohorts to apply the planks in a boisterous weekend. We shared in these occasions with our particular friends Patti and Jerry DesRoches, Barbara and Jim McCaig and Tom and Blanche Freeman, all building Brown-designed trimarans in the vicinity. The guys would almost throw the panels at the boat as one man with a pneumatic staple gun would bang them home; inside the upturned hull the ladies wiped up excess glue, their hair protected with bandannas to prevent contamination from wet Weldwood®. After a day of such frenzy there would be the usual pot luck feed and partying. Kids and dogs and homemade music augmented these scenes. Folk songs and folksy camaraderie would continue well into the night. At our place, dawn would find a ring of twitching sleeping bags around the smoldering campfire in the redwood cathedral. Coffee and a hearty breakfast would crank things up, and off we'd go for another day of communal construction.

It was heady stuff for us all, but especially for me, I think, because I was the one who had drawn the plans for these projects. The pressures of this responsibility were offset by excitement and anticipation of setting off to sea. I was taking the whole trip, beginning with design, then construction, and then – I was certain – to seafaring with a family crew. It was wonderfully complete except that we would learn that building was, by itself, no preparation for ocean sailing.

Furthermore, I was sometimes dismayed by building from my own plans. I actually followed them closely, as did most of my clients, but at times I had real difficulty understanding the drawings. I had built the boat completely in my head while producing the drawings, which were acknowledged as being among the most expressive and comprehensive available. The pictorials showed two or three views of every component in the structure, and they were surrounded by little notes to guide the neophyte builder, but every so often I would read one of those notes and say out loud, "Now what in hell does he mean by that?" This dismay helped me realize that plans drawn for neophyte builders need to be accompanied by extensive consulting services, and I had created a monster that was going to starve without my ongoing personal involvement. How could we ever get away?

Sailing Through Space...

While the boat was taking shape, our boys were growing up and our business was budding out, and all in a glorious setting! There were many occasions when we pondered the natural splendor of a lively creek in a redwood canyon near the California coast. One such occasion was the lunar eclipse of 1971. Of the many attempts made by people to witness celestial events undiminished by artificial light, say, from aircraft or mountaintops or isolated islands, I herewith suggest trying from the bottom of a box canyon. Something happens there at night that must be similar to the strange phenomenon of being able to see stars in daylight from the bottom of a well. Our canyon walls blocked off the metropolitan lumes of San Francisco, San Jose and Santa Cruz giving minimal skylight on the night of the eclipse. Fortunately the central coast was flushed with cold, dry air fresh in from the Aleutians.

We were joined that night by some valued non-boating friends, folks with whom we could socialize without talking shop. Bruce and Marcia McDougal, operated a nearby ceramic school, and Bruce Bratten was a venerated local roustabout. The five of us often packed away enough of the local varietal wines to float our boat, but this night we soberly assumed a vantage on the moon from the bottom of a big hole. The vista began with the man in the moon assuming his usual countenance as a far off face on a dime in a spotlight, but slowly the vista developed into a shocking celestial show that is often re-run in my theater-of-the Big Blind Blotch:

The subject is set in a canyon-rim frame that is bordered by the silhouettes of coniferous spires. It slowly slides into the partial shadow of Earth's atmosphere to be tinged on one cheek by spectral hues of blue. While growing apparently much larger it is shaded by Earth herself and thereby overwhelmed by sunset red and becomes startlingly globular. Huge now, we sense nonetheless that it is a mere bonbon orbiting our bowling ball, yet it comes so very close we fear a stellar smashup.

As we shiver there in the canyon spellbound by this sight, we reach up, stretching as if confident of feeling the old man's blotches and zits, of rubbing the wrinkles that are casting shadows all around the edges of his spherical face.

Beyond this nearby blushing ball we see the heavens, too, in three dimensions; actually perceive their – until now – unfathomable .depths. Considering two planets as neighbors in our own sun's light, we then perceive the stars as hugely distant suns, not tiny moons. This foreshortened projection of the moon makes the rest of what's out there – Milky Way and all – stunningly deep. We at last apprehend the enormity of our isolation in this place called space.

Then, as if by time reversal, one cheek of the otherwise red-faced man in the moon is tinged with celestial blue. He now rapidly recedes, pales, and recovers his usual countenance as a far-off dime in a spotlight. We are left cold, awed, enlightened and a little frightened. Do we really want to know how utterly alone we are on Earth?

That night's peculiar portrait of the heavens has stayed with me for reasons of its parallel with seafaring. Our project of building SCRIMSHAW was somehow akin to whacking out a space ship for traveling in the most vast wilderness still accessible to individuals. We became nothing more than cosmic mites now conscious of our inconsequence. Marooned on our mass of molten magma, which is skinned over by a rusty crust and two-thirds smeared with water, our intent was to go, and come to know, something of this smear, this hydrosphere, for it is apparently unique upon our Earth, not so far found upon any of the other orbs in multiverse.

But, like reaching up to touch the moon, the very notion of embarking on such an odyssey was scary. We became audacious to ourselves. Marooned here on a particle of stardust, we were contemplating the investigation of Earth's mid region, that frontier where its wet smear mingles with its lithosphere. We knew it had been done by families before; cruising with kids was not unique. It had started with the ancients of Pacific Oceania who moved the makings of entire villages from one island to another very far away; their equivalent of colonizing space. But could we do it? Ordinary gringos in a back yard-built bucket? Well, we were readying to try.

Print Power...

During the sixties the west coast multihull owner-builder scene was dominated by trimarans (although the catamaran would later prevail in popularity), and several small magazines popped up. These included TRIMARAN, TRIMARANER and TRIMARAN SAILING. They survived only briefly but gave the movement an air of legitimacy when it was badly needed.

I wrote occasionally for these publications, espousing the notion of "seasteading," a life style wherein a vessel's crew – especially a family crew – could be sustained by, with, and from their boat. It was being done, and not just in multihulls, by a few very resourceful and dedicated cruisers. Some sailed to foreign lands and settled in harbors where they had skills that could be sold ashore. Some chartered their boats to tourists, and others operated small businesses from on board such as making canvass work for other boats. They lived frugally but often very much enjoyed their endeavors. In my writing I emphasized safety, discouraged racing and tried hard to identify the purpose of my boats as for something more than showing off.

In 1968, Jo Anna and I published a slick catalog of Searunner designs. In the Catalog I again espoused the notion of seasteading, asserting that the boats were intended for the purpose. Soon we had the great good fortune to have our catalog briefly reviewed in The Whole Earth Catalog, and all of a sudden our plans sales increased substantially. Once finished, the cost of printing and mailing plans was small compared to their price, so finally all that eyeball-busting work was paying off.

We had been duplicating a set of leaflets to accompany the plans which guided our builders during construction. Nevertheless, phone calls, letters and uninvited drop-ins were taking over our lives, leaving little time for drawing new plans or working on our boat. As SCRIMSHAW slowly took shape it became obvious that we were never going to be able to extricate ourselves from our clientele without something that really answered all (almost all) of the questions. Furthermore our customers deserved more information, enough to get them through the seemingly interminable, truly complex, commitments they were making to our line of so-called Searunner Trimarans. So, with Jo Anna typing the manuscript, I began to try to write it all down, every scrap of know-how I had mustered from my schooner days and as a beginning builder making several of these boats, and counseling neophyte builders for almost fifteen years. I took a lot of pictures while building our boat and of others, nitty-gritty details of all kinds. I mined my own drawings for examples of typical practice, and wrote reams of how-to, trying hard to avoid the usual deadening gobbledygook of technical writing.

To this end I was mightily assisted by Jo Hudson, whose cartoon illustrations became icons in our publications, for they served to take the drudgery out of boatbuilding and the fear out of seafaring. Without Jo's cartoons, the Searunner lineup would have been just another also-ran.

When SCRIMSHAW, yet to be named reached the stage of three hulls completed and the main interiors roughed-in, it was time to move her parts and pieces out of the canyon to a place where she could later be transported to the water as a unit. This exodus involved not only moving out of our beloved canyon home but also borrowing a rickety truck and trailer for towing the boat over logging roads. Hauling the main hull first, son Steven and I came out of the woods only to have a breakdown on a narrow curve of the Coast Highway with no shoulder. We were rescued by Bruce Bratten driving a school bus; he towed us, the truck, trailer and main hull out of peril. We were then escorted through Santa Cruz by a red Cadillac convertible driven by the midget whose profession was to speak the voice of Donald Duck. The Caddie was piled high with hippies (friends of those who loaned me the truck and trailer) who dutifully blocked traffic at every intersection – regardless of the lights – while the midget excoriated those who objected to the blockage as a vociferous, angry and profane little duck. I remember thinking that this was probably the most hazardous voyage the boat would ever make.

We moved into a grand house near the center of Santa Cruz and settled Scrimshaw's components into a boat yard just blocks from the harbor with its four-lane launching ramp. We were really selling plans now, enough to start salting away a cruising fund, but the need for a real Construction Manual became increasingly evident. I worked on the boat when the weather permitted (she was never under cover) and when it rained I worked on the Manual. We were making progress, but there seemed to be just too much to do! Jo Anna and I knew that if we were ever going to take a big deal boat ride with our sons, we were going to have to go soon; otherwise they would become involved with their peers and not want to leave.

Yet we were committed to leaving! Why? On the face of it there was no reason whatever. We had a great place to live, a promising future, lots of friends, two great kids and two great dogs. Yet the call to adventure, to sailing and to escape was irresistible. After all, I was sending hundreds of people – many as families – out to sea in my designs in the same nebulous quest, and it seemed only fair that I should subject myself and my family to the same treatment. In order to get away we were even prepared to simply shut the business down and flee.

The Deal of a Lifetime...

In early 1971 I was approached by friend Tom Freeman with a proposition. He and John Marples had been talking, and now offered to run our plans business for us while we went cruising. They were already conducting ALMAR, an active procurement service for boatbuilders, selling spars, sails and a host of yachting equipment to back yard builders of all boats. Some of this equipment was manufactured by Marples and friends at the boat builder's collective in Alviso, an abandoned and sometimes-flooded cannery town at the very southern end of San Francisco Bay. There were all kinds of cruising craft under construction by owner-builders, including several Searunners, at this vibrant site. Couples and families with building projects there either hauled in house trailers or whacked out shelters in the cannery buildings, some of these habitations accessed only by high ladders to cliff dwellings scabbed into the giant trusses of the old industrial sheds. Colored lights, cool music, holistic food and the air of incense typified these residences. Working at outside day jobs and whaling away on their boats late into the night, these builders often helped each other, exchanged vital information and sometimes partied hard. The morning after one such party I awoke in an aerie pad to discover, while descending the seemingly endless ladder to the ground, that some wag had inscribed the lofty wall with a spray can to read, "Jim Brown slept here." I had arrived!

ALMAR was the source of a non-yachty line of marine hardware designed and built by John Marples expressly for Searunners. The line included running backstay levers, robust lifeline stanchions and the now rare and highly coveted aluminum winch handles whose castings were boldly inscribed, "MADE IN ALVISO BY HIPPIES." ALMAR's stuff sold well and served well, and it seemed appropriate that this progressive outfit should purvey plans for Searunners.

So we made a deal: Tom and John would handle our plans and consult for the builders, and we would split the gross income fifty-fifty. Starting immediately! The only hooker was that if I was going to bail out, they must have a definitive construction manual to answer most of the questions being asked by our builders.

All at once I had time! In a great spurt of activity we produced a big book called SEARUNNER CONSTRUCTION. I wrote furiously by hand on the beach, Jo Anna typed the camera-ready text on our new Selectric typewriter in our kitchen, Jo Hudson drew the cartoons at his mountainside home in Big Sur, Tom Freeman did the paste-up composition in our basement and – gambling our entire cruising fund of some ten thousand dollars – we had the book printed up in Berkeley. (Now long out of print, the book developed a cult following and was used by many builders of non-Searunners. Even builders who wanted boats other than Searunners built Searunners because of the book. I now regard that project as the favorite undertaking with our friends and, what's more, our arrangement with Tom and John allowed Jo Anna and me to take three years off at age forty! It was literally the deal of a lifetime.)

But For the Corks...

Now, at last, I could finish the boat! For ten months in 1971-2 I worked almost full time on SCRIMSHAW, loving it but hating the rush. We were committed to setting sail in the summer of 72 while the boys were eleven and twelve, believing strongly that if we didn't go NOW we would never get away. We set a drop-dead launch date of June 21st, the summer solstice. Despite the endless details of trying to finish a seagoing sailboat, ready to sail before the launching, we somehow made the date.

Early on that morning I backed our station wagon, loaded with equipment for the boat and supplies for the launching party, into my workspace. This was a maneuver I had performed many times, and I was preoccupied with planning the launching, but while backing up I was surprised by a commotion behind the car and saw a ghostly figure – someone wrapped in clear plastic – roll out from almost beneath my back wheels. It turned out to be a local boat bum sleeping off a bender. We were both shaken by the near thing, but he then noticed a carton of fresh orange juice, left for him in the plastic by his ultra-considerate girl friend of the previous night. He calmly offered me a swig, and we toasted the start of SCRIMSHAW's launching day together.

Then I noticed that the boat and the outer walls of the shop building were all plastered with poster-sized pictures of me making a panic face. I knew Tiny Tommy had been working that night on his printing press, and that this was going to be a lively day.

The move to the launching ramp went well, and so did the christening. In accord with a local, cliquish tradition at multihull launchings, we anointed the rudder with some "sacred wine" saved by friends Patti and Jerry from their rounding of Point Conception in their Nugget trimaran with a broken rudder years before. Jerry had dragged the wine astern in crashing waves, the plastic jugs serving as a movable drogue. He swung it from one side of the boat to the other to steer finally into shelter. This was our christening; we saved the cases of Champagne for another purpose.

As the boat and trailer descended the ramp, all the kids in the party wanted to ride the vessel into the water. Thinking that this really was a family project and wanting to begin by delegating responsibility to our young crew, I agreed to put them all aboard for the launch. But I instructed Steven and Russell, "As soon as she floats free from the trailer I want you guys to go below and look for leaks, okay?" Brimming with a sense of duty, they agreed.

So into her element she rolled... And came afloat! I'll never forget the moment, or the sound of the cheers.

Nor the moment after when Steve, the elder of our two, popped out of the forward hatch to say solemnly, "Dad, the water's coming in."

"Sure Steve," I replied laughing. "Cry wolf and nice try."

"No Dad, the water's coming in fast."

Chagrined, I waded in up to my chest to the bow and, with an effort I could never duplicate, climbed aboard dripping and draining. I jumped to the hatch and saw that Russ was working the bilge pump and two other youngsters were deep in the holds beside the centerboard trunk, each with his thumb stuck into one of the centerboard glands to stem the garden hose-sized streams that both fittings had been squirting into the bilge. I had left the caps off of these fittings.

Meanwhile the crowd had pulled the vessel over to a floating dock. Amidst the apprehension and merrymaking on the dock I confided to Jo Anna, "I left the caps off of the centerboard gland and can't find them. The kids have the leaks under control with their thumbs, but they're turning blue and I don't know what to do."

Jo Anna then reached into her purse and slowly extracted a small plastic bag filled with an assortment of corks. "Will these work?" she asked. "I saw them somewhere and thought they might come in handy." What a first mate!

With my glands firmly corked, we went on with the party, which grew to such proportions as to cause the floating dock to sink, soaking several participants. Tipsy and enthralled, we moved aboard that day and spent the next three years living in, with and from the boat.

But again, our beginning experiences with her were not auspicious. On our first sea trial we were just leaving the dock, close hauled against zephyrs moving slowly down the fairway in the harbor when a proud monohull about our size slid out of a side isle right in front of us. With no recourse but to turn and collide with another boat on an end tie, I chose instead to ram the intruder with a bang. SCRIMSHAW was undamaged but the teak toe rail of her opponent was smashed, and of course the boat was owned and steered by the commodore of the Santa Cruz Yacht Club. How to start out, eh?

Our next foible occurred at the end of our first hop to another harbor. Upon entering between the breakwaters at Moss Landing, after a rousing sail from Santa Cruz in a stiff breeze, we found that our diminutive outboard motor, of only four horsepower, was insufficient to push us against the wind up to the awaiting slips. As we were being blown out of the channel I dropped the anchor, which at once became fouled in a mass of weed, and we drifted helplessly sideways until ramming a waterside restaurant. The patrons watched us coming in wonderment until the collision shook their tables and sent them scurrying. Again, there was no damage and no blood, but my pride was weeping.

Doggedly, Jo Anna and the boys stuck with me and I stuck with the plan. In the wee hours I sometimes fretted about the wisdom of that plan, the intrusion on our lives and the risk of seagoing in a back-yard boat with a family crew. Was this commitment reasonable? We would find out.

By late August we had either sold or given away everything we owned that did not belong on the boat. Tom and John were running our business well, and our other friends became convinced that we really were going to leave... With no idea where we were headed and with no intention to return. The boys were game, and we wanted out of our involvements ashore. We wanted to be away from California's cultural craziness of the time, away from the bombardment of bad news about the economy, the government and the War. We wanted into the seasteading adventure.

When I say "we" I mean all of us. We could only fantasize the enormous change in our lives now beginning, and of course we all had apprehensions. Yes, Jo Anna and I had done this before in 1959 with our little trimaran JUANA, a junket that lasted only three months (Chapter 4), and I had been bitten by the seafaring adventure in my premarital schooner-bumming days (Chapter 2), but now we were a family! The boys were leaving their peers, I was leaving my career, and Jo Anna was uprooting her progeny. We were quite possibly venturing into harm's way, and we had no clear destination, no notion of the long-term consequences of bailing out and sailing away.

The enticement to go, however, was irresistible. By now we already knew something about the seakeeping properties of modern multihulls, and we knew that the thing about adventure was that it could be a whole lot easier to stay home. But after eighteen years of trying to get my affairs in order, I was finally headed back to my beloved Caribbean. This time we had a real boat under us, not some back yard-built contraption, and after ten years of driving our own business together we were not broke and Jo Anna was not – as she had been in '59 – pregnant! It all combined to suggest great portent. Surely our very own Shangri La was lurking somewhere over the horizon, and this was our chance to find it. Quite frankly we were scared, but we were also greedy to go.

Greed versus Fear...

It is mid August 1972, the night before departure. Steve and Russ are snuggled in their bunks after a very hectic day. Jo Anna and I are basking in the lamplight of our sterncastle, sharing the dregs from the last Champaign bottle saved from the launching party. She is thumbing the pages of one of the boys' comic books and suddenly exclaims, "That's it! That's how I feel!" Chuckling, she tries to read out loud from the story of some fictional gems. Supposedly these emeralds carry a curse for all who possess or try to steal them, including a character named Gryce, the currently aspiring thief. As the conclusion of this month's installment nears she slaps the table and guffaws, and then reads out loud:

"Many men had died from coveting those emerald orbs, but Vincent Gryce's greed was greater than his fear."

"That's exactly how I feel!" She laughs and slaps the table again. "My greed is greater than my fear!"

....

Illustrations for this chapter, narrated by the author, are available online at ...
www.OutrigMedia.com/books/atm-volume-one.html

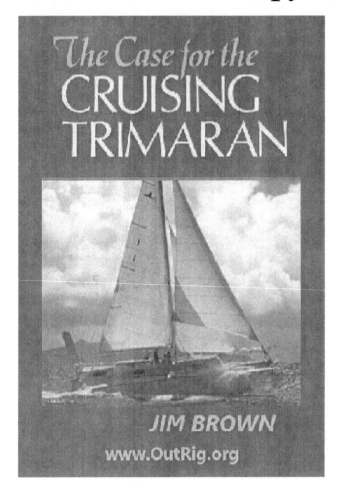

2

PROMISE MADE

1956

He is climbing up and barely hanging on, and it takes all the strength in his neck to keep his head from flailing painfully out of control. He is part way up the mast to where the yacht's motion, as she rollicks in the tradewind seaway, is greatly aggravated by his elevation, and the boat is heeled enough to swing him way out over water. To rest his hands he loops both arms over the cross tree above and wraps both legs around the shrouds below. With his limbs and torso thus restrained he tucks his chin down on his chest and cradles his head between scrunched shoulders. The warm wind is rinsing him clean through.

Yes, it was me there, the protagonist now appearing in these "formed hallucinations" I am trying to describe. Maybe they are really just like any geezer's snapshot memories of youth, but this one's watercolor hologram comes together with Caribbean bathing air. I didn't really go seafaring until my early twenties, but when I did... Well, something happened up that mast that often re-rents space in my cerebral tenement. It begins to explain how my family and I came to perch on that precipice at the end of Chapter 1. Indeed it only begins to explain, for that was in 1972, when the modern multihull was already well established. We do not return to that predicament until Chapter 7! Instead, what follows now, for roughly half of this volume, is an attempt to chronicle something of the early days of modern multihulls, of how they happened, and how they happened to me and my family, my clients and friends.

LA BRISA, the big steel ketch to whose mast I was clinging back then in 1956, had recently fled in panic from the pre-revolutionary skirmishes that were heating up in Batista's Havana. It was now near the end of our third night of sailing south. The boat was threading her way between isolated reefs lying way off the Caribbean coast of Honduras. She was well eastward of that great Central American promontory, named by Columbus as he finally rounded it in 1496, Cabo Gracias a Dios, "Cape Thank God."

This passage, around the west end of Cuba and down into the Southwestern Caribbean, is bounded by unmarked reefs on both sides. On our chart one reef's Spanish name, Quita Sueño, translates as "Nights of Little Sleep." The other is named Abre Ojos, "Keep Your Eyes Open." Cloudy weather had prevented celestial sights and made the night's navigation rather tense, but looking up past the masthead I now saw that the overcast had thinned and a few stars were fading before first light.

The yacht's owner and I had taken over the watch at 4 AM, and he asked ME if I could climb the rigging in these conditions. Glad for the chance to demonstrate some worth to my new employer, I said I thought I could. "Then go as high as you think safe and have a look around," he said. "You should be able to spot the island as the sky gets lighter, but there's no telling where on the horizon you'll see it. I think it's ahead to starboard, but we don't know exactly where we are, so it could be anywhere, even behind!"

Now the motion at my perch was so violent that I imagined myself to be a booger on the little finger of God, and He was trying to shake me off. Obliged to wait there for more light, I realized in full that during the night we easily could have struck a reef or even struck the island that I was hoping now to see.

On our American chart it was called by its modern Spanish name, Isla Providencia, but we also had on board the old British Admiralty chart, made from a 1691 survey which included in its wide margins several romantic pen-and-ink renderings of the Island as seen from different approaches. Each rendering showed the Island to be dominated by a huge volcanic megalith that was split wide open down the middle. The rock was called Split Hill, and the chart's title was Old Providence Island. The place was certainly remote.

I looked down, suffered vertigo, became agog at the sight. The wake was illuminated by multitudes of minute dynoflagilates, their glow-worm brilliance turned on by the turbulence of the hull's passing. Except for the wake, the sea seemed to be without surface. From my vantage the yacht appeared as a romping rendering of itself painted on velvet and black-lighted against the void of celestial space.

Besides the wake there was a deeper brilliance, a long, blue-white beam of phosphorescence streaming from the keel like a moonlit contrail. The west was still night's territory but the east was contested. No horizon was yet visible there, just a roiling muddle between sea and sky. Again I was not so much watching as being watched:

LA BRISA makes a violent pitch and that kid there tries to shift his grip with arms and legs. Finding no alternative position he continues clinging to the cross tree and shrouds. Stuck here inside this wind machine he marvels at its process of putting out real power. As the vessel's bow climbs a wave, the masts and sails rare back and the great fabric foils scoop up gulps of fuel that cannot get away. Then, as the bow falls from the crest, the spars, sails and rigging are thrust forward through the fuel too fast, spilling lots. The sound is alternately that of gulping and howling, and there is one complete reciprocating stroke every five or six seconds. He is located at about the sonic centroid of the sails so their arching vaults produce surreal acoustics. The gulps and howls, the gabble of the bow wave and the pulsing hiss of the wake, all echo in syncopated rhythm off the sails. It is unlike the string of detonations made by other engines he has known, for this machine propels its vehicle in a sequence of sublime surges. Looking left and right, and twisting to see forward past the jib, he surveys the scene hoping not to see breakers on a reef.

Now it passes, that brief meridian between nightset and dayrise, so crisp in the tropics. It sweeps through at about the speed at which Earth's girth whirls toward morning, one thousand and thirty seven miles per hour. Dividing east from west, light from dark, it leaves behind a high smear of heaven turning pink with purple wisps of doubt below. He mutters, "This is what I came for," and the wind inflates his downwind cheek to siphon the enunciation from his mouth as if spoken from deep within a whistlejug.

Now all appears in gloaming, and way over there the softest vapors at the bottom of the sky are punctured from beneath by something hard but split. It has to be... It can be nothing but the very top of Old Providence Island.

Of Protégés and Mentors...

Such a snapshot image now explains a lot of why I fastened onto sailing all those five decades ago. It lurks inside my rental like a burglar caught with no way out. Trying always to steal the show, he can explain neither how it was I ever went to sea nor why it came to be in multihulls. Like him, my answer was that I had failed at other things I tried.

After trying things like digging ditches, washing cars, selling clothes and checking credit, by age twenty-two I was rather down and out in Miami, an Ivy League flunkout desperate for direction. My only vocational achievement was in the new sport then called skin diving. Holding my breath I could descend to the reef sixty feet below and stay long enough to grab two lobsters or spear a nice fish and return to the surface still conscious but seeing spots. It was this prerequisite that fed me in the Florida Keys and then landed me a job on a large sailing schooner named JANEEN (later re-named POLYNESIA). We carried diving charters to the Bahamas, Cuba and Yucatan. I lived and worked in a crew of six Bahamians and Captain Mike Burke, founder of the soon to be famous Windjammer Barefoot Cruises. We sailed ten-day excursions twice a month with about twenty passengers at a time.

Coming from a weak but traditional yachting background I was soon sailing as mate in the schooner. This was a position for which I was pathetically unqualified except for my white skin. I served only with the monumental patience of the ship's boson, a brawny Bahamian named Fred McKenzie. It was Fred who taught me the ways of a windjammer, and in time I came to regard myself as something of a swashbuckling sailorman.

Beleaguered by the U.S. Coast Guard for safety violations, Burke was soon obliged to base his vessel in Havana and fly his patrons over from Miami. I had enjoyed the diving and the people of the Bahamas, but it was in Cuba that I came to know my first real foreign port, language and culture. The first authentic Spanish lesson was taught to me by a young woman named Josepha, my mellow girl friend in Havana who worked in a laundry. The ship needed laundry services and, well, isn't that how it happens? With two, five-day dates per month, Josepha and I became an item, and I suppose we cut quite a figure together, the tall, long blonde-haired Nordic with the also tall, long black-haired mulata. She guided me through the wondrous old city, always with her thumb tucked into my belt in back and me with my hand on her far shoulder grasping her heavy braid. She proudly presented me to her friends who, like herself, were all destitute but jivey, and we sometimes enjoyed evenings with them aboard JANEEN. The Cuban national libation, Cuba Libre (Free Cuba) was then made with the very best of rum, and real CocaCola, the stuff that still carried a touch of cocaine in the old pinch-waist bottles.

Despite Havana's party atmosphere I began to fathom the plight of the common inner-city Cuban, who struggled daily but with good nature under Batista's military fist. There were armed guards everywhere, and the elite lived with big dogs behind high walls topped with glass shards, their gates, windows and doors all barred with steel. Even to a New Yorker like me, the contrast here between rich and poor was troubling, but not as threatening as the machine guns. To get to the water taxis, rowing skiffs manned by old men, for going out to JANEEN, Josepha and I had to pass the Navy building, an imposing edifice on the Havana waterfront whose four corners were decorated with dome-shaped concrete pill boxes at ground level. Each three-quarter dome had a continuous horizontal slot all around with the muzzle of a water-cooled machine gun protruding from the slot. The helmeted gunners inside, whose heads could be barely seen, had a 270-degree scope of fire, and they seemed to have been ordered to swing their guns at pedestrians passing by at any pace faster than a stroll.

During one of our layovers in Havana, Josepha and I traveled by train to the far eastern end of the Island to visit her mother. There in Oriente province, the country people also faced a daily struggle to subsist. In contrast with the high-rolling humor of the Island's elite, its tourists, bankers, pornographers and gamblers, a repressed but latent peasant anger was evident.

I had failed Spanish 1 twice at Dartmouth and now, as Josepha reached me with "the loving tongue," I began to sense a deep delight in discovering that a second language is actually an alternate reality, another consciousness, a different life. The new life I was experiencing with this vivacious-yet-steady Cuban woman was, compared to my struggles in academia, transcendental. Besides the intimacy and the carousing we shared, there was the percolating conflict between the Cuban rich and poor that I found deeply troubling, and the poor were more authentic, more lifelike in my view. These common people were both threadbare and generous, a paradox I had not previously known, and they spoke engagingly of living so close to the bone. This "two-tongues, two lives" aspect of language was unexpected, for never had I heard it mentioned in the halls of academia.

Big Tin Cat...

It was also in JANEEN that I found my first multihull mentor. Years later I would consider him the bravest trail blazer of all the postwar multihull pioneers. He is little known, even obscure in the multihull literature extant, and his name was Wolfgang Kraker von Schwartzenfeld.

On one of those diving expeditions in the schooner, Wolfgang joined our crew. His credential was that he had fancy camera gear and the Captain needed photos for a brochure. Soon I learned that he was also a good diver, and that he had crossed the Atlantic in his own boat. It is the details of this latter episode that dragged me by the nose over that Tradition Pass and into Multihull Territory.

I barely saw Wolf's boat in Miami, but was offended by its crude concept; it had two hulls! About 32-feet long, they were made of thin sheet steel welded over a pipe frame. Set fifteen feet apart they were joined together by a spidery bridge of welded pipe truss work, and this bridge was covered with wooden slats and chicken wire. The cockpit was a shipping crate lashed to the slats, and hatches led down into the hulls where there were tank-like accommodations. His hand-sewn sails were set on a crooked pipe mast, and the overall results had the weight of a big tin can. Obviously the thing had been built mostly of scrap, and when I asked Wolf to translate its German name, GERüMPEL, he said it meant either confusion or rubbish. This so-called "catamaran" honestly confused me. How could such a crude contraption cross an ocean?

While working in the schooner with this guy Wolfgang I soon realized that he was no phony. Initially he was flummoxed by the complicated rig of the big windjammer but in some ways such as in sail trimming and navigation he knew more about sailing than I did. The schooner jolted Wolf as much as his catamaran jolted me.

JANEEN was 151-feet long, twenty-two wide and drew almost fifteen feet of water. She had eight double cabins and a gracious saloon all finished in raised-panel English oak. There was a twelve-berth focs'l for the crew, a cushy deckhouse for the passengers, and a monumental Gardiner diesel engine with six separate cylinders the size of grease drums. Each had its own blowtorch for pre-heating the cylinder head, needed to start the great machine.

Rigged as a Marconi staysail schooner she had a 26-foot bowsprit and a very long overhanging fantail. Using a double-reeve wire halyard with eight parts of topping purchase, it still took eight men to hoist the mainsail on a steel mast 176-feet high. When wet, this mainsail, which was made of flax, took sixteen angry fists to furl. The rig was clean and modern for a ship her size but was still a proverbial cat's cradle of lines and cables. There were running backstays on both masts with four-part tackles on their whips, a working jib that was set flying – its halyard and sheets made of cable as thick as your thumb – and a gollywobbler that Freddy called "de sky blottah," for that sail surely did blot out the sky.

Wolf caught on quickly and we began to work well together shepherding the divers and driving the ship. He made more cruises with us partly because JANEEN was so sensational to sail. We were both repeatedly amazed by the power of this vessel; when close hauled she just knocked tradewind waves aside and when reaching she would schoon at 18 knots in a 20-knot breeze. Downwind she went like a train although jibing that huge main boom was a challenge which if not met with proper handling of the running backstays could result in dismasting.

On one of our cruises we booked a passenger named Jeannie Miller, a very game and becoming young woman who also took quickly to the ship... and to Wolfgang. They hit it off hot and heavy, and the three of us formed close friendships and a tight diving and sailing team.

However, our time in Havana made us wish for other harbors, other lands. We soon took berths in the ketch LA BRISA from whose mast I was to sight the providential Island. The yacht's owner, a German-Colombian businessman named Hans Hoffman, and the three of us were the only hands aboard. It was in this boat and this crew that I unintentionally embarked on a career-long voyage. As my account will reveal, it has been a passage through boisterous seas, over shoal waters often riled by the winds of tradition blowing hard against the inexorable current of change.

Our Triumvirate...

Three days after our arrival at Old Providence Island Hans Hoffman's business obliged him to return to Bogota. He was the Cessna aircraft distributor for Colombia, so he simply summoned a seaplane which took him away to Cartagena and left his crew alone for a month with the boat, the island and the islanders. It also left us with one another.

The people of Providence had a rich cultural and genetic heritage. Descendants of the British pirates who sacked the Spanish Conquistadors, who of course sacked the Aztecs, Mayas and Incas, these islanders were also part African and part Carib Indian. They had been rather isolated on this island since the days of the Spanish Main. They fished their wide reef, raised a few cattle, and fed their 'chickens coconut. Outlying reefs and steep shores almost surrounded their very real estate, but there was also an occasional white beach. Thornless jungle crowded the moist places, and unlike many small islands, this one indeed had moist places, even mountain streams, for its split volcano core protruded skyward just high enough to tear the bulging bellies of passing tradewind clouds.

With the yacht's owner away, the three of us now began to get to know each other. Both Wolf and I were tall, long haired and thickly bearded, our blonde manes bleached by sun and brine to pale yellow. But we were different in other ways; I was, and still am, lanky, with just enough meat to cover my knobby armature. I have a protruding brow and chin and small pale blue eyes that can hardly be seen behind thick glasses. Except for the glasses I'm told I look something like the man on the Indian-head nickel. I still talk too much, and back then I could be funny, even though I was running from adolescence and academia, toward something not quite yet identified. I loved learning about boats and the sea.

Wolf's build was almost skeletal, his rickets the result of malnutrition in his youth. His face was gaunt, and his deep blue eyes made him resemble some portraits of Christ. He was still learning English, so was often quiet, always considerate and willing to do anything for anyone. His thorough approach to keeping and operating the yacht, plus his focus and forethought, gave him a stolid worldliness. It also gave me and Jeannie great confidence in him, so Wolf was the acknowledged leader of our group.

Jeannie was tall and athletic, with wavy dark hair that swarmed around her pretty face. She had brown eyes with pronounced lashes, and eyebrows that were naturally darker than her hair. Her expression was remarkably warm, but she was running too, from an unsuccessful marriage and toward adventure. She brought stability and routine to the crew, and was as much a part of the boat as its anchor. All three of us were in our early, invincible twenties, and we kindled one another's ebullient optimism.

The islanders, who spoke both West Indian English and some Spanish, welcomed their visitors. They called Wolf and me Las Piratas (the Pirates) and Jeannie La Magnifica. They escorted us around, invited us into their homes, and took us out fishing in the local sailing smacks. Occasionally I had sharp sensations of deja vu in this place, to the extent that I wondered if in another life somewhere I had been an islander.

A Name To Remember...

Our days at Providence were filled with many undertakings. Wolf and I helped the islanders rebuild an old dock, and Jeannie introduced the local bakers to her sourdough starter. Hoffman had left a list of things he wanted done to the boat, like scraping the teak deck down to new wood, re-varnishing the masts, and painting the cabin sides and top. There was rust to chip and paint, and the hull's bottom had to be scraped free of marine growth by diving. But our evenings were relaxed, actually charmed. Sometimes we went ashore to visit newfound friends. Jeannie noticed that the Islanders' little board-frame houses, with their myriad cracks, emitted the evening lamplight to define them as giant woodcuts that were cut through and back lighted. On board, the ketch's main saloon was our private netherworld, a safe and homey retreat into familiar surroundings. Jeannie and I joked a lot, but that was the extent of our flirting. I was the odd-man-out in this threesome, so I made a point of giving her and Wolf the space to be committed lovers. Early morning was their time, so I often left the boat at dawn to snorkel or hike or fish:

I grab a grapefruit from the galley and a fishing rod, and board the dinghy. While rowing out to the reef I encounter Ricksey Higgins, a youth I have met ashore. Ricksey also has come at dawn to fish. He paddles a dugout canoe, and uses two hand lines at once. Immediately he begins yanking up little snapper. I am using Hoffman's sporty rod and reel, casting lures from our fiberglass dinghy, and catch nothing. Ricksey pulls his canoe alongside and says, "Das de wrong bait, mon. You gots to use rivah lobstahs." He gives me several of the pincer-headed grubs, which he says he has collected from underneath the boulders in a stream. As he shows me how to put one on the hook, a great black presence soars beneath our boats. I gasp at the giant ray as it swoops through a steep, banking turn, slicing the surface with one curling wingtip. It is followed by a seemingly endless, fine line tail that scribes the creature's track. The thing flies by again, banking to show its profile. I can see that its head is molded into a nacelle as part of its body, its body is molded into its wings, and its wings are part of everything except its tail. It is the most striking sea critter I have seen. Unnerved, I ask, "What kind of ray is that?"

Ricksey laughs and says, "Das de cow ray, gots a nose look jus like Bossy. Dey harmless mon, no stinger. We call dem searunner."

"Searunner," I repeat. "Searunner."

Never Seen the Sea...

Wolf's English, now that he was living with Americans, advanced to the point where he too could tell jokes. In the lamplight of the cabin, with the day's work done and the dishes washed, I talked about my early childhood on a Wyoming ranch, a Vermont farm, and later in New York City. I lamented my wasted years at school but confessed guilt for having let my parents down. "They so hoped I would succeed at business school," I said, "and here I am, wandering the Caribbean as a boat bum. Well, I've never had a greater feeling of belonging in my life."

Jeannie downplayed her past in Miami as a married commercial artist and confessed she had booked passage in the big schooner immediately upon finalizing her divorce. "Sailing is saving me from becoming a suburban matron," she said.

Wolf had mentioned little of his life in Germany, and I suspected his reticence had something to do with the war. At my request one evening he began to talk about himself. English was difficult for him, and his accent was thick. Jeannie had heard only bits of his past, so now she urged him to share his story. "We can understand you just fine," she said, "so relax and tell us how you came to America."

At first, Wolf's account was brief, matter-of-fact: "I vus youngest of ten childs. My family vus rich, and ve lift in Bavaria. Vhen I vus little, Nazis takes all za money andt all za landt, andt Voor takes all my family except my mozzer andt vun brozzer." His declaration made me feel that my own life had been almost synthetic by comparison. Wolf continued by explaining briefly that he had left from Holland in his catamaran alone and somehow made it to the Canary Islands, Barbados, and Miami where, as he said to Jeannie, "I meetet you."

Jeannie snuggled him and said, "Jim should know more about your trip."

"Where did you learn to sail?" I asked.

"In my boat."

"You didn't know how to sail before?" I asked with surprise.

"No, I never see ze ocean in my life until I leaft Hollandt."

"Now wait," I said, "I believe what you say because I know you, and I've seen your boat, but I can't understand how you could cross the Atlantic in that thing, and no sailing experience?! And why did you leave Germany, go sailing in the first place?"

"I haf to go avay."

"Why, Wolf? What happened?"

He went on to explain that when he was twelve or thirteen, going to school in Munich, he realized that he had seen the War at an age that made it very intense for him, but he didn't know why it had happened. He was studying French and English, and he read a French book about the War. He didn't know what to believe, and his confusion led to an interest in philosophy. Later, when working in a restaurant and studying philosophy at university, he was even more confused. "I know somesing is vronk. I know zere is more to my life besides vhat ozzer people sinks of Germance." After a difficult pause, Wolf continued in a very tired voice, "Zere must be somesing else in me besides kill and burn and hate, and vin and lost." He had to find out, he said, what other people are, and show them what he is. He implored us that he didn't want to fight anybody. "Andt za trouble is, Jim, za more I findet out, za more I know some people sinks of me the same I sinks of Hitlah!" He covered his face with his hands.

"Nobody could think of you that way," said Jeannie, comforting him.

We all were quiet for a long moment. Then Wolf said, from behind his hands, "I cannot liff viss ziss. So I tell myself to go andt show ozzer people vhat I am." He made a muffled sigh, which ended in a barely audible "Ach." Then, "So, here I show you vhat I am."

"I know what you are," said Jeannie, putting her arms around him and her head against his chest. Wolf returned her embrace, quaking back emotion.

"So do I," I said. "You are our friend." Jeannie and I looked at each other, wondering what to do next.

Soon Wolf brightened, and said, "So I decidet to trrr-avel!"

I asked why he decided to travel by sea, and he explained that he had no money, and did not wish to beg or impose for hospitality. He needed a mobile place to sleep and cook his food, a habitable vehicle that did not require fuel.

"But why a catamaran?" I asked him, "Of all things..."

"I spend dace in Berlin Museum," he replied, "studyink boats. And I findet out about za Polynesiance. So I sinks, if zey can do all zat viss catamarance in Pacific, why can't I do same sing in Atlantic?"

At some urging from me, Wolf proceeded to offer an account of his voyage. He began by sailing on a pond with two aircraft wing tanks joined as a catamaran. He then found his way to Rotterdam where, with the help of an old machinist who wanted to travel but knew he never would, Wolf built larger tanks: the hulls of his hopeful catamaran. There on the banks of the Rhine, where there were other sailboats to observe, Wolf worked half time for the machinist, joined his new hulls together, and eventually outfitted the craft as best he could.

When at last he was ready to embark on his philosophical quest, the Rotterdam Harbormaster denied him clearance from the port. It was neither the construction of the boat nor the fact that Wolf had never seen the ocean in his life; it was the catamaran configuration of the craft. So offensive was the contraption to the Dutchman's nautical sensibility that Wolf was restrained from leaving. A spell of illness, which he sweated out alone on board, provided time for the authorities to forget about him. Once recovered, he left Holland by way of a side canal at night and, in stages, crossed the ocean to America.

The first leg of the journey took him across the English Channel to the shores of Suffolk. "I vas so sicksea zat all I could do vas let za boat takes me." Two days later, he heard surf at night and dropped anchor. Waking to daylight and the sound of knocking on his hull, he emerged from his bunk to see people staring up from below his boat. They were standing on the sand, and his boat was perched high on a pile of rocks. In this way, Wolf learned of the tides.

After weathering a three-day storm in the Bay of Biscay, he was run down by a freighter. "I vas asleep, but ze hit makes me, how you say?... Knockout? Andt I vakes up in vasser, but still in my boat. I put my sweater, all coveret viss grease, in ze hole, andt bails out, and zen comes anozzer storm for sree more dace, andt ven I am in Rabat, Norse Africa."

He was befriended there by a newspaperman who published his arrival (I saw the clippings) and helped Wolf with repairs. Wolf sailed from there to the Canary Islands. "Now I know how to sail, so it vas a goot trip." He was joined there by his brother Heinz, who recently had been released from a Russian prison camp. He brought a little money saved by their mother, and together the two of them made a neat 30-day crossing to Barbados. Wolf's brother chose to stay in Barbados, so Wolf, alone again, cruised up the Antilles to Miami. This was probably the first modern – meaning lightweight –multihull to sail trans-Atlantic.

The spell of Wolf's account prevailed for long moments in our silent, lamp-lit cabin. Jeannie and I were dumbstruck.

Moonsing...

Suddenly we heard a drum and someone singing. We scrambled for the deck, where the music seemed to be coming from everywhere, reverberating softly from around the quiet little bay where LA BRISA lay anchored. Soon it seemed the sound's source was to seaward. Looking out, our eyes were led along a dense avenue of flashbulb-popping wavelets toward the moon. Brightening as it narrowed away, this path appeared blocked by a barricade at its far end, where hollow swells rose up and collapsed on the reef, their curling crests topped by veils of cold, silver steam. The soft rattle of that surf mingled with the song, and everything else was ink. Then, as if entering by a side street, a little silhouetted smack slid out onto the glitzy thoroughfare, its translucent patchwork sails metering the moon according to their many weights of rag. Protruding from the vessel's sheer were several figures moving to the beat, heads swaying, hands clapping. There came the straight glint of a bottle being raised. "Let's invite them over," Jeannie said excitedly. Wolf reached inside the hatch to the switch panel and flashed the mast lights. We waited.

"Here they come... they're coming!" Jeannie said. I ducked below to get our bottle of rum. It was not where I thought it would be, and by the time I found it and regained the deck, a wet rope was thrown up to Wolf, a sail came sliding down, and LA BRISA was boarded.

The music never stopped. While the drummer climbed up, handclapping held the beat. Singing kept the melody as a battered guitar was passed between the lifelines. There must have been ten islanders, but some stayed aboard the smack to bail, scooping phosphorescent bilge water from between the ballast stones. All sang and swayed together, including the bailers, who discharged their glimmering result exactly on the downbeat, giving swish to the rhythm like cymbals teased with the brush. I removed the bottle's cork, tossed it overboard, and passed the rum around.

Everyone on deck was dancing. Some islanders went below to look around, passing through the yacht's interior while wiggling in time.

Through the music they all spoke with us a little, and when I asked a young woman if they did this often, she said, "Oh yes! We alltime moonsing when de weddah nice." And then she asked me, "Which pirata you be?"

"What?"

"Ah haa! I means, what be yo name, sweet honey?"

"I be Jim," I said, and we danced.

"I be Eeeve-alyn," she said in a soft voice, spinning herself completely around slowly, fetchingly. "An' you, mistah Jimsieboy, you mus comalong moonsing wiff me sometimes." I was kindled by her advance, for she was a long-limbed siren. "But tonight," she concluded, "dat lil bow-ut be fullup, an' leakin'? Baahd! Ha-hHaaaa! Oh, sweet honey..."

The song wandered as aimlessly as the dancers, all changing partners, with same-sex couples common but Jeannie popular with the island men. They wandered through and over the ketch as random solos were sung for each verse, often repeated. But everyone joined the chorus as if it were an anthem. Before the bottle was empty, they left as theatrically as they had come, singing, "Way-up Suzyanna, Prov-i-dence is de place where I belongs in. Roun' de bay of Prov-i-dence."

Seafall...

Back in the cabin, we now finished the rum, and dwelled deeply in the spell left by our visitors. "What a great way to live, this cruising life," I volunteered. "Times like that, with relative strangers? We couldn't ask for more."

Wolf added, "Zat's why I trrr-avel for. Ve all show zem vhat ve are, and zey show us what zey are. Nussing fake in between. Ve are velcome on za islandt, and zey are velcome on za boat. Ve all haf boat andt ocean, moon andt vindt. Iss rrr-eal life!"

After a time, Jeannie said, almost apologetically, "If there's one thing wrong with this life, it's that this boat belongs to someone else. Hoffman is a good enough guy all right, to leave us with his beautiful yacht. And he says we're going to sail to all those great places, like those Islands off of Panama where the women paint their bodies. And that old walled city in Colombia. Well, I hope we get there, but let's face it, we may not. After all, we really are nothing but his floating domestics, and he's apparently got a lot of other things on his mind. We're not really free. I get the feeling we need a boat of our own."

Wolf said nothing, but dragged out his sketchpad and turned up the lamp. He was always drawing something, usually a boat. After a moment he said, "Ze only sing vrongk viss my catamaran is it needs anozzer boat in between."

We all laughed, not understanding what he was trying to say, so I said to Jeannie, “Here we are, in the cabin of this juicy yacht, anchored in what must be about the nicest cove on the nicest island on earth, with the whole scene to ourselves, and yet you’re telling us we're not really free?“

“Not the way we would be in our own boat,” she replied. “There would be nothing like that kind of freedom.”

“I vus really free on my catamaran,” said Wolf, “Decidet everysing myself. But I vus alone for a longk time. I always vantet someone to share my travelingk.” He grinned at Jeannie.

“Okay,” I said, “Jeannie has expressed an outrageous idea. It’s very appealing. But how the hell are we going to get our own boat?” I looked at Wolf's sketch and chuckled.

"Vhat ze hell you laughing at for?" he asked, chuckling too.

"Vhat ze hell you drawing at for?" I replied.

Showing his sketch to me, and speaking with guttural, trilled rr's, he answered, "Trri-marran." We all crowded around the drawing.

“Ve must built zis sing out of fiberglass,” he concluded.

When three logs burn together, their individual heat radiates to the others, and they make a conflagration. The "triple cat," as it was called at times that night, was sketched out and sketched over again and again. The fanciful boat was designed by committee, and so not finalized, but at least we made a plan of action. When we got back to Miami, Jeannie would get on with the airlines as a stewardess and save money. Wolf would return to Germany, finally responding to repeated requests from the TV station that had provided his camera equipment. He would submit to interview shows, and save money. I would go to somewhere to work in a boat factory and learn about the new stuff called fiberglass, saving money. And when we were ready, we would all meet again in Miami to build our boat.

Even though the plan itself was brainstormed, hypothesized, fantasized and then left hanging in mid air, our commitment was cast in concrete. We would build our own "trrimarran" and really go sailing. We didn't know how or where or when, but we knew why; because we wanted to be free, really free, in a way we had only now begun to understand. And now we knew we could.

The Promise...

So enrapt was I by this notion that I couldn’t sleep. I went back on deck, to watch the moon glitter on the steaming swells. Of course! Anyone could build a boat and hit the briny trail. I had just never realized it. But I tried to be realistic. The prospect of the three of us hanging together, and pulling off such a caper over time, seemed fanciful. I was odd man out in our crew, and needed my own companion, but there weren't many girls like Jeannie in the world. Poor Josepha would be challenged by this life. and even if I should find a mate, then what? Two couples on a small boat? Not likely for long.

But so what? If we couldn't pull it off together, I resolved to pull it off alone. I could learn about building boats! I could learn about triple cats! If Wolf could do it, without any experience at all, I could do it myself. Feeling the forging die of fate smack down upon my being, I muttered to the moon, "And I will, dammitall, I will!"

....

Illustrations for this chapter, narrated by the author, are available online at ...
www.OutrigMedia.com/books/atm-volume-one.html

“Conversations With Jim Brown”

Multihull Nautical History & Lore From a Master Storyteller

Discover the tales behind 20th century’s multihull revival, visit historic ports around the globe, and sail on waves aboard classic vessels ... whether riding in your car or simply relaxing at home!

Multihull pioneer Jim Brown personally narrates and also engages in conversations with other designers, sailors and boat builders from the past 50 years – including historic figures within the movement. These fascinating recorded audio discussions will open up your understanding of multis and the unique heritage shared by “multihullers” on oceans and inland waterways throughout the world.

Topics include:

- **Sailing Stories** - cruising the world, favorite destinations, unforgettable experiences, adventures & famous boats ...
- **Multihull Development** - who were the pioneering designers, what attracted them to multis, reasons why certain models were created & notable design features ...
- **Spartan Cruising On A Budget** – low-cost blue-water travel around the world ... before high-tech, high-dollar yachts (or even GPS and long-range satellite communications), family situations at sea, in search of one’s own “Shangri La” ...
- And much more!

These conversations are being recorded and made available to multihullers around the world in downloadable mp3 audio format.

For more information on how to listen to these historic multihull audios, visit www.OutRig.org or www.OutrigMedia.com today!

3

THE SKIPPER

1957 > 59

Sausalito, as seen from out in San Francisco Bay, first appears as a scruffy harbor front town, but on closer examination the waterfront marinas are stretched beneath a classy bedroom community that clings to the steep slopes of an often fog-capped mountain ridge. To the south, which is on the far left, there are two huge, disembodied towers that thrust above the fog. They are festooned with great cables that swoop down into cloud. It is The Golden Gate Bridge.

My deal with Wolf and Jeannie was that I would learn about fiberglass. We wanted to build our own boat of this then new material, and not a lot was known about how to work with it in larger craft. I heard that there was only one company in the United States using fiberglass to build a substantial cruising sailboat. it was located in Sausalito, California, a town just north of the Golden Gate that I'd never heard of. I arrived there in the summer of 1957 having crossed the country by motorcycle, and was promptly hired on at the Coleman Boat and Plastics Company.

Factory work was a jarring contrast for a boat bum but it proved to be a crucial experience for what was to come. This company was developing a manufacturing process for the forty-foot full-keel sloop called Bounty Two. The original Bounty had been a popular prewar design by Philip Rhodes for traditional wood construction, and it had been adapted here for fiberglass as the pioneering Bounty II. The commercial premise was that molded fiberglass could take the requirements of experience and skill out of boat building thereby transforming a costly custom yacht into an accessible consumer product. To demonstrate this premise, Coleman's would hire unskilled labor; Embarcadero wharf rats, North Beach Bohemians and even boat bum bikers. Consequently, the firm was dubbed by its employees, the "Coleman Bloat and Spastics Company." It was a great place to work. The production process was developmental. Any employee who had a good idea was given free rein to experiment. Know-how developed there contributed much to the fiberglass revolution in boat building but Coleman's eventually went broke. I learned about more than fiberglass. I learned that trailblazers can easily expend themselves in finding the way only to have others later pave their footpaths with thoroughfares. The real skill in pioneering, as in business and life, is survival.

Sausalito was still recovering from having been a shipyard town during World War II, where dozens of Liberty ships and thousands of landing craft were produced for the Pacific campaign. At War's end the original harbor front land owners, two aging Portuguese fisherman brothers named Arques, inherited a mile of shipyard junk from the Government and promptly undertook to make a living from it as "unimproved" housing. Semi-squatters were allowed to set up residence in the old tool shacks and wharfinger's cabins and aboard the many beached hulks of rusting ferryboats, decaying lumber scooters and still-floating ammunition barges. Toilets discharged directly into San Francisco Bay. For thirty dollars down, two roles of garden hose, a propane bottle and several extension cords I set up housekeeping in a blocked-up landing craft, got to know my eccentric neighbors, worked at the boat factory and on weekends rode my BSA 650 on the nearby mountain byways. From my houseboat the view of Alcatraz and San Francisco was glorious especially at night and the Sausalito social scene was scintillating. For a while there I wished for nothing more but soon began to feel boatless.

The news from Miami was good. Jeannie got on with an airline and with her regular income she and Wolf rented an apartment with a back yard where Wolf was building a trimaran out of, yes, war surplus wing tanks. This was to be his means of returning himself, his cameras and all his photos and movie film (including those taken of us as a triumvirate) to Germany. He was to appear there in a long-planned television adventure series, and the TV station that had given him the cameras before he left Germany now wanted them, and him, back. He would be adequately paid. We were all performing according to the master plan hatched that magical night at Old Providence Island.

A few months later, Jeannie wrote that Wolf had launched his wing-tank trimaran and made a fast passage to New York from where the trade winds could sweep him across the 3,500 miles of North Atlantic to Europe. We eagerly awaited news of his arrival.

The Initiation...
At this time I began to learn of other activity in multiple-hulled boats. The first news was of small day-racing catamarans being developed in England and Australia, but the tip that got my attention was of a forty-foot Hawaiian-built catamaran named WAIKIKI SURF that had sailed across the 2,400-miles of Pacific to Los Angeles in 1955. The passage was made against the trade winds, and a real gale had developed in mid ocean but the upstart boat and crew had made the trip in less than sixteen days, a feat that was regarded as beyond human experience at the time. The designer and builder of the craft was said to be named Brown, Woody Brown. Like many traditional sailors I couldn't help regarding the whole story as bogus.

Then I learned that this Was not the first Hawaiian catamaran of seagoing size. There had been a 38-footer, named MANU KAI, launched in 1947 by the same Woody Brown. It was originally intended for taking tourists for joyrides off the beach at Waikiki, but the boat had also competed well with monohulls on inter-island races. This made me want to go to Hawaii to find out more, but I was working and trying to save.

Then came yet more word of another Hawaiian catamaran named AIKANE (Friend in Hawaiian), this one very nicely designed and built by a friend and associate of Woody Brown named Rudy Choy. It too had sailed across from Hawaii to Los Angeles, and its owner had asked to enter the 1957 trans-Pacific yacht race to Honolulu. All I heard was that he was denied official entry by the race committee, and so decided to "accompany" the monohull fleet back to Hawaii unofficially. Leaving hours after the proper entrants, this catamaran arrived off Honolulu more than a day before the official winner, a famous ketch more than twice the length of the catamaran. This was downright humiliating to the yachting establishment, and I now suspect the incident initiated the mono/multi schism that would become a divisive part of yachting for the next fifty years.

With the impatient tutelage of my shipyard neighbor Don Kogut, an assiduous student of yacht design, I now learned that this upset was nothing new. Going back as far as 1878, the venerated Nathaniel Herreshoff, dean of American yacht designers, had also been prohibited from racing his developmental catamarans against the spangled fleet of the New York Yacht Club. He had humiliated them once with his futuristic catamaran named AMERYLLIS and was promptly banned. That incident appeared to have effectively halted multihull development until after World War II. However, with this news of AIKANE and other activity in small day sailing catamarans I suspected that this time, multihulls were not going away. I had to find out for my project with Wolf and Jeannie, and for myself. In a fit of great extravagance I flew to Hawaii, met Woody Brown and sailed with him in one of his Waikiki joy riders named ALII KAI, And I came home dazzled but frightened.

Woody was a wonderfully affable host, ebullient, even effusively enthusiastic about his boat, and he gave me a demonstration of its speed from which I'll never quite recover. We left from the Waikiki beachfront, sailed right out through the surf while dodging surf riders enjoying the beneficent swells breaking on the outer reef. Rounding Diamond Head far enough to feel the gusts for which the Hawaiian inter-island channels are infamous, my first impression was that the boat did not heel to these gusts to spill excessive wind but instead stood up to convert all that wind power into raw, head-snapping acceleration. She went streaking through the waves like a seaplane on takeoff.

But she was cranky. In the hardest gusts she would not head up into the wind. Even with the tiller bar held hard down the boat kept driving off, actually running away to lou'ard despite the efforts of the crew. When pushed way beyond what I assumed would be the point of boat crash, with one hull almost flying free of the surface in this 38-foot boat, the sheets were finally released to bring the runaway under control. Woody and his Hawaiian crew felt this was the greatest fun, and expressed their joy rather vocally but I was shocked into silence. Beating back to the beach, I noticed that the boat was very slow in tacking, requiring that both the jib and the rudder be backed, and coming out of the tacks she was sluggish and aimless. Furthermore it appeared to me that her interior could not be made livable. Thus it happened that my initiation into modern multihulls was a hard hazing. I was frightened by so much speed with so little control. I just didn't understand what was going on. I later learned that the boat's behavior was partly explained by the fact that MANU KAI and the other Hawaiian Beach cats were just that; intended for operating to and from the beaches. Of necessity they had no keels and, most significantly, shallow rudders. Yet these guys had taken them to sea with historic results!

Neither was I taken with Hawaii. It was physically fabulous but too discovered, too expensive and too Americanized to give me the thrill of foreign travel. Of course I didn't see enough of it or stay long enough to give the place a fair shake, and I've been back since and loved it, but at the time I was too jolted by raw speed to feel a future for myself or my friends in Hawaiian catamarans. Maybe it was my schooner background. Looking back I realize that, like most initiates to this new phenomenon I was too well washed by my schooner experience, and its traditional maritime heritage, to identify with this new phenomenon.

Perhaps more than with other choices, when we choose a boat we select an identity for ourselves. I was still a schooner bum at heart.

Lost Leader...

On returning to my Sausalito landing craft there was a letter from Jeannie. Seven weeks had elapsed since Wolf's departure from New York, and there had been no word of his arrival anywhere. The Coast Guard had put out an "overdue notice" to shipping, but there had been no "sightings." We were both stunned. While we waited we continued corresponding but there was not much to say. The very thought of him dying in the sea was painful for us both and the hard part was not knowing. We didn't even know how to contact his mother in Germany or his brother in Barbados. It seemed impossible for him to disappear because his boat, even the pieces of his boat, could not sink. He was traveling in shipping lanes so it seemed the most likely disaster would be collision with a ship. We could not imagine him surviving without contacting us. This limbo went on for weeks.

I began to contemplate building a cruising boat for myself. With great trepidation I told Jeannie of this plan. I finally asked if she would consider a visit to California. She declined, saying that she'd had enough adventure for a while and was enjoying her job and her house. In the end we each found that the best way to recover from having lost our leader was to pursue our individual lives in earnest.

(I lost track of her then and have not seen or heard of her since. Jeannie Miller, if you're reading this, where are you? As described in Volume Two, it was 35 years before I would see Wolfgang again. No photos of our earlier time together had survived his wing-tank capsize in the North Atlantic.)

The Ancients...

My multihull education continued. Don Kogut undertook to clue me in on their historical background, and I soon realized that multihulls emerged very much within a global context. Long before the time of Christ, Pacific mariners devised the three basic multihull configurations still in evidence today. These vessel types now are called catamaran, trimaran and proa. All utilize two or three very narrow hulls, originally dugout or even solid logs, so narrow that they are easily driven even through rough water. One such narrow hull alone would be unstable (tippy) even while at rest, so the ancient architects spaced at least two of them wide apart and joined them together with outrigger beams and platforms. With this arrangement and much development they achieved vessels having good seakeeping properties combined with remarkable speed and, coincidentally, safety. These vessels were composed entirely of vegetable fiber and so could not sink even if flooded, capsized or dismembered.

I was quite amazed by what the ancients had done with these boats. Kogut gave me things to read that described how the early Polynesians and Micronesians made planned voyages of thousands of miles exploring much of the Pacific basin. In this vast wilderness, by far the largest single space on Earth, they colonized all the habitable islands thereby disbursing themselves over a wider area of the planet than any other race in their time. Much of this migration transpired during the same era, (the first and second millennia B.C.) in which the Phoenicians, the earliest European seafarers, felt their way around Africa in monohulls, always within sight of land. Our own rich maritime tradition is largely euro-based, yet if "traditional" means old, multihulls are the most traditional of all seafaring watercraft. However, the Pacific vessel types were (and still are) poor load carriers. Their narrow hulls easily outsailed the ponderous square-riggers in which the first Europeans arrived in the Pacific in the mid 1600's, but the multi's could not support the weight of cargo and cannon. If they could have, we might not be speaking English today.

Multihulls of ancient design are still operating now in the Pacific and Indian Ocean Islands – even as far west as the east coast of Africa. These stone-age craft, amazing lash-ups of sticks and string, were seen sailing on atoll lagoons at motorboat speeds by servicemen during World War II. To some extent the modern multihull was born as just another of the cross-cultural exchanges resulting from that war.

As early as 1662 there had been efforts to update the ancient Pacific multihulls but not until the decade beginning with 1945 did the essential ingredient of "modern" multihulls appear. Working more or less independently, inventors in such far-flung locations as Hawaii, Britain, California and Australia all struck upon the component that had not been present in the type since the Stone Age; it was light weight. Many of the ancient multihulls were wonderfully light for the materials and tools available to their builders, but the advances in materials science during WW II now became commonly and inexpensively available to anyone. Things like plywood, fiberglass, light metals, waterproof adhesives, synthetic fibers for sails and cordage, and stainless steel rigging wire... All combined to bring unprecedented strength, lightness, stiffness and efficient use of wind power to these sprawling seacraft. Now the postwar pioneers were in position to literally re-invent the multihull and make it "modern." A smattering of experimenters – unregulated and often untrained and so unfettered by the constraints of traditional marine architecture – began to apply to multihulls what they knew of aeronautics, mechanical engineering and the new materials But it took more than materials and experimenters. Let's pick up the story again in 1957:

"Live Buoyancy To Loo'ard"...

Arthur Piver ("rhymes with diver") began sailing in his youth aboard his father's fine 60-foot schooner Eloise. In his teens, the vessel traveled to Hawaii where he was attracted to the single-outrigger surfing canoes of Waikiki. Art became an avid surf rider in the days of wooden surfboards and he believed that the growing popularity of surfing was going to be responsible for the coming of an age where young people were no longer afraid of the ocean. "I grew up knowing that a big wave was something to be enjoyed," he said.

In his mid forties Piver built a small sailing catamaran from one of the many kits offered by Skip Creger, who is acknowledged as a true multihull trailblazer. However, Piver said of his first catamaran, "The thing would go like stink on a reach, but it wouldn't come about, wouldn't go to windward, and was prone to diving the lee bow. It would trip on its own nose, and its upwind stern would somersault diagonally over its downwind bow. I thought I could do better than that."

He subscribed to the journal of the Amateur Yacht Research Society (AYRS), a grapevine for watercraft inventors worldwide. Piver learned there of the work of one Victor Tchetchet, an eccentric, jovial Russian artist and boating hobbyist living in New York. As early as 1945, Tchetchet built the first of several boats that may be called modern sailing trimarans. (Tchetchet coined the term "trimaran" (long before Wolfgang used "trrri-maran" that night at Providencia. "Catamaran" apparently descends from the Austronesian "katu maram" meaning logs joined together). Dr. John Morwood, director of the AYRS, offered certain recommendations to Piver on how the trimaran configuration might be improved, and Piver realized from his catamaran experience that the outrigger hulls of Tchetchet's boats were not long and buoyant enough to resist diving the downwind bow. In a succession of almost frenzied experiments during 1956-7 Piver and his friend Fred Jukich built and tested several small prototypes thereby arriving at the basic trimaran configuration still in use today. His 16-foot Frolic had long, very buoyant bows on its outboard "float" hulls, a serious dagger board to resist side slipping leeway when going to windward, and shallow ends on its main hull to facilitate turning. The float hulls were mounted rather high to barely touch the water's surface when the boat was turning head-to-wind while tacking, and this greatly improved maneuverability. There was a deep vertical rudder for crisp steering, and the mast and sails were mounted rather well aft on the vessel to further discourage depressing the bows. This craft was crudely built of plywood, glue and nails, and its mast was made of a discarded TV antenna. Sails were made of transparent plastic film stuck together with tape, and the hulls were painted with a mixture of leftover house paint, "vomit yellow."

But this was essentially the "perfect" double outrigger canoe. With a reference from Don Kogut I contacted Art Piver and sailed in this boat. I was amazed by its ability to ram right through the raucous conditions in the Golden Gate. San Francisco Bay has about the strongest sailing winds, day in and day out, of any sailing center in the world. This wind, when blowing against the roaring tides of the Gate, sets up a chop that looks like little Matterhorns; the waves are steep, very close together, and have three sides on them. When they break, their crests fall down all three sides at once and are seemingly replenished like fountains from within. Piver's little Frolic could go bashing through that stuff at alarming speed under complete control. It was like dirt-bike racing over knee-deep potholes, but this collection of little plywood boxes held together. And it was responsive, forgiving and fun! Perhaps most important it was inexpensive. Weighing only 200 pounds it was light enough to be manhandled on the beach or on a trailer and it could be built by a clever scrounger for about a dollar per pound.

Because Piver and I both had schooner backgrounds we had something to talk about besides these little trimarans. I told him of my time in the Caribbean, and he remarked that I was the first experienced sailor to be attracted to his work; we were copasetic from the start. I was a bit put off by his persistence in calling monohulls "ordinary boats," and by his branding of ballast keels as "technical absurdities," but I began to understand the multihull concept in his terminology "live buoyancy to loo'ard." He explained, "Instead of gaining stability by carrying a huge pendulum underneath the boat, which does more to pull it down than stand it up, we've got the loo'ard float lifting up. It's live buoyancy instead of dead weight. Of course, catamarans operate on the same principle, but they're narrower overall than trimarans, They need two centerboards and two rudders, and there's really no good place to step the mast or attach the headstay. The cat might be faster on some points of sail, but the trimaran is more intuitive to sail. It just makes more sea sense to me."

It did to me too. Perhaps because of my monohull background I liked the notion of a real boat in the middle with "training wheels" on both sides. After the worry of trying to sail JANEEN, with her fifteen foot-deep keel, in Bahama waters I was enthralled with the multihull's shallow draft. Right from the start I felt that its real difference was its unique combination of shoal draft with what I could see were exceptional seakeeping properties. (It is that combination - not so much its speed - that I believe continues to distinguish the multihull to this day.)

Arthur's demeanor ashore was that of a solid businessman and family man but once away from the dock he became animated and boyish, leading the way to a wacky brand of camaraderie that was infectious. He had a lovely home in nearby Mill Valley, two lively teen-age daughters and a very gracious wife, but no sons to sail with him. For a time there our friendship became rather thick, and I undertook to help him sell the rudimentary plans he was drawing for his upstart little vessels. We both felt like proselytizers with a worthy cause.

There were other Piver disciples early on, young men like Lauren Williams who eventually did most of Piver's drafting; Don Kogut whose light weight and quick sheet work made him Piver's crew in many small boat races; the Viking-like Rich Gurling who eventually sailed with Piver on many ocean voyages; and Piver's long-time "bosom buddy" Fred Jukich, an absolute wild man in a boat and no Mr. Milquetoast ashore.

Soon I joined this fraternity by building a Frolic for myself just to have a boat on San Francisco Bay. I knew next-to-nothing of boat building but watched Art and Fred fabricate their Rube Goldberg boats, and figured I could do as well. They knew little of working fiberglass so I was able to assist, which brought a level of permanence to our otherwise disposable creations. Soon there was a little fleet of these nifty new watercraft dashing about on the Bay. We all felt like we knew something nobody else had realized: multihulls really work!

From Sausalito the challenge of sailing in the Golden Gate is always available. With my Frolic I soon took up the practice, initiated by Piver and Jukich, of chasing inbound freighters through the Bridge, surfing their wakes at break neck speed while whooping and hollering to the dumbfounded crews of these huge commercial vessels. This kind of sailing soon suggested that a larger trimaran of similar configuration would make a very capable seagoing boat. We all suspected it but nobody talked about it.

When my paychecks from the boat factory began to bounce I took to building houses in the High Sierra. One day while working in the snow, the original commitment with Wolf and Jeannie came back to me strongly; I was seized by the desire to go back to the Caribbean and I had to go in my own boat. I imagined that by adding one more sheet of plywood to Frolic's sixteen-foot length the resulting hull would be 24-feet long, and that seemed huge by comparison. I thought it would be enough boat for a long mostly coastal voyage down the western seaboard to Panama and points east.

Returning to Sausalito I discovered to my surprise that Piver already had drawn a 24-footer but it was intended only for day sailing with a crew of four. One such boat had been completed, and he gave me the name of its owner. I contacted Carlton Eugene, an auto upholstery man in San Francisco. His boat was rather roughly but adequately built for $600 in materials. We sailed it out the Gate to Mile Rock and the Potatopatch shoal where conditions are often raucous. Carleton's was the first of Piver's Nugget class trimarans, and seeing it sail right through gruesome overfalls in the Potatopatch was all I needed. Feeling the bottom, these waves literally turn somersaults, conditions that would even razz the big schooner... except that JANEEN, with her fifteen-foot draft, could never get into the Potatopatch. She'd be lying on her side at the edge of the shoal half full of water with seas bursting against her windward bilge, her crew stranded a mile from shore.

Nugget convinced me that if equipped with a little cuddy cabin it could become as seaworthy as any small open boat could be. It had the great advantage of being beachable, which I took to mean that its crew could conceivably find refuge somewhere along almost any shore.

When I expressed this opinion to Arthur Piver he thought for a long moment and finally said "Jim, you know what you're doing, so I suppose you could sail a boat like that anywhere." It seems now that the seafaring trimaran marks its own conception at that moment. I rented space in Fred Jukich's sign shop and started building my Nugget trimaran. I did not know what I was doing.

A Doctor On Board?...

About four months later when the boat was half finished I met Jo Anna Holderby, a comely folk songstress and schoolteacher who was looking for adventure. Our first date was a calm moonlight sail in Frolic. It was a fortunate introduction to sailing for a girl from Kansas, and after that she could take anything. For me it was the most propitious boat ride of my life. "Jim-n-Jo" couldn't get enough of each other. In a few months we married at the courthouse, lived on a houseboat, launched our boat, christened her JUANA and began preparations for a voyage.

Before we shoved off in August of 1959, Jo Anna told her gynecologist that she was going on a cruise to the Caribbean. He asked, "Will there be a doctor on board?" She replied that she'd find out, and simply declined to see the doctor again. She said that if necessary she could give birth anywhere, and I agreed to stop anywhere when the time came. We would "make it" one way or another.

On this junket we were joined by friend Dick York, an avid sailor who - like each of us - simply abandoned his life in California to set off on an adventure from which none of us intended to return to Sausalito. When our other friends realized we were serious about embarking on this voyage in this boat, especially with Jo Anna in her condition, they made quite a fuss. One old salt said angrily, "You'll have to swim for your lives!" It didn't matter. Because we had the boat, the world's door was ajar and we could not resist. We sailed out the Golden Gate and turned left.

Horses And Bulls...

It is July, 1959, and JUANA is rushing southward in headlong surges down the slopes of big, blue-black water dunes. To prevent her from swapping ends, Dick and I are trading short, tense tricks at the tiller. Jo Anna, now in her fifth month is bracing her belly with her knees against the ceiling in her tiny bunk. We are all in our mid twenties, and all spellbound by what must be the most terrifying thrill on this planet... surf riding in the open ocean.

To us, JUANA is a little double outrigger, her center hull about as long as a limo but her cabin no bigger than a Beetle's. A real back yard-built contraption, she may have looked like a giant water spider, but she was built like a hollow plywood glider, and now she is truly soaring on the sea. We didn't know it at the time and we wouldn't have cared, but this is the first time a "modern trimaran" has ventured offshore.

Just yesterday we had sailed out through the Golden Gate and turned south for Mexico. Until this morning we have been locked in the netherworld of fog, dodging fishboats and navigating by noises. At first light I relieved Dick at the helm and we could see the great moro of Point Sur on the central California coast. From our position about two miles out, Big Sur now looks like voluptuous draperies, hanging folds of Earth in richly blending hues. The summits of the Santa Lucia range are being highlighted in silver by the still-occluded rising sun behind. The redwood canyons are still somewhat obscured by white vapors hovering in staggered strata, and the rounded ridges of this, the steepest coastal slope in the contiguous forty-eight, look like they are plunging into the surf. Zephyrs are increasing with the sun and finally are blowing the fog away.

By late morning now, a sunny summer gale is building through twenty-five toward thirty knots of very steady wind from dead astern. With plenty of fetch the waves are stretching out and mounding up. Most of their crests are topped by the frothy cornices that sailors call white horses. JUANA seems to play with them by almost backing up, letting them rush down upon her and then, at the last second, she simply sprints away. This causes us some consternation. It's not just her speed, it's the strange sensations that she sends to us. It's like riding in a fast elevator but the building is lying down and rocking end-to-end. As she lunges toward the trough ahead it feels like dropping from the top floor. We accelerate in a tongue-swallowing surge, but our speed through the water drops to nearly nothing. The helm goes mushy, the wind falls calm and the sails go limp, yet we outrun that snorting steed that canters right behind. What's going on?

Now we're slowing way down, like coming to the bottom floor, but our speed through the water is phenomenal. Spray flies everywhere, great fans peeling from the three prows. The sails slam full of wind, the steering gets crisp and we go bucking over mixed potholes and speed bumps in the long valleys between waves. Now she's going to try diving into the back of the wave ahead...

Ah! She never does. Time after time we expect to nosedive but the bows always rise again and sometimes we even... Yes! We are climbing the hillock ahead even as it tries to flee. We make the crest and perch – almost pirouette -- and then hurl forward "over the falls." Plummeting into roaring, deck-deep spindrift, we soon squirt out ahead to ski pell-mell before the roiling avalanche. Again spray flies... we're decelerating again... bucking again... climbing again... hurling forward again...

Tonight we are still surfing in the open sea and the sensations are not just confusing; they seem beyond normal human experience. It is overcast with no visible horizon and no moon or stars to steer by. I fixate on the red glow of the compass but the white horses all around have turned iridescent blue from phosphorescence in the water. Sometimes I am overcome by vertigo and its accompanying nausea as the boat convinces me it is soaring in long climbing spirals toward a red beacon set among tumultuous blue-white galaxies.

Dick takes over, and in my bunk below, the noise is terrific. The plywood hull, only one quarter of an inch thick, is streaking through spindrift that is just beyond my ears; it's like being inside a big guitar that is dragging down a gravel road. Lying on my back, arms at my sides with my hands against the trembling skin of the hull and my feet against the transom, I hear the waves approaching, lifting the stern and feel the crests slap my soles to catapult me head-first forward and upside down. The long surging dives seem never to pull out but instead plunge ever faster and steeper into weightlessness.

After two days and two nights of this we rounded Point Conception, called "The Cape Horn of the Pacific." That was not riding white horses, rather running with bulls. By morning we were all very tired but much relieved to sail into the more protected waters of the Santa Barbara channel. Jo Anna emerged from her crypt to eat a hearty breakfast and enjoy the ride. We all agreed that we were sailing in a very capable boat, and after some discussion now, we began to understand our JUANA.

On downwind headings she could sail as fast, or even faster than, the waves, and the disorienting fluctuations in boat speed, over the bottom, through the water and before the wind, were being caused by strong opposing currents within the waves themselves. Sailing in normal boats had not prepared us for this because the speed of most single-hulled vessels is limited by their wide, deep and heavy hulls. Except for some modern racers, single-hulled sailboats can neither surf with nor overtake the seaway. When observing the phenomenon of waves from such boats, it is obvious that water at the wave crests is rushing toward the troughs, but it is not obvious that water in the troughs is also rushing back underneath the crests. Finally it became clear to us that white horses result where these currents collide; crest water, pushed forward by the wind cascades over the top of trough water on its return cycle under the cascade. Our narrow-hulled – but outrigger stabilized, lightweight boat was running through both of these naturally reversing currents at about the same speed as the seaway was advancing over the ocean floor. There was lots more to learn about our little trimaran, but this was our first initiation into what would soon become a new kind of seafaring.

....

Illustrations for this chapter, narrated by the author, are available online at ...
www.OutrigMedia.com/books/atm-volume-one.html

4

YOUR BOAT IS GONE

1959

The foreground is cluttered with cactus and the background is a desert seascape. That's me there, lost. I am scrambling in scree half crazed with guilt, Jo Anna is not visible for I have left her sitting in hot sand two miles away, Dick has vanished into a wall of haze, and we are all stranded in Mexico without funds or boat.

After visiting Ensenada, the first Mexican port south of San Diego, we continued down along the desert coast of Baja California. It was August. The weather was hot. The wind grew light. We spent many mornings drifting in flat calm, made a little progress in the afternoon sea breeze, and sometimes managed to keep steerageway at night on catabatic zephyrs coming off the land. We had a light southbound current helping us along, but in all we were making very little progress. The reason was clear; we were sailing in exactly the wrong time of year for these waters but had knowingly chosen to do so because waiting for November's trade winds would have put us too close to Jo Anna's birthing time. We were foolish for another reason; this was also the time for Mexican hurricanes. However, ours was a coastal voyage and I assumed that if the weather turned foul we could always find refuge even if it meant beaching the boat. Our craving for the unknown future was irresistible so we had sailed despite good reason to stay home. Now the cosmic reality of Earthly weather systems and human gestation were disabusing our naïveté. At this rate we could not reach Panama before the baby arrived.

Early one afternoon we spotted an oasis ashore. There were fields of sugar cane and groves of tall date palms. A few miles inland a village could be seen. On our chart the place was identified as Todos Santos and we assumed there must be something cold to drink in there. In truth we were all desperate to get off of the boat if only for an hour or two. There was no harbor, just an open roadstead by a rocky promontory that separated an endless beach stretching northward from a craggy coast to the south. The wind was calm so there were no waves but a long swell was running. Occasional sets of heavy surf boomed onto the beach where we saw several fishermen working on their skiffs. As we surveyed the situation one such skiff approached us from seaward. Propelled by a lone man rowing, it came alongside and we saw several large sharks in its bilge. The fisherman assured us they were dead and he offered to take us ashore.

We anchored JUANA well outside the surf line in about fifty feet of water over a sand bottom. I had to join two lengths of anchor line together to achieve plenty of scope, but sand was the very best holding ground for our lightweight anchor. In the skiff we kept our feet well clear of the business end of the sharks while the fisherman expertly shot the surf. We were welcomed ashore by a very friendly group of peasant fishermen, but with no dinghy of our own I felt strangely separated from the boat.

We were driven by jeep to the village of Todos Santos which revealed itself as quintessential old Mexico with dirt and cobblestone streets, adobe and stone buildings, a sun beaten cathedral and reserved but amicable people. The place was remote, some fifty miles west of the district center of La Paz over a very bad road. The town had been a sugar center, now obviously depressed, so the locals seemed pleased to have visitors. We enjoyed our cold drinks and a hearty, Mexican meal at the Hotel California, a crumbling adobe structure of great colonial charm gone by. (Now restored, this establishment is popular with today's Baja tourist throng, but it is incorrectly thought to be the setting of the seventies rock song of that name by The Eagles... "You can check out any time you please, but you can never leave.")

One thing led to another culminating in a lively party in our honor. The participants came dressed in everything from fishermen's rags to colonial finery. There was music and dancing. The men encouraged Jo Anna to imbibe their very dark beer, which they maintained was good for mother's milk. For Dick and me there was mescal, the local cactus liquor. We spent the night in the hotel, feeling that our trip to foreign lands and real adventure had begun at last. We were right.

While having breakfast next morning we were greeted with surprise by a man who had been at the party the night before. He spoke English and said, "Oh, I thought you were gone. Your boat is gone." We raced back to the beach and stared at where our JUANA had been anchored the day before. It was now bare water.

A group of villagers had climbed the rocky promontory and were staring and pointing out to sea. Dick and I made to climb the headland to have a look for ourselves but not before Jo Anna stopped us to say, "I've got to remind you guys that our thin pack of traveler's checks is on the boat."

"Don't worry Babe," I replied with false confidence, "the boat's got to be someplace."

Dick and I left her on the beach while we scrambled up the goat trail to the headland's summit. From there the view up and down the coast was clear but to seaward it was blocked by a line of haze about a mile out. Pointing earnestly into the haze, one of the shark fishermen insisted he could see the boat. Neither Dick nor I could see anything where he pointed. Our English-speaking friend arrived with binoculars and even those failed to reveal what the fisherman said he could see. At this point I became suspicious.

The locals became insistent. They explained that this fisherman had spent his life looking for the fins of sharks on the surface of the sea, and that his eyesight was stronger than anyone's in the village. To demonstrate, the little man turned his severely weather-beaten face to me, pulled down the lower lids of his eyes, and stared intensely into mine with the bottomless black pupils of his own. His gaze was convincing and he said imploringly, "Ojos fuertes," strong eyes. He then offered to borrow an outboard motor for his skiff and take us to retrieve our boat. I was still suspicious. It seemed just possible that this could be a ruse to remove us from the area. I felt sure the boat had been securely anchored with plenty of scope in the line for these mild conditions and would not have moved by itself.

In the end Dick and I arranged for a double search. He went with Strong Eyes in the skiff and I hiked down the coast to search the crags and coves. From atop the next outcropping to the south I watched the skiff with Dick and Strong Eyes proceed diagonally southwest into the haze. In the big blind blotch now, I watch them disappear...

For the first time in months I am utterly alone. Scrambling over one cactus-studded ridge after another I am trying to gain positions from which to observe all the shoreline including the rocky points. I am hoping not to sight the remnants of JUANA churning among surf-scoured boulders. In the occasional cove I gape with intense anticipation at the beaches where our floating home might be stranded or pulled up safely on the sand. I cannot help suspecting that someone has taken the boat to where it could be hidden or looted. It is hot, I have no water, I am in sandals, and the cactus and spiny brush is everywhere.

Running and sliding, falling and resting, scrambling and running again, by mid afternoon I have found nothing and seen nobody, not even the skiff to seaward. The wall of heavy haze still hangs a mile or two offshore but the coast itself is baking in light with an eerie yellow intensity. The desert looks more and more like endless heaps of hot slag, and I am dizzy from dehydration and the gravity of our predicament. A corrosive sense of guilt pervades my consciousness, guilt for leaving the boat unattended overnight in an open roadstead, guilt for leaving Jo Anna alone on a hot beach, guilt for sending Dick offshore in a skiff powered by a borrowed outboard, and guilt for leading our expedition into the wrong piece of ocean at the wrong season. "Why!" I cry out, "What has made me do this?" Another ridge, another point, another beach.

Suddenly I feel the chill of dehydration, and realize the sun is slipping into the haze. "Got to get back before dark," I mumble, short of breath, and I hear the strokes of my own heart as a thudding vibrato in the words. On the return hike desert shadows soften and lengthen to reveal the earth's anatomy with relief. I am aware that I am looking at what our planet is really made of. Almost naked of natural growth and human influence, the desert's heaving conformation gradually reveals itself as charming, even lovely. The late afternoon light suggests an early scarlet sunset developing behind the offshore haze. It imparts a mood of intense serenity, even confidence, that I find inspiring. "People live around here," I say out loud. I'm thinking that surely we can live here too. Perhaps in time the boat will turn up somewhere... a fishing boat will find it drifting. On the other hand maybe a fishing boat has towed it away. I tell myself, "In any case we're going to survive!"

On arriving back at the long beach I find Jo Anna sitting in the sand, her chin on her forearms as they span her knees. In the rosy light we greet each other in a wordless way that confirms the boat has not been found. At least we are back together.

"I'm worried about Dick," I say.

"These guys spend their working lives out there," she replies. "He'll be all right."

"Have you been here all day?"

"No, the man with the binoculars took me to his house. His wife and daughters were very kind, but when it cooled off I wanted to come back here where you could find me."

"These people have been so welcoming," I say, "so helpful in our dilemma. I'm ashamed of suspecting them of taking the boat."

"Look up there," she says, pointing to the headland, "If someone has actually taken the boat, I don't think it could be these people. They are still up there looking out to sea." I can see several of the younger villagers up on the promontory. One of the youths is shouting in our direction. Something about "pajaro" comes to my ears. He cups his hands like a megaphone and shouts, "Como pajaro." Now they all turn our way, flapping their arms.

"What's that about?" Jo Anna asks, and again come shouts of "como pajaro."

"Something about birds," I say, and slowly the meaning comes to me. I jump and cry, "They're saying our boat looks like a bird!"

We gasp and exchange looks of incredulity, trying to readjust from our loss to our reprieve. I drop my shirt and sandals and run for the surf. Diving through the second wave I swim hard in the sea and in my head. When I am spent and treading water, Strong Eyes comes around the headland in his skiff; he is standing regally in the stern holding his hat over his heart. Dick soon follows sailing JUANA in a blessed evening breeze from off the land. I shout. He steers for me.

As JUANA approaches, the sight of her astounds me. Never have I seen a more breathtaking sailing scene. My bird, the red haze shining through her sails, is soaring directly overhead to put me underneath her starboard wing. I grab the wing netting and she practically yanks me aboard. Giddy with both exhaustion and jubilation I bellow, "My boat! My boat!" On the verge of breaking down I splutter to Dick, "Good for you and Strong Eyes."

"There's no way he could have seen this thing," Dick says. "It was at least ten miles out to the southwest and it was really hazy all the way. I think he just knew where it was, where it would have drifted on last night's land breeze and the southbound current. But we went straight to it and he still insists he could see it."

"What about the anchor?" I pant.

Pointing to the line draped in the netting, he says, "It's on the bottom here somewhere." At once I realize that only half the line is there, only one length of the two I tied together. "Don't tell me!" I wail. "My knot came out!" Flushed with chagrin, I grab my mask and fins and jump overboard. In failing light I search the bottom for the other line, thinking of how I had attached a "farthing weight" at the knot. Such a weight is useful when anchoring in deep water to sink an anchor line at its midpoint. This absorbs the shock of the boat heaving against the anchor in a swell. I had tied a bowline bight in each line, one square-knotted through the other, normally an extremely secure knot. But I had also hung the farthing weight in one of the bights, and somehow – I could not imagine how – the dangling weight must have opened the knot. That's the only explanation, my mind tells me. In any case she somehow went adrift, and without the night's land breeze to carry her out into the current, she probably would have gone ashore on the headland's rocks and been reduced to splinters in the surf.

"Wow, are we lucky," I mutter through my snorkel, totally unable to enunciate with the mouthpiece in my teeth. Then, "There it is!" Our other line is stretched out on the sand fifty feet below, its anchor end disappearing into the sand. I choke on water leaking around my mouthpiece from trying to talk to myself. I surface and cough and then shout to Dick, "Over here."

I hyperventilate and dive. Pedaling hard for the bottom and popping my ears all the way, I enter that spacey netherworld of the deep free dive. The gasses in my gut compress, my sinuses throb and squeak, and as I reach the line I emit a peeping little fart. On the way up I am pulled diagonally downward by the line. Realizing that I must veer toward the anchor, at length I burst through the surface gulping air and seeing spots. The line is in my hand. "We've got everything back!" I sing to the sky.

Well, all we could do was leave. We hastily arranged for Jo Anna to be brought aboard. She arrived in Strong Eyes' skiff with a full load of fishermen all wanting to see the boat. JUANA was quickly jammed with people. Despite my impatience with their curiosity at such a time I tried hard to be gracious. They appealed to us to come ashore again for the night but the lesson had been learned the hard way. I refused to leave the boat in this anchorage unattended for another night. Their extreme generosity combined with their obvious poverty had left me adrift in conflict. I owed them so much but was anxious to be away with our miraculously reincarnated boat. We paid shamefully inadequate respects to Strong Eyes and abruptly put to sea. Before dawn we realized that we had jumped from the desert's frying pan into the ocean's cauldron.

Forty Men Of Fortune...

I am standing outside the open door to the manager's office, my bathing suit dripping on his floor. In one hand dangles my mask and snorkel; in the other my swim fins. The manager of the tuna cannery is talking rapid Spanish into the microphone of a huge short wave radio. The replies are interrupted by frequent zaps and mutters but I hear the word chubasco more than once.

I wait, pleading to fate that this man will help us. Through the window of his office I see JUANA heaving to her anchor in the swell. At times she is almost obscured by breakers on the beach. When a big one bursts, clouds of steam are blown sideways by the wind.

The man signs off, turns to me, eyes the puddle in which I stand, and without a word of preamble from him or pleading from me he says in English, “We must to put your boat on de beach.”

“Yes sir,” I say. “It is very light, less than a car, no keel, but we will need some help.”

“We have forty men here. You come to de beach in one hour.”

“Oh, thank you sir! But the waves are very strong, especially the undertow. The boat must not be washed back out and turned sideways under the next wave.”

“We know this beach. You have long rope?”

“Yes, anchor rope.”

“Make it ready with no anchor, throw to men.”

“Ah! I see. We will be ready with the rope.”

“Good, one hour.”

I didn’t even know his name then, but realized that he was offering us salvation. Tremendously relieved but still anxious, I thanked him and headed back for the beach. I now noticed that the ramshackle cannery was pressed hard against the rocky spine of Cape San Lucas, the very southern tip of the Baja Peninsula. The tail end of this spine wagged past the cannery and each vertebra stepped off into the sea until the last three stood detached and defiant in exploding surf. Crouched behind the shelter of these earthly bones the cannery’s long wharf swayed on spindly steel stilts above waves that curled around the Cape but did not break until almost on the steep berm of the beach. Here they quickly reared and pounced angrily on the sand.

The bottom of this little bay was like a well, deeply scoured close inshore by currents where the open Pacific meets the Sea of Cortez. A hundred yards behind the beach atop a long dune there stood a string of houses made of mostly wattle and thatch. Outside the crashing surf JUANA continued her bounding dance at anchor.

More Blessed To Receive...

After leaving Strong Eyes at Todos Santos we had sailed all night in a strange slowly building breeze from off the land. We were going fast but there was no sea so steering was easy. Sometime in the night as I steered, Dick slept in the stern bunk and Jo Anna in the bow. I was muttering to myself. "What does `thank you' mean?" I must have said.

Jo Anna, her head just four feet from where I crouched at the helm, stirred and answered, "I was just thinking about that."

Surprised by her voice I said, "Didn't mean to wake you, Babe."

"I was awake," she said. "And I was thinking that 'thank you' means you can't offer much of anything in return for whatever it is you've just received."

"I gave them all the cash we had, for gas and all their trouble," I replied.

"You said thanks in the best way you could by inviting all those fishermen to come aboard and look around our boat. They know they saved it for us. It was a great gift, but sometimes I think it is more blessed to receive than to give. Especially if you receive it well."

"Yeah," I said, "our stopping there was a big occasion for them, too, and they couldn't believe I built this thing. If we could just have offered them something they really need."

"It'll be our turn to give someday, somewhere else, and we just have to remember them," she said.

Premonitory Signs...

There were no beacons visible ashore but before dawn the waves built up and I guessed we had passed the end of the Baja peninsula. Grateful for the wind, we continued steering southeast for Banderas Bay on the Mexican mainland. It was over three hundred miles away and this was to be the longest offshore hop on our way to Panama.

Looking eastward in the false dawn we saw only overcast, but to the southwest there was a crimson gloaming. Soon high wisps of pink appeared and then beneath them a huge squat tower of cloud that resembled an enormous stadium, its uppermost bleachers illuminated pink. Dick noticed a very long swell running from the direction of the stadium, its crests so far apart that when looking down the long valleys we could barely make out two crests at once. Jo Anna checked the barometer and quietly got out our dog-eared copy of the Sailing Directions for this area, written for commercial shipping. She began reading out loud:

"Premonitory signs of the existence of a tropical cyclone may be discovered from the appearance of the sea swells, the barometer change, and the clouds. The sea swell affords one of the first hints. At sea it is noted as a long unbroken wave, usually with a time interval between crests much longer than it is in the case of ordinary waves. In the tropics the barometric pressure and other weather conditions tend to remain the same from day to day. However, on the approach of a tropical storm the barometer falls slowly at first and then more rapidly as the center draws nearer. The appearance of high, feathery cirrus-type clouds indicates the outer edge of the storm. The cirrus clouds are often brilliantly colored at sunset and sunrise..."

At that point we faced a critical decision; keep running eastward for the Mexican mainland, or beat back for the tip of Baja? According to the Sailing Directions, the harbor at Cape San Lucas offered no shelter from a southerly storm. I was strongly tempted to run for the mainland and safe harbor but realized that by the time we got there conditions might be such that no harbor could be safely entered. I knew that by returning to the Cape we could probably get ourselves to safety ashore, but the only chance of saving the boat was to find help in putting her on the beach. The Mexicans had been unreasonably kind to us at Todos Santos, and I could only hope we would receive similar assistance at San Lucas. I felt chagrined for being their dependants, but we headed back.

Close reaching now, we had a building wind coming forward of abeam, but occasionally JUANA would catch one of the southerly swells and surf wildly upwind. This increased our apparent wind to the point of overpowering the boat. I feared mast failure, which would leave us truly helpless, so we handed the mainsail and continued under jib alone. After crawling for about ten miles against these now-manageable conditions we approached the dramatic rocks of Cape San Lucas and anchored in the open bight to their east.

Anda Le!...

Entering the surf I was thrown back twice before getting past the abrupt break line. On the way to the boat I realized that without the fins I probably could not have made it. Once on board I found that Dick and Jo had stowed everything possible in plastic bags, stuffed them into duffels and tied the duffels into the boat. We carefully trussed Jo Anna into all three of our life jackets, the extra two padding her abdomen. We joked nervously that she looked like the Michelin tire man.

Now we noticed that women and children were gathering on the beach. They were completely obscured when the waves felt the bottom and mounted up. As each swell ponderously lifted itself and then fell, it looked like a long gray warehouse under progressive-charge demolition. It collapsed deliberately from one end to the other in a long roar and a cloud of water dust that swept toward the cannery's wharf. Then the people on the beach reappeared and were soon joined by a gang of men streaming from the cannery.

Dick took the helm. I hoisted the jib only, pulled up the anchor and coiled one length of its line ready to throw. We tried to time the swells. We were all ready to bail out if the boat was hurled upside down. Dick waited for a set to subside and, with our hearts in our throats, pointed our bows for the beach:

All at once we are hurled forward on a wave so steep that it sucks out all the water from in front of itself. The boat pirouettes on the crest as Dick sculls hard with the rudder to keep us heading in. We are half buried in the crashing crest and our bows overhang bare sand. We strike and stop short, nearly pitching me off the bow. Spindrift surges over our stern and on ahead up the beach. I hurl the line into a forest of hands waving above the crowd of faces all urgently expectant; many are yelling out. Men are in the water alongside, now struggling to stay upright as the backwash digs sand from beneath their feet... and from beneath JUANA. She slips back, sinks down and begins to turn sideways. Men grab the crossbeams, the line goes taut, the boat straightens and before we can even jump off it glides forward several yards on the next surge of swash. She stops again. Dick and I jump out as the boat is surrounded by eager men who literally lift it forward and ahead, not stopping until almost clear of the swash. Tremendously relieved I open my arms to the crowd and holler "Gracias! Gracias caballeros!" Everyone laughs and cheers.

Now Jo Anna emerges from the cuddy. Free of life jackets but obviously showing, she nimbly slides down onto the sand. The only sound is of the surf and of wet clothing snapping in the wind. Then comes a collective gasp. The women exclaim and promptly usher Jo Anna aside while darting glances of disapproval at Dick and me.

Shaking their heads and exchanging smiling grimaces, the men surround the boat. Their foreman directs their positions at the crossbeams and along the line. At his cry of "Andale!" some eighty soaking sandals driven by as many soaked and sinuous legs begin to churn against the sand. The boat moves slowly but without hesitating up and over the berm. Picking up speed it leaves Dick and me running helplessly alongside as there is no place left for us to grab on and assist. Onward up the beach they drag and push our JUANA its V-shaped bottom plowing a deep trench in the sand. About a hundred feet from the dunes they stop, smile at us, and in unison walk toward their houses. Dick and I are left befuddled by our great good fortune.

Soon four of the men returned carrying shovels and long pipes. They each commenced digging a deep hole near the boat. Dick and I offered to dig but they declined, pointing to the houses on the dune where others were also digging. Some were throwing ropes or cables over the roofs of their houses. "They've been through this before," said Dick, "and they take it seriously!" Our men kept digging until they were in the holes deep enough to require throwing out the sand over their shoulders. They put one pipe in each hole and back filled. To these pipes Dick and I spiderwebbed the boat down to the beach with our anchor lines.

With the boat thus secured and its stout canvas cover lashed over her open cockpit, we were approached by the cannery manager. He introduced himself as Luis Bulnes. He led us to a small house adjacent to the cannery where Jo Anna was waiting. "You can spend the night here," he said. "Our maid lives here but she is away. I don't expect this storm to be as bad as the one four years ago, which blew the roof off of the cannery. Parts of it were found three miles away! But the forecast for this storm is that it will pass into the sea of Cortez, which puts us on its more favorable side. But you must be ready for anything. If this building is damaged you must try to get into the cannery."

"We were going to try to cross over to the mainland," I said. "Coming here has probably saved our lives and your men have certainly saved our boat. How can we thank you?"

"This place is very lonely," he replied. "My wife and I will be glad to have some company, but the storm isn't over yet.

But For The Knot...

During the long night the wind wailed and the clouds burst and the waves crashed with sufficient force to seismically shake the beach and the little house in which we sheltered. Unable to sleep, I once tried to reach the boat but quickly became lost. Pellets of briny sand were driven between clenched eyelids and into nostrils, striking almost hard enough to break the skin. Unable to breathe, I returned to shelter by crawling, holding my breath and feeling my way. Back inside I found my mouth was coated with sand, and I was forced to imagine the horror of being out at sea. But the wind finally abated and by the dawn's early light our boat was still there!

When I walked down to have a look at her I found that the wash from the largest waves had swirled around her just enough to settle her in the sand about half way to the water line. At that point I loved my boat as if it were a living thing. I also realized why we, and it, had survived. It was because my knot in the anchor lines had come untied at Todos Santos. If it had held, we would have left there early in the day and, with the favorable wind, been too far from San Lucas by dawn to return here to Cabo San Lucas. Heading east for the mainland we would have sailed directly into the path of the cyclone.

During the next several days while the villagers put their lives and houses back together we stayed in the maid's cabin as guests of Luis and his wife Conchita. They were sometimes joined by the local doctor, a young intern serving his obligatory year in the boonies. He was quite concerned for Jo Anna, saying that no matter how naturally she might give birth this was her first child and San Lucas was no place for her to have it. When she failed to become alarmed he became insistent and we realized that even though he obviously dreaded the responsibility of attending a Gringo mother he just might be right.

One day Luis asked me bluntly how much money we had. When I told him about seven hundred dollars he said, “Oh Jim, it is not very much. And besides I don’t think you should continue sailing on this coast at this time of year. These storms can come up quickly, and the Gulf of Tehuantepec, south of Acapulco, is a terrible place in these months. And really Jim, you should not go farther from the States with Jo Anna in her condition.”

When he left I remembered that seven hundred dollars was the amount that Jo Anna had cleaned out from her account at the California Teachers Retirement Fund. It was our only nest egg. That and our two close calls in two days made me face the fact that our sailing trip was over. My boyish dream of wondering the Caribbean with a never-ending stream of pals and gals was no longer tenable. I was soon to be a father, and my family was in a difficult position. Our only asset was our boat, and it too was in a difficult position.

But For The Gas Station...

Now that the storm had passed the weather was nice and I contemplated sailing the boat across to the Mexican mainland hoping to find a safe harbor for storing her there. But the wind was calm and leaving her anywhere was troubling. Any secure location was likely to be costly and I had no idea when I could return to retrieve her. Again Luis saved the day. He told me that out in the desert behind the cannery there was a gas station. “Go have a look at it,” he said. “Nobody has ever used it for anything.”

With nothing but concrete walls and roof – no pumps, no doors and no road – it was painted bright green and its big PEMEX logo proudly announced the product line to the cactus. It would make a great boathouse.

Luis explained that in order to secure a fuel distributorship, the cannery had been required to build the gas station. “This is Mexico,” he said wryly. I was glad of it. Furthermore he told of a secure storeroom in the cannery where we could stash all our belongings from the boat.

Despite my shattered dreams, we were set for returning to Sausalito. Considering our circumstances that didn’t sound so bad.

Unloading the boat and organizing its equipment made me realize what a complex undertaking it is to prepare even a small boat for ocean voyaging. We were faced with a monumental collection of clutter all of which had to be maintained and packed for either storage or luggage. Selecting items for the latter was critical, for when we arrived "home," what we carried would be literally everything we owned.

The Way Back...

Much of the road to La Paz, a hundred miles across the mountainous desert, had been washed out by the storm. After several days it was decided to attempt the trip in the cannery's dump truck. With Dick and six or eight locals in the back, Jo Anna and I rode in the cab with the driver. Even with the truck in its lowest gear proceeding as slowly as the driver could manage we were all severely jostled. Sometimes we braced our hands overhead to prevent banging our heads on the roof of the cab. Jo Anna brought her feet up onto the seat to support the weight of the baby with her thighs. She was now nearing her seventh month and we were very concerned by this jostling.

There was great damage in La Paz. Practically all of the stately palms lining the harbor front had been uprooted, and the top story of the town's most substantial building, the Hotel Los Arcos, had been literally blown off. But the hotel was open! We booked a room and Dick took off on his own for a walkabout on his return to California.

While the local airport runway was under repair, Jo Anna and I enjoyed La Paz for several days. Almost every night we dined on filet mignon at an unbelievably low price. One evening while paying our check in the hotel bar, I was approached by a young Mexican man who tried to tell me something in Spanish. When I failed to grasp his rapid Spanish he seemed aggressive, and I expected trouble. Finally he said in English, "Your wife is the most beautiful woman I ever see." Indeed she was glowing with motherhood and I was very proud to be her escort but again I was ashamed for suspecting the locals of anything untoward.

We made our way by DC-3 to Ensenada, by bus to San Francisco and on to Sausalito. Arriving there in late September, 1959, we stepped down from the bus with our luggage but virtually no money, no job, no car and no place to live. But we had friends! Jo Anna stayed with them while I hitched a ride up to the mountains looking for work. While I was with friends in the High Sierras, Jo Anna called to say that her water had broken and the doctor was going to induce labor. Friends kindly loaned me a car and I sped back to the coast arriving just in time. Our first-born son Steven arrived early; over five weeks premature. He spent his first few days in a glass box. Feeling deprived of our parenthood we peered helplessly at our son in his isolett.

But For The Foundation...

Otherwise these were busy days. On the first of them I found work at Bud Lowry's boat yard in San Rafael. They magnanimously advanced me two weeks pay with which I bought a fifty-dollar car and rented a fold-up bed apartment with a large closet for the nursery. On the second I went to work sanding boat bottoms, a nasty gig that was to bail us out more than once.

A friend who sold baby-care equipment gave us a bassinette, a crib and a feeding table, all "blemished" items which lasted us for years and which we later passed on. Others donated baby clothes, bedding and diapers (yes, the kind you rinse in the toilet, soak in a pail, wash and dry ad nauseam). When the big day came to bring Steven home from the hospital we were set up pretty well except that our medical bills were horrendous. We were referred to the Babcock foundation, a charity that loaned money to people distraught with medical debt. The Foundation settled with the hospital and in time we settled with the Foundation. Talk about luck!

With Steven's head in my hand and his body outstretched on my forearm, his feet barely touched my inner elbow. He lost weight at first but soon nursed hungrily and I marveled at his vitality. He was the primordial unifying force in our family. Today at six-two he and his son Noah are my best crack at immortality.

For "Jim-n-Jo," it was a little hard to give up our Caribbean expedition. We felt lucky to have apples and oatmeal but we were counting on mangoes and papaya. At least we were all together safe and well, and we handled the disappointment by planning how to get our boat back from Mexico. We suspected that its tiny hold contained some kind of private treasure, but little did we know it also held the makings of many other boats and expeditions.

....

Illustrations for this chapter, narrated by the author, are available online at ...

www.OutrigMedia.com/books/atm-volume-one.html

5

INAUSPICIOUS STARTUP

1960 > 63

A shallow fog has bright moonlight shining through. It's almost as if the masthead is in the clear, but from on deck we seem suspended in the center of a universal eerie glow. As we ghost along in this fluorescent cloud, suddenly we hear surf. Knowing that we are in the vicinity of the Tres Marias Islands we approach the surf sound gingerly, soon hearing a gentle swell breaking against rocks on either hand. Straight ahead we also hear the sound of wavelets sliding up and down a beach. Continuing as close as we dare, we anchor and retire...

Four months of sanding boat bottoms had now put us in a position to "go get JUANA." Sailing her back from Baja, a thousand miles against the wind, was not an option because of her small size and the time it would require. The alternative was to ship her back and we had no idea of how to arrange for that in Mexico, but it was clear that she must be moved from San Lucas to a shipping point.

I contacted my boyhood friend Russell Miller. We had done a fair bit of adventuring together, and he had recently returned to his parent's home in New York from a two-year trip walking, hitching and working his way around the world. His folks were hopeful that this experience would settle him down to a serious career but my phone call destroyed their hopes at least for the time being. Russ soon joined us in California and, with Jo Anna's complete support for this attempt, Russ and I left her with the baby and set out for Cape San Lucas in February 1960. We found JUANA secure in the gas station. Some poor Mexican had snipped a single strand of stainless steel wire from her rigging, probably for use as a fishing leader. I hope he landed a big one. Otherwise the boat was just as we had left her.

Again we were assisted by the locals in carrying the boat back to the beach; this time we could pay them something. We scrubbed her down, launched and re-provisioned. Luis Bulnes again assisted us at every turn. He suggested we sail to Manzanillo, a shipping port some 500 miles farther south on the Mexican mainland. Russ and I embarked in perfect weather, enjoying just the kind of sailing hoped for on the previous trip. I learned never again to go into the wrong piece of ocean at the wrong time of year, missed Jo Anna and Steve, and promised myself to give them a real boat ride some day.

On our second afternoon while surfing in moderate waves our lower rudder gudgeon broke. Hanging over the heaving stern deck to work below the surface I lashed the rudder to the boat and tightened the lashings by jamming a catsup bottle into them. Very fortunately, the lashing held, and the wind dropped at sunset. Ghosting along until midnight in that moonlit fog, we then heard that phantom-vision surf and anchored. We had only the slightest notion of where we were, but were blessed with calm conditions.

At sunup we found ourselves snugly situated in the center of a spectacular cove. Surrounded on three sides by a high escarpment, the beach was well protected so we decided to make a more permanent rudder repair by sailing Juana ashore. This accomplished, we played Robinson Crusoe for the rest of the day. I wished very much for Jo Anna's presence and again resolved that she would experience this kind of cruising. We saw absolutely no one but later learned that we had landed on a strictly forbidden, maximum-security prison island.

Our next stop was at Yelapa, a wonderfully secluded Indian village (now a bushy resort) just inside the westernmost promontory of Banderas Bay. It was our first sight of truly tropical Mexico, complete with mountain streams, a waterfall, coconut palms and proud, receptive native people. Pushing on we ran for Manzanillo in the most perfect sailing weather yet enjoyed. JUANA surfed almost continually among fat white horses all running at a gentle canter.

We found Manzanillo an agreeable place for a shipping port, and one evening we came together with members of the local 21 Club. After dining and wining to excess with them, we invited the membership aboard for a nightcap. Celebrating Mexicans crowded every square inch of JUANA's little decks. After operatic performances of bawdy songs, they departed and we retired. Feeling woozy at sunrise I arose to relieve myself and discovered one of the members had remained on board; he was asleep in our portside, severely sagging wing net with his butt steeping in the sea.

We were befriended by the skipper of a banana boat anchored in the harbor. The skipper was awaiting orders as to where to take his cargo. If that proved to be San Diego, he offered to carry us and JUANA, but he expected to be sent to Acapulco instead. One morning while we were having breakfast with him a board his ship he noticed a deep sea fishing vessel entering the harbor. He said, "Look! There's a big tuna clipper. She looks loaded with fish and she's headed for the bunkering pier. I bet she's going home to San Diego."

Once the clipper HIGH SEAS was taking fuel, Russ and I moved JUANA alongside her and were assisted in tying up by one of the Portuguese crew. We explained to him our need. We were told to wait, and while doing so we saw several faces staring down on JUANA from the ship's bridge. In minutes the Captain approached us and said brusquely, "Ah boy! You going home? I going home today. Cost-a me no more you come or you don't come!"

In this way we were offered a free ride for ourselves and our boat back to San Diego. Much relieved, while the Clipper was fueling, we quickly ran into town and invested our shipping money in a small truckload of the best of Mexico's alcoholic libations, loading the loot carefully into JUANA's outer hulls.

So that no shipping manifest was necessary, the Mexican authorities insisted that the clipper leave the harbor before hoisting our boat aboard. Outside the breakwater, the ship rolled easily in the swell while JUANA was suspended from its cargo boom. With me and Russ aboard the trimaran it began to swing wildly, its mast in conflict with the clipper's boom. In some confusion, the clipper's crew managed to rotate JUANA to clear the conflict, but she was bashing menacingly into the side of the ship. Fortunately no one was hurt and little damage was sustained... mostly to the wooden clipper from the trimaran's sharp, fiberglass-reinforced bows. We eventually came to rest on a pile of rope fenders on the clipper's deck.

The 160-foot HIGH SEAS was loaded with 180 tons of fish, returning after a relatively short expedition to Chilean waters. The Portuguese crew, homeward bound on what promised to be a lucrative trip, was extremely generous with me and Russ. For example, the cook had plenty of stores remaining and exclaimed to us, "Any time day or night, anything you want, steak, ice cream, whatever, you just let me know." After our steady diet of canned stew heated over JUANA's camp stove, we eagerly accepted his unreasonable kindness. The mate moved to a spare bunk in the captain's cabin so that Russ and I could have the mate's cabin to ourselves.

Over the next five days, as the ship plowed its way northward against steady wind and waves, the crew twice spotted flocks of sea birds in the distance, indicating schools of fish, probably tuna. Steering for the birds, rapid preparations were made for catching more fish. This was not one of the modern "purse seiners" that harvest whole schools at a time (including turtles and porpoises) with giant nets; rather it was one of the old-fashioned "bait boats" still operating at the time. These vessels capture fish by chumming with live bait and catching individual tuna by hook and line.

As our ship approached the school, rapid orders were shouted from the bridge to the crew. Large basket-like containers, made of steel frames and cyclone-fence wire, were hinged inside the vessel's bulwark. These were now swung outboard, outside the bulwarks, and the men climbed into them and stood ready with their short, stout fishing rods. As the ship rolled in the gentle swell, the men were sometimes knee deep in the sea and only waist-deep in the baskets.

There was a huge tank mounted on the vessel's stern. A hatch in its top was now opened to reveal millions of swimming minnows, which the clipper had harvested previously with its bait net. As we entered the tuna school, one man began scooping out minnows with a handled net and scattering them into the water to attract the tuna. The crew now began casting artificial lures. The lines were short (no reels). The sea now teemed with tuna and sharks, the air was macerated by birds, and all were agitated into a feeding frenzy. The steel baskets protected the men from the sharks:

Big fish are flying through the air! They slam against the high wall of the bait tank and writhe in the scuppers with shocking displays of energy. Yellow fin tuna averaging about 40lbs are striking viciously at the men's lures but the fishhooks on the lures have no barbs. When a fish is yanked free of the surface its struggles throw the hook instantly but the fish continues its flailing trajectory into the scuppers while that lure is immediately cast again and struck again by yet another fish that follows its predecessor through the air and into the scuppers. With six men fishing, soon there are a thousand pounds of prime food in the scuppers.

There is no "playing" the fish by the fishermen, for the catch must be jerked quickly away from the sharks. Now the size of the fish increase to the point where one man cannot yank them free of the surface. The crew is obliged to change to "two-pole rigs" having one lure attached by lines to two poles used by two men. In the delay of changing over, they lose the bodies of several big tuna to the sharks, pulling in nothing but the heads. Huge fish are flying through the air, slamming against the bait tank and vibrating violently in the scuppers. Eventually the men resort to three-pole rigs as tons of fish accumulate.

When finally the school wises up and dives, the exhausted men turn to stowing the catch in holds filled with sub zero brine. To toast their good fortune, Russ and I share with them a portion of our contraband...

Before leaving Manzanillo I had tried without success to contact Jo Anna. Concerned for our safety, she contacted the Coast Guard for any reports of our whereabouts, and the next thing she knew the news of our demise was on the radio and in the newspapers. As the ship approached American waters we were able to contact her by radiotelephone. Of course she was much relieved to hear from us but also much embarrassed to have sounded a false alarm. Over the radio, Jo Anna and I freely expressed our love for one another, this to the enjoyment of all within hearing of the marine operator.

In San Diego the customs inspector was much interested in hearing the story of our trip and considerately avoided inspecting inside JUANA's floats. However, in order to fit her onto a trailer for the overland hop back to Sausalito, I was forced to amputate the cross beams with a saw. Once home again with my wife and child, I spliced the boat back together and returned her to the water and enjoyed sailing her in San Francisco Bay. Because she had actually made a voyage, she caused a little stir among local sailors. Relieved of the responsibility and risk of offshore sailing, I began seriously to drive the boat hard for the first time. Unburdened by the weight of cruising stores, her performance was quite satisfying, and we took many of our friends, and infant Steven, for blustery rides.

Cats and Counter culture...

Jo Anna and I moved from the fold-up bed place to a classic houseboat at Waldo Point, Sausalito. This is now an ultra-yuppified houseboat compound; yes, since we were there in the 50's-60's Sausalito has gone seriously uphill. I went back to sanding boat bottoms but soon, with a reference from Arthur Piver, I was offered the opportunity to build one of his 16-foot FROLIC trimarans for one of his plans buyers. I opened a little boat shop in the Arques shipyard and thus became self-employed. Baby Steven was growing well, and Jo Anna and I took to parenting and serious socializing. One contributor to this cause was our supply of Mexican booze. When Russ Miller and I bought the stuff in Manzanillo, it was an investment, clearly to be sold at a profit, but in the end we and our friends just drank it all.

Piver arranged for me to write an article about our trip for the editors of SEA, then a popular California-based yachting periodical. In truth, our aborted adventure was a serious defeat for me because we had not made it back to the Caribbean, but Piver managed to turn it into a positive PR ploy, something he was to do often with his own setbacks. He was building for himself a thirty-foot trimaran, enormous compared to JUANA, and between my article and Piver's other writings, and his new boat, trimarans now began to attract some real public attention. At this point JUANA's ocean voyage had been the only one made in a trimaran, and because of this I found myself quite suddenly to be an instant expert in this fledgling field. This result was completely unintended and made me slightly uncomfortable with being a horse's mouth. But hey, Piver began paying me a royalty on plans that I sold for him, which was better than sanding boat bottoms.

His 30-footer was to become the prototype for his popular NIMBLE class of which many hundreds were eventually built. This first one he trailered to New York in pieces, assembled it there and sailed, with the help of two crew, to England via the Azores. It was the first trans-ocean voyage in a modern trimaran, 1961.

(To set the record straight, our 1959 cruise to Mexico in JUANA had been a coastal run, not an ocean crossing. The Hawaiian catamarans of Woody Brown and Rudy Choy had made substantial crossings in the 1950s, all in the Pacific, and Eric de Bishop had crossed all three oceans in a plank-built catamaran in the 1930s. Therefore, our trip in JUANA and Piver's crossing in NIMBLE was unique only in that they were sailed in trimarans.)

Except for the GERüMPEL of Wolfgang Kraker von Schwarzenfeld (Chapter 2), I knew nothing of what had transpired in the Atlantic. Again thumbing through Don Kogut's pile of old magazines I learned that in 1956 a young Englishman named James Wharram had crossed the Atlantic from England to the West Indies in his 28-foot catamaran TANGAROA with two girls for his crew. They had sailed almost literally in the wake of GERüMPEL. At 28-feet, Wharram's cat was very simply and inexpensively built. It was the first of his "Polynesian" catamarans, but he then had build a forty-foot counterpart, the RONGO, and crossed the Atlantic east-to-west in her in 1958, three years before Piver's first crossing in that direction by trimaran. Compared to the almost aeronautical "Hawaiian" catamarans of Woody Brown, which were intended for taking tourists for joy rides, Wharram's "Polynesian" cats were utilitarian, Showing sophistication of another kind, they were intended for vagabond cruising and living aboard. With their high underwing clearance and modest rigs and sail plans they were extremely safe. They were not nearly so fast and powerful as the "Hawaiian" cats, nor arguably as livable as Piver's early trimarans, but they led the way for the soon-to-come eruption of back-yard building of both catamarans and trimarans. Wharram openly practiced polygamy with his crew, of up to five wives at once, adding controversy to the mono-multi schism. The countercultural aspect of multihulls was to play an increasingly central role in years to come.

Back To Front...

With two exceptions, it was catamarans to first cross the threshold from back yard to front yard building. The first exception was that of Cox Marine in England who, in the very early sixties began producing in plywood the early trimaran designs of Arthur Piver. Following closely the plans that Piver was offering to individual builders, hundreds of Cox Marine boats were built and sold inexpensively. In my view they were little different from those produced by the back yard builders of the time.

Another exception was the early trimarans designed by San Francisco artist Lou MacQuillard. His small, owner-built trimarans were contemporary with Piver's FROLIC and ROCKET, and indeed were faster than the Pivers, but not nearly as maneuverable. Then Lou designed a 50-foot cruising trimaran, very beautiful and way ahead of its time, for quality production in Japan. But again because the effort was premature for the market, only one vessel was built and imported.

As it happened the first truly noteworthy, if not commercially successful, front-yard venture was achieved in catamarans. Beginning in the early 1960's Rudy Choy and consummate craftsman Alfred Kumalae were joined by Californian Warren Seaman. Warren was a very accomplished sailor who had helped develop the Malibu Outriggers, fast, tacking single-outrigger canoes (not shunting proas) built of plywood for operating off the ocean beaches of Southern California where there were few natural harbors. But Choy, Seaman and Kumalae now formed CSK Catamarans, and with the help of their friend Vince Bartelone, a gifted draftsman and artist, this group created a stable of elegant catamaran yachts for discerning, well-moneyed clients; actually the first true yacht-quality multihulls. The contrast between these boats and the owner-built vessels of the day was usually dramatic, and furthermore the CSK boats were fast! Their owners enjoyed competing in long-shore and offshore races having classes exclusively for multihulls. It was these fixtures in the Pacific, together with the trans-Atlantic races now being entered by multihulls, which set the stage for the blizzard of hard-core ocean racing multihulls soon to come.

Beginning in the 1950's there were also several hotbeds of small, day-racing catamaran activity especially in England. The Prout Brothers, working with kayaks and canoes in their father's Cornwall boat shop, joined two decked canoes with a platform and a sail, and soon evolved the Shearwater catamarans. These became the first production-built multihull daysailers and, together with the home-built Malibu Outriggers were the predecessors to the coming Hobie Cat phenomenon. Indeed the "beach cat" in all its many speed-intensive iterations (something over 200,000 vessels produced) has since become the most ubiquitous of small sailboat types worldwide.

Both endeavors, racing and cruising, were now on the multihull table. The common postwar availability of plywood and fiberglass was making it relatively easy to build the light weight structures for both types. Note that this materials-driven evolution was applied early on to both the sophisticated "Hawaiian" cats and their utilitarian "Polynesian" counterparts. Similarly the now emerging home-built trimarans all used the same materials and skills to build. Now the gem was showing all its facets - racing, cruising, twin hulls and triplets, back yard and front yard, daysailers and seagoers. These distinct aspects of early modern multihulls all emerged in the same period but in different oceans, and the emphasis on racing and cruising would soon trade between these regions but eventually become mixed and world wide.

Unseamanlike?...

The revelation in early racing multihulls was not very interesting to me personally. First of all the motive seemed to be nothing more than competition and I wanted something else. I wanted to travel, to cruise with companions, to live aboard and find the worldly freedom that I knew was latent, to a very high degree, in both catamarans and trimarans. Their potential for low cost owner-building and their shallow draft opened up a whole new realm of accessibility and cruising freedom.

Furthermore I was uneasy with the very notion of racing multihulls offshore. My reticence – call it chicken – stemmed from the belief that the multihulls potential for speed was best used as a reserve for safety. If the boats could go so very fast in such very rough water, it seemed obvious that simply slowing them to something like half-again the normal speed of an equivalent monohull would produce an exceptionally seaworthy, comfortable, and safe seagoing platform. Racing, on the other hand, implied that this margin of safety would be sacrificed to competition; the racers sailed without reserve. Nevertheless, in 1964 Piver was preparing to enter the first OSTAR. This was to be a single handed transAtlantic race run from England to America, across the north Atlantic against prevailing winds. I considered single-handed racing to be downright unseamanlike because at times the vessels must be sailed at flank speed with no one on watch! I wanted no part of this. Furthermore the multihull action in Sausalito was getting a bit cultish and we wanted out.

Mountain Boats...

When Steven was about a year old, Jo Anna and I moved south along the Big Sur coast to live on the landward site of that same coast that had first given us the terrifying thrill of surfing JUANA in the open sea (Chapter 3). The only place that we could find to live in this rugged, frontier-like region was a rather primitive one-horse barn. Located at the end of a precipitous canyon road, it was on the brink of the upper limit of the redwoods and just above the elevation of the usual summer morning, coastal fog. The place had been crudely modified for human habitation by the landlord's renaissance son. He had tired of the solitude so the place was now available for minimal rent. We moved in, tidied up and settled down.

We lived in a netherworld whose beauty and power were almost demoralizing. Today my phantom visions of that time swirl with straw-colored mountain ramparts, almost anatomical in shape, lying restlessly in blazing sun. The canyons were crowded by giant living columns holding up a dense boreal realm above a dim, shadowless and nearly naked forest floor. The steepest coastal slope in the contiguous forty-eight, this region combines plunging creeks, roaring rivers, dripping fogs, suffocating downpours and crashing seas with parching droughts, gleaming beaches, dark canyons and hanging mountains... all a cataclysmic zone of separation between continent and sea.

For us, a simple trip to Monterey for supplies and laundry involved 120 miles of driving on dizzying grades and curves, yet the vistas from the highway were so spectacular that we never tired of the trip. Our neighbors were living there for the region's natural beauty, and for the privacy its isolation provided. I think it was because we were a family that we were welcomed and accepted by these normally reclusive, frontier people. I began working for our landlord rancher restoring buildings. We were doing well on about $200 per month, largely because Jo Anna arranged our needs so as to require a trip to town only every three weeks, and because of the region's ready supply of venison. We had no place to garden but we made our own beer.

I was soon offered the chance – in this unlikely setting - to continue with my boat building. A contract came my way from one of Arthur Piver's plans purchasers, and the tolerant rancher, Ralph Newell, agreed to my renting a portion of another of his barns. I began building a boat much like our JUANA. For the time being JUANA herself was stored in Sausalito, and while I created her likeness on a Big Sur mountainside we reveled in our canyon home and delighted in Steven's learning to crawl. We didn't know or care that I was beginning the next phase in my unintended career as a "yacht designer."

The Fear Fighter...
Living in a barn was sometimes cold and dank, but it had certain advantages. When the weather was nice we could open the barn door, thus exposing one whole side of the house to the great outdoors. A level patch of ground had been hand-graded just outside the door, to form a small patio, the cut lined with stonework. The area was ideal for enjoying a bit of repose beneath the pungent bay laurels while looking right into the upper canopy of redwoods whose roots were far below. Before the morning fog cleared we looked out upon its sunlit top, a gleaming "snowfield" smothering the sea. It did not smother the sound of the surf, which nibbled at our mountain some seven hundred feet below.

One morning before the fog had completely cleared from the forest, our dog Bosco (a 105 Lb. German Shepard/coyote cross) dove off the patio and raised holy hell in the fog below. In the ruckus we heard a heavy scrambling, and soon made out two men climbing on hands and knees, apparently mindless of the dog, straight up toward our place. Jo Anna took the baby inside and I propped my trusty rifle inside the barn door. Soon two young men bounded over the edge of the patio, breathless, and seemed for the first time to notice Bosco; his alarm barking now changed to menacing growls as he awaited some word from me.

"Are you Jim Brown?" one of them asked. I nodded. "We want to talk to you about trimarans."

In this way, Jo Hudson and I came together for a friendship that has spanned fifty years so far. It has included lots of collaboration over Jo's inimitable cartoons as published in my boating books, and it has involved not yet enough sailing together in his seven trimarans of my design. It has also contained perhaps a bit too much rowdy fun. Jo has done a lot more sailing than I have, crossing the Pacific some six times to experience the seasteader's life in such places as Hawaii, the Marquesas Islands, Fiji, Tahiti, Australia and the New Hebrides (now Vanuatu). With the exception of Hawaii, I have never sailed to any of these destinations.

At the time of our meeting, Jo's accomplice was one Michael New, a Trinidadian living in Big Sur with his friend Joan Baez. Jo, who was and is a life-long resident of the region, was in cahoots with Michael's sister Jenny. The four of them occupied a rustic cabin on the grounds of Slates Hot Springs, a crude geothermal spa later to become the world famous Esalen Institute. Jo and Michael ordered plans through me for Piver's 30-foot NIMBLE trimaran. The check for $150 was signed by Joan Baez. She was just becoming known as one of the hallmark hip-political voices of the sixties, and when the check arrived at the Piver household the two teen-age Piver daughters, Nancy and Dixie, knew all about Joan Baez. They were thrilled to have her autograph, and very disappointed when their parents insisted that the check be cashed because, for one thing, $30 of it had to be sent to Jim Brown.

Jo and Michael began building their boat on the grounds of Slate's Hot Springs within easy sight of – but totally without launching access to – the sea. As the project progressed, our respective families engaged socially in this unlikely shipyard setting, and on occasion we all were casually entertained by "Joanie." Her precise, driving guitar and her throaty contralto voice with its almost mathematical vibrato (both obviously the result of training in the classics) could almost blow the walls out of that "crummy little shack" where the two couples lived. She delighted in razzing her man by singing "Michael row the boat ashore," but in the end never set foot on their boat for she had a dread fear of nausea. She called me "mister boat;" no matter how prophetic I am glad it didn't stick.

Jo Anna was pregnant with our second child. As her time approached, we encountered a communication problem. If she were to feel contractions and I was across the canyon at the boatbuilding barn, only half a mile away as the crow flies but much more by road, she needed some way to get my attention. I coached her in how to prop the shotgun against the thick, soft bark of a redwood and sound the alarm. This was never necessary, for when I came home one evening she was feeling pangs but insisted we relax with Manhattans before starting the trek to the hospital in Monterey about an hour away. We arrived in time, and our throng was soon joined by baby Russell, just seventeen months behind Steven.

Big Sur, Big Man...

When Jo Anna and I began having trouble with our well-worn 1949 Chevrolet station wagon, I was referred to the Big Sur Garage, Don and Gretchen McQueen, proprietors. I knew of the establishment for it was located adjacent to the post office in the bottom of the Big Sur River valley. Upon entering the very tidy workspace I saw two huge, booted feet protruding from beneath a car. Conversing with a muffled voice somehow attached to the feet, I described my wagon's sticking valves and in response was asked where I lived. When I explained, the voice said, "Oh, you're the guy building boats up there on the mountain. I've heard about you." Slowly the huge feet and their proportionately endless legs and their proportionately massive torso emerged from beneath the car. The man propelled his mechanic's creeper by walking his heels and elbows on the clean concrete. When his head finally appeared it remained resting on the little pillow of his creeper. I saw that his wide face was smiling and his smallish eyes gleamed from behind thick glasses. Then he sat up nimbly and said, "I'm going to sail around the world some day." I was a bit jolted by this opener, but Don and I made fast friends, our wives soon did the same, and before long we were all four building a boat together. It was the first Piver-designed 40-foot VICTRESS trimaran to begin construction, and in time the project dominated the narrow parking area between the Big Sur Garage and the River; it became a tourist attraction.

Shortly after Russell was born, we moved from Newell's mountain down to Walker's Camp in the Big Sur River valley. Our comfortable rented cabin was close to the job and perched on a high bank above the River's flood plane. In flood season (January to March) the River sometimes roared past our windows with such force as to tumble the boulders in its bed. This geological phenomenon, called saltation, is a manufacturer of sand and the producer of a most ominous sound... the deep growl of rolling boulders heard from beneath the hissing surface of the torrent. I had trouble sleeping with this rout for two rainy seasons because the location of our boat project was vulnerable to flooding. (Years later, the one-time site of our project plus the McQueen's house and garage were obliterated by a flood-caused landslide.) For the rest of the year, however, we enjoyed living deep within the redwoods by that river, with our kids growing and our boat coming along. Except, of course, for that night I was awakened by the sound of something heavy pacing on our roof. In summer the boys' slept in bunk beds on a screened porch from where the pacing sound seemed to be coming. I went quietly to the porch, listened in confusion, and finally turned on the light. All I saw was the hind feet and long tail of the mountain lion as it leaped from the roof into the darkness. Afterwards the boys slept in their interior bedroom.

Both our project and Jo Hudson's were visible to the stream of summer tourists who threaded their way down the Big Sur Highway in the pleasant months from August to January (after the fog and before the rain). Many of these gawkers stopped to investigate, causing serious interruptions to our work. We put up nasty signs, asked for donations, and handed disc grinders to those who disturbed our dialog with the tools. They kept coming. It was to this dilemma that Jo Hudson addressed his first cartoons and shared them with us. His humanoid characters, outlandish settings and wry fun reached our little clique with the effect of turning desperation into comedy, thus spurring our frenzy to get the boats built. (Later his work was published in my Searunner Construction Manual and the yachting press; it helped thousands of greenhorn would-be mariners to accept the duration of boatbuilding and transcend the fear of seafaring.)

But For The Boulder...
As Jo's and Michael's project neared completion, the original plan to launch the craft at Limekiln Creek, ten miles to the south, was foiled by a big slide that buried the access road to the beach there. The launching obstacle seemed insurmountable. However, the Big Sur Highway had been built by The CCC Boys in the 1930's as a depression-era make-work project, and the old wooden trestles that crossed the canyons were now being replaced with concrete spans. Jo's father owned a mountainside in the area, one that descended steeply to the beach, and the bridge contractor was in need of beach sand for backfill around the pylons of the new bridges. The contractor asked Jo's father for permission to bulldoze a road down to a beach to obtain this sand. Jo's father said, "Sure, so long as you launch my son's boat in the process."

The road was dozed, but at one tight turn the dozer encountered a house-sized rock embedded in the uphill bank. If the rock was dislodged it promised to take a big chunk of the mountain with it to the beach, so the road was cut close around the base of the rock...

The proud new trimaran SOUTH WIND (named for the direction from which come the winter storms that pound this coast) is ready to launch. Together with its construction cradle, it is lifted by the contractor's mobile crane and loaded on a big flatbed trailer with its main hull well off-center. One outboard hull is cantilevered out over the cliff so that the other will clear the big boulder in the bank.

This ungainly rig is now towed by a cement mixer truck filled with water ballast to gain traction on the steep one-mile grade to the beach. The whole shebang comes within inches of tumbling into the canyon as it swings wide around the giant rock, and the boat comes within les than inches of the rock itself. I am thinking that this is probably the most hazardous voyage the boat will ever make.

With the load now on the beach, the track crane is brought down that same road; it lifts the boat and cradle off the flatbed and gently places it on wet sand just above the surf at low tide. A thirty-foot, clear-heart redwood timber (salvaged from one of the old trestles) is lashed with one end against the boat's cradle and the other end into the dozer's blade.

Using a kayak to punch out through the surf, Jo and Michael have set an anchor out beyond the break line. Now they are both on the boat's bow ready to haul on the line. The dozer idles in readiness while Jo watches the surf for a long, breathless time. After a big thumper swirls around the cradle he hollers, "Now!" The dozer advances, relentlessly thrusting the timber against the cradle. As the boat, gingerly skids down the beach, a rock under the sand is uncovered by the cradle and commences tumbling under the boat and breaking up the cradle. Small waves Jill around the boat and the dozer. The dozer retreats, the boat lists and settles, and our hearts thump.

Now a six-foot wave breaks just before the boat and lifts it clear. Jo and Michael haul frantically on the anchor line but as the wave subsides the hull grounds. As the vessel climbs another breaker the crew holds fast on the line and then hauls away as the boat swims clear of the surf.

Sometime during that night the rock, together with its chunk of mountain and section of road, all plunge to the beach.

SOUTH WIND was subsequently sailed to Australia.

I was learning lots from working with Don McQueen. He could make almost anything, from a radio for our boat to a bridge across the Big Sur River. The union hall in Monterey had offered him journeyman cards in nine trades if he would join the union, but he respectfully declined. Instead he delighted in teaching his skills to those who worked around him, and he was an inspiring teacher. Besides our boatbuilding we were building houses and hauling wrecks. The Big Sur Highway was treacherous at times, with hurricane force winds, dense fogs, flash floods and unpredictable rockslides. Don had the only towing service in the region. Of his two highway wrecking trucks, one was a real brute capable of dragging things like semi-tractors out of canyons. He also drove the only local ambulance.

Without A Trace...

One day, Gretchen McQueen received the news that there had been a shipwreck on the coast some fifteen miles to the south and the big truck was needed for salvaging its equipment. We went to the site and could barely discern a tiny white speck on the shore some 600 feet below the highway. The survivors, two young men, had climbed up to explain that they were sailing down the coast in, yes, a 24-foot Piver NUGGET trimaran when the craft began taking water at night and they couldn't find the leak. They panicked and turned for the beach. Surviving the surf they discovered that the smallest grain of sand on this particular beach was about the size of a basketball. The boat was badly damaged, having been hurled over rocks to above the high tide line. It was loaded with a great deal of valuable diving equipment, which the survivors hoped somehow to retrieve:

From the highway Don examines the slope with binoculars and suggests that I descend with the survivors to the boat and lash all the equipment onto its deck. So the two youths and I drag the towing cable, joined of several pieces for sufficient length, down the mountain. The going is so steep that I can't imagine dragging the boat back up, and just before the beach we are obliged to climb down through the crags of a thirty foot cliff. Not knowing what else to do we secure the equipment – a big pile of dive tanks, wet suits and duffle bags of other gear – on deck with a spider web of lashings. Then we rig a harness around the vessel, so as to tow from its after crossbeam, but lead from its main bow. I use hand signals to communicate with Don that we are ready; I can't see him but he can see me through his binoculars. When we are ready he commences to drag the boat across the beach.

After only a few yards of smashing over the rocks the main hull bottom opens up to admit a bushel-sized boulder, which rolls inside the boat. With moans from the boys and crashing from the boat the boulder slowly grinds its way out through the stern leaving mangled pieces of the hull in its wake. But the platform of the boat remains intact. I am amazed.

Once across the beach the load encounters the cliff. The cable, which now leads down onto the boat from almost straight up, lifts the bow and the boat dutifully scales the cliff while hanging like a model on a string. At the top of the cliff it teeters on the edge, leaving more fragments of itself lodged in the lip and then begins the long, slow drag to the highway.

Don has to pause three times to strip excess cable from his winch, and during one pause I scramble well ahead of the load and rest in the sage, not too near the cable. From my position I cannot see the highway or the beach or the boat. The young survivors are attending to the lashings on their gear so I am seemingly alone on the mountain.

When the cable again begins to move I am soon aware of the approaching sound of heavy scrapes and groans in staccato spurts. I smell crushed sage and see the tops of yucca plants snap from sight. Now the three bows of a trimaran are parting the brush and inching their way in short jerks up the mountainside. It is eerie, yet the scene seems to give new meaning to the term "beachable" as applied to these boats...

Once up on the road, the two young survivors managed to hitch a ride for themselves and all their gear in a big, empty pickup heading south. Don realized there was little chance of getting paid for his towing so he accepted the boat as his fee and the boys took off. We examined the wreck and found there was precious little of its hardware that we could use on our much larger boat. The bottoms of all three hulls were gone and the topside planking was shattered at the butt blocks but amazingly the decks, connectives and crossbeams were intact. If seen only from above, the structure looked undamaged and we marveled at what it had withstood. In the end, however, we were obliged to take axes and sledges to the thing and break it into little pieces, which we loaded onto Howard Welch's stake truck. Howard, the local garbage man, hauled the wreckage to the dump.

Months later Don received a call from someone at the Coast Guard who was trying to trace the whereabouts of the boat and its crew. "The boat seems to have vanished without a trace," said the guardsman.

Don laughed and said, "It sure did! The only thing left of that boat is a scrap of its hull that shows its name (which I remember as being RAINBOW CHASER or some such) and that scrap now decorates Howard Welch's garden."

The guardsman then explained that the diving equipment had been stolen and the boat had been "borrowed" from its unfortunate owner, the father of one of the survivors. To Don and me, the important thing was that the boat had saved their butts. Like all the early trimarans it was whacked together by an amateur builder out of quarter-inch plywood over a spindly frame. All of it was stuck together with water-mix glue and little galvanized nails. Yet those scoundrel kids had ridden it through the surf onto dry land, their bodies unscathed if not their pride. Then the boat had endured an incredible stress and strain against a mountainside without being totally destroyed. We were satisfied.

While building our boat I became acquainted with one Harry Dick Ross, a local pillar who was then married to Eve Miller, former wife of the region's most famous writer Henry Miller (Henry had left the area before we arrived). But it was Harry Dick's late wife who had written the folksy, haunting and unofficial anthem of the region, "The South Coast... is a wild coast and lonely." (The term "South Coast," as used by the local people, was a common alternative to the postal name Big Sur, which stemmed from the Spanish Rio Grande del Sur or Big River of the South.) Folk music was storming the country at the time, and as the song became well known we chose its title as the name for our boat.

As SOUTH COAST took shape, the form of her three hulls were straight out of Piver's plans, but the lack of detailed information in the plans as to other features of the boat tended to encourage improvisation. With Don's agreement I developed certain aspects of her decks, superstructure interiors and rig. I found this level of "creativity" to be extremely satisfying, and others seemed to like the looks and logic of the differences in our boat relative to the stock Piver conformation. It was in this way that I first exercised my predisposition for design, and I am ever grateful to Don McQueen for providing me this opportunity. Without the experience of working with him, and living with the cause and effect of heavy stress and strain, and without exposure to his knowledge of materials, and certainly without his transfer to me of basic woodworking and drafting skills, I would never have become a designer of anything tangible. He was the teacher I never found in school.

Ah! Audacity...
While Piver was away for months in 1963, racing in the Atlantic, Don and I were visited by one Chuck Folden, a professional aviator who flew crop dusters and fire bombers. Folden had just purchased plans for a 35-foot Piver design and was told to visit our project for consultation. Having made no commission on his plans, I was reluctant to spend time with Chuck, but he noticed the differences in SOUTH COAST and pressed us for details. At Don's suggestion, we agreed to design for Chuck an entirely new boat from scratch.

Suddenly Don and I were partners in this fledgling industry. Don had never really sailed, and I had never even taken a high school course in mechanical drawing! But Don had. He loaned me his instruments and coached me in their use, and I "imagineered" my first seagoing sailboat. The result was the 38-foot OFF SOUNDINGS-class trimaran of which several were eventually built.

When I ponder this move today I am struck by its audacity. What explained my willingness – with no formal training and little experience – to specify down to the last detail the configuration, structure and outfitting of a supposedly-seagoing vehicle? Moreover this thing was to be built by rank amateurs and operated on the bounding main by absolute greenhorn lubbers. From where came this audacity?

Perhaps there are three answers: First there is the extent to which a young man will become aggressive when he has little kids growing up. Next comes the power of naiveté wherein one is driven to do things because he doesn't know why he cannot. But most important is the blatant fact of ego. How totally intoxicating must be the stimulant of flattery, the submission and confidence conveyed when one person selects another as the designer of his boat? Indeed the designer/client relationship still seems unreasonable to me, and I regard the fact that many of my clients have started out as friends and stayed that way as my most precious yet inexplicable achievement.

However, my transgression onto territory which Arthur Piver considered his own had real repercussions. When he returned from voyaging in his own 35-foot LODESTAR I gave him the plans I had drawn for OFF SOUNDINGS. I suggested that perhaps it could be added to his stable. Had he accepted it would have forged a continuing partnership for us. His response was a polite negative whereupon our once-thick friendship abruptly ceased to exist. My mentor had kicked me out of the nest, which is just what a good mentor must inevitably do to his audacious protégé.

Similarly, my relationship with Don McQueen began to crumble. He was having difficulties in his own life, and I was voracious to design independently. We realized that our original notion was pathetically naïve. Our two families – one with two little boys – were simply not going to fit into one SOUTH COAST and sail off into the sunset. Gradually, and without any yelling at each other, we dissolved our partnership. Don took the boat (he had paid me to build it and paid all the bills) and I took the design business. There was angst for us both but we remain friends today for we sailed through some rich stuff together. Now Jo Anna and I were free to move to Santa Cruz with our boys, and it was there that I hung out my shingle as a multihull designer. Ah! Audacity. What would life be without it?

Inauspicious Startup...

I still regard that first design, the 38-foot OFF SOUNDINGS, to have been a rather successful compromise cruiser for its time; unless one is designing pure raceboats, compromise is the name of the game. I have always considered a cruising vessel to be a very highly specialized yet multipurpose workboat, its design inevitably the result of a lot of push and shove. But my first attempt to be a "player" in marine architecture seemed to bring great misfortune to some of my early clients. Chuck Folden, who commissioned the OFF SOUNDINGS design, built it in Mexico but never sailed it. The engine of his crop duster tore loose on takeoff. The insecticide tank burst in the crash and Chuck's wounds were dashed with poison. He spent many months aboard at Tampico recovering but never regained the drive to finish his dream. The second was built by Mark Hassall, perhaps my most illustrious client, for he eventually built three of my boats and circumnavigated in two of them, but his OFF SOUNDINGS was destroyed by shipwreck only nine months after launching. Bob and Ann Steg built a solid version of the class and began their world cruise only to have the vessel burn at dockside in Australia; a kerosene refrigerator set the boat ablaze while they were shopping. Maitland Dwight fell into his hull during its construction and broke his back. Then, just before the launching of his OFF SOUNDINGS, our pharmacist friend Bob Pietrobono agreed to help a friend OF HIS deliver a power boat from Monterey to San Francisco. A navigation error caused the boat to founder on the breaking reef at Half Moon Bay. Being close to the refuge of the harbor, Bob had just removed his float coat and loaned it to his shivering friend; the friend survived but Bob drowned.

In contrast, the late Commander E. T. Sullivan, USN (ret) built his OFF SOUNDINGS at the Navy base at Sasebo, Japan, a facility he had commanded during the occupation. Sully came to love the Japanese, and he was haunted by guilt from the aftermath of Hiroshima and Nagasaki, a guilt that literally drove him to drink. In his retirement he sailed his boat some 60,000 miles with a young Japanese man named Norio as crew. Only when Norio confessed that he wanted to leave the boat to get married did Sully swallow the anchor and leave the sea to weaken and eventually die from his conviction. I loved him for the purpose to which he put my first design. Still and all, these events did not constitute an auspicious startup for my unintended career among the multihulls.

....

Illustrations for this chapter, narrated by the author, are available online at ...
www.OutrigMedia.com/books/atm-volume-one.html

6

THE MULTIHULL CONTEXT
1964 > 68

What made modern multihulls happen? Was it just the new materials? The light weight? Were they just a product of the times? Or was it that these new/old watercraft suddenly satisfied some basic human need?

In my attempt to understand the context from which modern multihulls emerged I have been aided by my friend Dan Larned, an amateur historian of considerable depth. Jo Anna and I first met Dan in 1962 when he escaped from prep school near Los Angeles and blew into Big Sur with his dog, the two them riding a Lambretta. Today we live within a day sail of each other. He sails a 25-foot racing trimaran that streaks through the water with such ease that it often leaves us and his dog spray blown and speechless. But when we sail in SCRIMSHAW, my 38-year old Searunner, it is easier to talk. With the anchor holding, the stew simmering and the wine pouring, we occasionally enjoy discussing the last half century.

We fondly remember the buoyancy and optimism of the fifties, when multihulls started really to happen, but Dan reminds us that the decade also had its problems - brooding racial tensions, the Korean War and the budding threat of nuclear annihilation. Nevertheless, the developed world was still high from having quashed the despots in Europe and Japan. By the late fifties even the defeated economies were booming, and Americans felt they could do anything and solve any problem with technology, wealth and will. "We thought we were a special people," says Dan, "and we were ready to pay any price to make the world a better place." As the sixties began we were headed for the moon and building a Great Society. Multihulls were acquiring some notoriety as a sub-cultural splinter in the backside of yachting.

By the early seventies, however, "We had lost our first war, and to a provincial enemy, yet," says Dan. "We had also discarded the gold standard thereby devaluing (desecrating?) our sacred dollar. We had retreated from a major technological challenge, the supersonic transport, and we had realized that at least some problems like poverty, bigotry and apathy, defy solution."

With our second glass pouring in the cockpit and the smell of stew wafting from the galley, we reminisce about the years of Kennedy, Johnson and Nixon, the assassinations, the Cuban missile crisis and the very lucky fact that The Balance Of Terror with the Soviets actually worked; it prevented our mutual annihilation. Dan speaks of his two tours as a Ranger in Viet Nam, of the land mine that nearly cost him his legs, and of returning home to find that the American war hero had been culturally vilified.

Having been declared 4-F because of my poor eyesight and broken bones, I reminisce about the wild ride I had experienced at home; the progression from Bohemians to Beatniks to Hippies; from peace and love to protest and confrontation. As Jo Anna and I became increasingly sympathetic to progressive causes we were nonetheless dismayed by the rampant defiance of authority, by elements like the white racists, the Black Panthers, the violent students and the angry police. The trimaran EVERYMAN sailed into the Bikini nuclear test zone. Then came the riots in Detroit and Los Angeles, the Chicago Democratic Convention and the killings at Kent State. It was during this progression from buoyant optimism to ballasted reality that the early-modern multihull thrived. Was there any connection?

I think for some of us there was, at least those for whom the captivation of the sixties led finally to escape. For example, when Ronald Reagan, then governor of California, ordered the National Guard to assault anti-war activists in Berkeley, we began selling lots of plans. The foment of the times certainly stimulated one's sense of bursting the boating envelope, of pioneering a new order and affecting the future. Few of us were cognizant of the ancient cultures and traditions that modern multihulls represent. We were enrapt by their novelty, their development and their speed but were generally ignorant of their ancient origins. With the possible exception of designers Woody Brown and James Wharram, who were to some extent inspired by ancient Pacific sea craft, modern multihull enthusiasts were only casually aware that all three of their configurations, catamaran, trimaran and proa, were given by the Ancients. In modern times, multihulls were the anti-yachts, flying in the face of tradition whereas their forbears stemmed from the oldest tradition of all: survival. Driven by the pressures of overcrowding and persecution in eastern Asia, the designers of many ancient multihulls apparently built their boats as escape vehicles, and it is here that I choose to draw a similarity in modern times.

Perhaps it was simple paranoia but I still suspect there was some logic in the minds of we who, when faced with the strange antithesis between the hip and the political at home, opted instead for freedom and adventure at sea. We chose to consolidate our assets in a “cruising machine” that we could build ourselves, that could move without fuel, that could swerve around geopolitical hot spots and could carry a microcosm of our own culture, our own food, music, family and friends. We would sail the wide waters to some unspecified sanctuary that surely must await discovery somewhere. It is easy to call this utopian but more insightful, I propose, to see it as survival.

Some of our vessels were born as slapdash prototypes, some as utilitarian vagabonders, others as spiffy yachts. The modern catamarans and trimarans (and later proas) were embarked upon a blustery sea of almost frenzied development. They were usually built something like the wooden aircraft of WW II with a very spindly skeleton covered by a very thin skin with the total structured weight divided more or less equally between the two. Anyone could get plywood and fiberglass and learn to work with them using carpenter’s and painter’s tools. Very lightweight structures of amazing strength and stiffness could be produced in back yard settings by untrained builders. Unlike the ballasted monohulls of the time, multihulls had no massive weights to be moved during construction or launching, and most important the projects were relatively inexpensive, especially if one did not account for his own labor. As Arthur Piver wrote, his trimarans could be built “...for the price of an ordinary automobile.” They were sprawling things, requiring a large covered workspace in some climates, and most amateur builders could not work fast, so their projects often took years especially if they tried to make them yachty. Nevertheless, more than any other vessel type, the 1960’s multihull was accessible.

There were several other features that attracted attention early on. The wide-track multihulls did not heel over like monohulls, and heeling, besides causing discomfort and inconvenience even to experienced sailors, is also a major cause of fear for beginners. Of course the ballast keel in monohulls is what causes them to pop back up after being knocked over by gusts and crests, a Shmoo-like principle that has stood the test of time. (Remember the Shmoo, that inflated, bowling pin-shaped toy with lead shot in its base so that it could not be toppled? Are they still around?) But sailing in a “shmooboat” is initially scary and takes some getting used to. As Arthur Piver used to say, “You cannot reason with fear.”

Furthermore the cruising monohulls of the time were heavy! Their hulls were necessarily built like fortresses because the lead in their ballast keels often comprised half their total weight (much more than half nowadays). This roughly doubled their weight relative to multihulls and meant they had to push aside something like twice as much water to get through. Another factor is that heeling spills excess wind power from sails...that is, excessive relative to the stability of the boat. It was this blatant waste of driving force that Arthur Piver called, "A technical absurdity." By standing up to the wind without much heeling, the early multis converted "excess" power into abundant propulsive energy, and that energy was then coupled with their narrow hulls.

How narrow? Well, the main hulls of the trimarans of the sixties were roughly half as wide at the waterline as those of monohulls; the monos needed breadth to gain what stability they could whereas the shape of individual hulls in a multihull did not need even to consider stability! (In this respect multihull design is a perverse cop-out compared to the challenge of designing monohulls.) Trimaran floats and catamaran hulls were one third or one-fourth the breadth of monohulls. This narrowness meant they could slice through waves instead of trying to push them aside. Moreover the narrow hull forms did not make waves, not anything like the typical bow wave pushed ahead and stern wave dragged behind by monohulls. The result of these combined aero-and-hydrodynamic differences – light weight, low wave-making and abundant power – all combined to give even the early multihulls the potential to go very fast even in very rough water.

However, multihulls do have several factors that increased resistance relative to monohulls. They have to part the water surface in two or three places instead of one; they have "interplay" wavemaking between their hulls; they can have more wet surface especially in rough seas; and they have more windage relative to comparable monohulls. Even so, these factors are easily overcome by the multis far more efficient use of wind power, and today the same efficiency is evident in motor-driven multihulls.

Nevertheless this stability and velocity had its downside: It was bottoms up... the potential to capsize. Right, multihulls are not Shmoos. They can turn turtle. There is not space in this book to present all the arguments in the case of capsize versus sinking. Suffice to say that most modern multihulls cannot sink and most ballasted monohulls cannot capsize. These days it seems nobody talks much about preparing for either type of calamity, which I think is a great mistake. Fifty years of experience now indicates that both capsize and sinking can happen to the best boats of either kind and that one is about as likely as the other. How likely? Very remote in cruising craft, shamefully common among the racers. On the multihull side of the issue only one argument is irrefutable: the aftermath of capsize is greatly preferred to the aftermath of sinking. There is evidence that the crew of a capsized multihull can survive for months by staying with the boat. Conversely, when a monohull disappears from the face of the earth its crew is relegated to a life raft if they have one, and either way their chances of survival are much reduced.

The increased stability and velocity of the early multis also imposed physical loads on the structures that were unanticipated. Failures were common, especially of masts, rudders, centerboards and under-wings. Successive trial-and-error refinements in both form and structure were required, and these were not just adaptations. No, these were more like integral mutations, thousands of experiments in the space of a decade, their results naturally selected in the evolution of a new genus of boat. Moreover, these successive refinements were made not by governments or corporations but by barnstorming individuals. There was no supervision, no regulation and no restraint. As with most pioneering, the atmosphere was charged with creativity and pluck, but there was risk and loss. Races were unfinished, cruisers overdue, boats wrecked, lives lost and backlash ensued, but the momentum was inexorable. It was in this period that I hung out my shingle as a multihull designer; for now it was clear that there could be some truly new creatures on the water, in the wind, and under the sun.

Oh sure, multihulls also offered the good clean fun of sailing, the beat-your-buddy business of racing, the chance to identify with something culturally fresh, and the fantasy of easy money made from building boats and selling plans. But the main enticement of multihulls for me and for many of my clients was their ability to permit the ordinary workaday dude to hit the briny trail and "know the world." In the face of instability and disillusionment at home, we cried, "Let's split this pop stand."

Not all of us did. The motive for having a cruising sailboat was often not so much actually to go, but to be able to go. Today I regard this "escape-vehicle" or contingency motivation to be largely responsible for much of boat ownership. What else can explain the square miles of marinas, really just flooded parking lots jammed with gleaming units of disused wealth? Please forgive my cynicism, but pure "recreation" cannot fully account for the millions of vessels large and small, power and sail, which spend 99.99 percent of their lives just sitting there "able to go."

Most of those who went, who voyaged to foreign waters and stayed even for years at a time, eventually returned to live and work somewhere under the Stars And Stripes, but often they kept their boats for many years. I did.

Stepping Stones To Searunning...
Jo Anna and I and our two youngsters moved from Big Sur to Santa Cruz in 1964, the same year that multihull ocean racing cranked up in earnest with serious offshore fixtures in both the Atlantic and Pacific. I was not much interested in racing, although some of my clients would be later.

Santa Cruz, located about 70 miles south of San Francisco on the coast, was then a small retirement and gardening community, but it had a compact man-made harbor and the University of California was soon to begin construction of its premier campus there. The sixties were lurching into revolutionary stride, Jack and Bobby were gone, Martin and Malcolm were soon to go, and back yard trimaran designers like myself had popped up all over, mostly in California but also in England, Europe and Australia. We all competed for the same market share, and while that market was rapidly expanding there was still a fair bit of intramural backbiting in our most unprofessional profession.

My own behavior in this commercialization of the multihull is a part of the story I am not proud of. It was partly our petty competition that caused the whole multihull phenomenon to gather into camps whose banners were the logos of their respective designers. If we had all gotten together and agreed to focus on promoting the multihull phenomenon as a whole instead of individual designs, I believe the entire marine community might have responded without stigmatizing multihulls as outcasts. Instead we seemed to revel in our image as the underdogs of yachting, and without the cultural foment of the time wherein the establishment was routinely challenged and the challengers often admired, I suspect our "movement" would have advanced even more slowly than it did.

It seemed slow enough at the time. The traditional yachting community was predisposed against multihulls, sometimes with good reason. First of all, some monohull yachtsmen realized that this phenomenon just might mature into something more than a threat to their speed records; it might even become a serious player in the marine marketplace. And second, the appearance of many multihulls and the behavior of their sailors sometimes offended yachting's genteel and exclusive sensibilities. Not only did many multihull sailors exhibit very lubberly handling of their craft, but often the craft themselves were sailing aberrations. This was particularly true in the Piver camp, where the demand for new designs was so strong that their construction drawings could not be sufficiently detailed to discourage improvisation by the builders. This improvisation, by those who had little or no "sea time" on which to base their creativity, would become the nemesis of the Piver trimaran phenomenon and of course it reflected on multihulls in general. The sprawling platform of both the catamaran and trimaran tempted builders to cover it with superstructure in the interest of increased interior accommodation space. Not cognizant of the consequence of these excesses on windage, weight and sea kindliness, these builders were inevitably disillusioned with their boats' performance. The traditionalists scoffed, "Multihulls won't come about, won't go to windward and can't get out of their own way." They were often right.

Furthermore, whenever the chance arose for multihull sailors to blatantly overhaul and pass, even sail circles around, their single-hulled counterparts, that chance was taken with sometimes vociferous glee. Or else we'd go charging through the monohull racing fleet, their crews lining the weather rail, all decked out in poopie suits and being doused by sheets of spray, while we were loaded down with kids and dogs, our barbecues streaming hamburger smoke and our wakes trailing music and laughter. We did not endear ourselves to the (sailing) establishment, which for "progressives" was typical of the times.

These obscure wrangles in the almost sectarian yachting world were occurring at the same time as the civil rights struggle and two wars, one "cold" and the other getting hot. A growing segment of the culture was engaged in collective hallucination and un-matrimonial bliss. In this global context, multihulls were but a symptom, a minor rash reaction to the main systemic malady of a society seemingly afflicted with the consequences of excess.

Of course I'm speaking of just one quadrant of the sixties' multihull mania, the "cruising quadrant." I knew little of the beach cat scene, which because of the small size of the vessels was confined mostly to daysailing. And I knew little of the Wharram cats, although they were akin to my own cruising trimarans in their appeal to owner-builders and seasteading romanticists. I also knew little of what was happening in the waters of the Atlantic and Australia, where multihull ocean racing was often done in cold waters and angry seas, whereas in California the races were generally subtropical sleigh rides to Mexico and Hawaii.

With this rather limited view of the multihull phenomenon as a whole, Jo Anna and I rented a little old house at 2301 Seventh Avenue in Santa Cruz about two miles from the harbor. It was a comfortable place steeped in the palpable happy spirit of the former inhabitants. Steven and Russell started school, and Jo Anna started our business. Without her diligence in answering mail, keeping files and metering the miserly money we made, there never would have been a Searunner Trimarans. At times I was driven back to boatyard work, doing bottom jobs and fiberglass repairs at three dollars per hour, but we soon had sold several sets of plans for my first design at $350 each. The plans were printed by our new friend Tom Freeman, a returning veteran and native of Santa Cruz who had just opened his own printing business in town. Tom and his new wife Blanche taught me how to draw for the printing process, and the four of us soon became close friends.

It was Tom who made me realize that selling plans in numbers was a function not just of how well the boats were designed but of how well they were promoted. He helped me publish the first little commercial flyers about my boats, and their effect was an immediate boost in plans sales. Once the work of drawing the plans was done (and it was many months of work), each sale was almost pure profit, so it seemed. I was soon to learn, however, that the real cost of doing business was in consulting for the builders, a task that mounted with each sale. To reduce this consultation it became important to provide detailed instructions with the plans, and here again Tom Freeman showed us how to print these instruction booklets at minimum cost. Was selling these high-profit rolls of paper a greedy racket? Or was it honest opportunity? It didn't matter, for we were off and running and it was lots of fun.

The Blowout Launching...

The first of the 38-foot OFF SOUNDINGS designs to be completed was built by Mark Hassall near Santa Barbara, California, and launched in 1965. A brief account of the launching – and the subsequent shipwreck – of this vessel are included here to illustrate the rather frantic multihull activity of the time.

Mark Hassall's boat shop was the driveway and garage of his rented house at Oxnard, California. His neighborhood bordered a large tract of undeveloped land belonging to the University of California at Santa Barbara. I helped Mark in the final construction phase of his boat, and quickly learned that the best way to help this guy was to get out of the way; otherwise I was going to get hurt. His level of productivity was frenzied. He knew what he was doing and could do good work fast, but faster-yet was better. Unlike many owner-builders Mark wanted to sail, not build.

On launching day, the boat was trailered through University property to a wide, gentle beach of hard sand. Starting at low tide we unhitched the towing jeep from the trailer at the upper limit of the swash and waited for the water. There were many celebrants on hand, the sea was calm, and we discussed the launching procedure as if we knew what we were doing. We lashed the rudder to the stern deck to avoid damaging it during the launch, intending to hang it on the transom upon reaching deep water. However, by the time of half tide, a stiff breeze had risen and its accompanying waves quickly buried the trailer to its axels so that there was no chance to roll the trailer seaward manually as we had planned. Gradually the waves jostled the boat enough to begin breaking up the construction cradle in which it rested on the trailer. The boat listed and settled (yes, shades of Jo Hudson's surf launching of two years before). With a dozen people in the water, up to their necks in the crests, pushing and lifting on the boat, and a few too many riding on deck as crew, a big wave finally washed the boat off the trailer sideways, breaking the fin from one float, wiping out the steel fender and blowing both tires... I'll never forget the muffled "whomp" and swirling steam of those underwater blowouts. With my eyes closed but my big blind blotch agape I can still see every move of what happened next:

On deck we are knocked from our feet, but at last the boat is free of the trailer. A report from below confirms that she is not taking water, and Mark cries, "We've got to get to the sails!" The fifteen-knot breeze is blowing along the beach and down the valleys of the waves, so we quickly hoist all three sails of her ketch rig and sheet them home. In fits and starts, the boat comes afloat on the crests and drops roughly onto sand as the crests pass. We are making nothing but leeway, sweeping sideways down the beach in jarring hops. Presently the boat lifts and surges ahead as well as sideways, staying afloat between two passing crests. Grounding again, I wonder how we will control the craft if indeed it ever gets past the breakers, for I realize now that we have no rudder.

She surges again, grounds again, surges again and skips, then skips again and finally, with the grace of a pelican, bobs over the outer breakers and into deep water. We are all panicked but ecstatic when I realize that the ketch is slowly heading up into the wind whereupon it is bound to tack itself and sail right back to the beach! "Slack the mizzen!" I yell, and as the drive comes off her stern Mark's boat lies almost in irons but by backing the jib we coax her to bear away to seaward. We steer her with the sails until well offshore, when we drop all sail and two of our number enter the water to install the rudder. We then proceed gleefully, enjoying the ride to the marina at Oxnard arriving just at nightfall...

It took me until late that night to realize it; any boat that can sail herself from hard aground in a crashing surf, right out through the breakers, and then be steered with her sails to safety... That just has to be a pretty good boat. But I resolve to discourage surf launchings; Mark's and Jo's have been enough.

Off Soundings, On Rocks...

Mark lived aboard and sailed his boat for only nine months before meeting Bonnie, who would become the focal woman in his life. On her first weekend cruise with him, they sailed the 25 miles across to Anacapa Island, an extremely steep protrusion in the open sea, and anchored in a tight cove. During the night a front passed, the wind changed and by morning they were backed up by storm seas close against the rocks with two anchors holding but no room to spare. The boat was bucking on the reflected waves within the cove, the anchors were threatening to drag and the engine was balky, refusing to take a load. So Mark hoisted sail, got one anchor up and was trying to cut the line to the other when the sails filled, the boat charged and the anchor line ran out of scope. It yanked the vessel onto the wrong tack just as the line was cut and the new boat charged full bore up onto the rocks. The seas deposited the trimaran some ten feet above high water with the bottoms ripped out of all three hulls but the platform intact (yes, sounds like the little NUGGET we dragged up the mountain in Big Sur).

Bonnie and Mark were able to step off onto dry land but the prospect of rebuilding the hulls in this location was nil. They stripped the craft of everything that could be used in replacing her and awaited rescue. After a week of surviving on the contents of the wreck, a fishing boat carried them and all their gear back to Oxnard. On the way home, Bonnie said to Mark, "You know, between us we're four thousand dollars in debt. You owe two thousand on the boat and I owe two thousand on my car. But I do have an apartment with a garage. We can put all this stuff in the garage and we can go to work. We'll have to make the money to build another boat so we can sail around the world." They did.

Pops the Pagan Priest...

My second design was a 34-footer we called MANTA. Our initial client was Commander Tom Le Dew, a navy weatherman who built his boat at the hobby shop on the Monterey Naval Air station. I worked on the project with him at times, and shortly after the vessel's launching (by a crane from a wharf, thankfully) I was invited to join Tom's crew for the passage to Hawaii where he had been transferred. This was an important chance for me to demonstrate the ocean-crossing ability of my designs, a factor heavily promoted by my main competition at the time, which was of course Arthur Piver. By '66 Art had crossed both the Atlantic and Pacific in his trimarans, and these achievements put the undeniable stamp of "ocean tested" on his work.

Also in Tom's crew were: Bob Pietrobono (who was still building his OFF SOUNDINGS at the time, a vessel he would never have the chance to sail because of that power boating accident described in chapter 5); my particular friend Jim McCaig (a scallywag and former B-29 navigator who was building a MANTA); and a young Catholic priest who we came to call Pops. Tom was a devout person and one of the several all-around great guys I have known, but he figured he had been a bad boy at some point in his life, an incident he never discussed with me. But he clearly felt that if he should die in the sea on this voyage he would need the supernatural assistance of a priest in order for him to make it into heaven. So, despite the fact that a crew of five in that boat was excessive, Pops was signed on. A fine and mellow man, Pops had never sailed, much less been to sea. He held mass in the cockpit at sunset, a feature which surely did augment the offshore experience, although the born again pagans among us soon tired of the droning repetitions of "Lord I am not worthy."

About three days out when we entered the trades and started really sailing in ocean rollers, Pops made a confession: He was unable to defecate or urinate. He insisted there was nothing wrong physically, and I realized that he was truly terrified by the sea, so much that he could not relax his sphincters. We had a problem.

When provisioning for the passage, Tom's wife Nancy – a delightful, dear, and yet demanding dame – insisted loudly, "There's going to be absolutely no booze on that boat!" We followed orders, except of course for Pops who brought a small supply of "alter" wine used at mass.

Poor Pops spent hours trying to pee. All wrapped in his brand new yellow foulies, he would kneel on deck, his head bowed and his arms reaching over the lifelines to hold his painful pecker as the boat surfed along in the dark and Pops prayed. He, and we, were in trouble.

Jim McCaig, that rascal, found the alter wine, dragged Pops into the cockpit, and while I steered we cajoled the reluctant priest into guzzling and giggling until finally he wet his pants. While changing in the bucking boat below he purged himself from both ends and the crisis was over. Pops became the best helmsman on the crew, and left us in Hawaii talking of having his own boat some day, and went on to be defrocked for taking up with girls. Bless you, Pops. You are worthy, dammitall, and I wish you fair winds wherever you sail.

The Broken Wing...

In the mid sixties I became involved with a budding corporation called Santa Cruz Marine. We had facilities near the harbor in the large shed of a defunct lumberyard where I began to build a 27-foot trimaran of a rather racy nature. It was believed by management that this performance emphasis would lead to repeat production and commercial success. This was one of many undercapitalized ventures into front-yard multihull production in that time. It seemed everyone was getting into the multihull business, for surely these new contraptions were going to take over the boating world.

CARAVEL, as we called her, was far too radical for her own good, and ample evidence that when going beyond the "modified Pivers" of my career so far, I really did not know what I was doing. Her construction was rather tedious, but once built she proved fast and fun. However, she was cranky at speed and prone to structural problems. Her main hull was very chesty with a long, flat outrun (which made her squirrelly off the wind), and her floats were extremely asymmetric (which caused her when power-reaching to run away to loo'ard despite even Herculean efforts from the helmsman. But she had a deep daggerboard and a tall rig, and would climb to windward at least as high and foot at least as fast as racing monohulls twice her size.

We had the chance to demonstrate this ability when the Monterey Bay Yacht Racing Union permitted us to enter their annual Around the Bay Race, a 50-mile triangle in open sea. The first leg was a long beat to windward against the usual summertime northwester which in those waters is light in the morning, blows steadily at fifteen knots by noon and often builds to thirty by late afternoon. We felt that if CARAVEL could handle these conditions respectably it would help us to sell others like her.

With Jim McCaig as navigator and a young friend as crew, I can see us starting from Monterey on a summer Saturday afternoon:

Hanging back to avoid conflict with the official entrants at the crowded start, we cross the line last in a fleet of some twenty monohull yachts all larger than CARAVEL. We quickly climb through the fleet except for the "mechanical rabbit" we must chase, the famous 50-foot Eight Meter yacht ANGELITA. She is a former Olympic champion, well kept, well crewed, and a gorgeous sight at the dock and under way.

As the afternoon passes the rest of the fleet disappears astern and we nip at ANGELITA's heels for twenty miles. Both boats are bashing into white horses but the relatively little CARAVEL makes heavy weather of it in the cold and wet. At one point McCaig is riding the weather float like it was a horse, his feet hanging over both sides while his hands grasp the two trunk handles mounted there for the purpose. As the boat drives through an angry crest, water is driven up the sleeves of his slicker with such force that it pours out at his neck.

Try as we might we cannot get past the Eight Meter on her windward side for when we try she pinches up to leave us stalled helplessly in her wake. At dusk as we near the weather mark off Santa Cruz, McCaig's keen navigation tells us that both boats are coming in high on the mark, the result of ANGELITA's crew pinching to keep us behind. With room to spare to loo'ard I bear off and struggle into ANGELITA's lee. From perhaps a quarter mile abeam of her, and with the setting sun touching the horizon directly behind her gleaming sails, her sleek silhouetted hull creases through the crests with a magnificent gait. It is one of those glorious, indelible sights of sailing. However it is now apparent that she is being driven over hard, heeling so steeply that at times, when she is in a trough and we are on a crest, we look almost straight down from the top of her mast at the plan of her deck, its lee side obscured by seas boiling past the cabin trunk. Amazed, we see that the foot of her headsail is scooping whole washtubs of water from the crests. Revealed in brilliant backlight they swash way up the sail to pour out at its leech. Clearly the crew is desperate to hold us in their lee, but finally we have taken the "safe loo'ard position" in clear air. Close reaching now we slide ahead but realize that this is still a horserace, for the off-wind legs will be sailed in the lighter airs of night and ANGELITA'S spinnakers, and her far greater length, could carry her to victory while we lollygag with no special downwind sails at all. Nevertheless we are delighted with the upwind achievement of our little boat.

Turning our attention briefly to locate the weather mark we then look back, look again, and find ANGELITA gone. I stand on the cockpit seat and soon spot her hull half a mile away. She is stalled among the waves, her mast, sails and rigging trailing in her wake. For me, her broken wing is a kick in the groin.

We finished that race at Monterey in the wee hours, tired and depressed. The committeeman minding the finish said through his megaphone, "That's nice but you don't count." The official winner, a 40-foot Kettenberg sloop, finished some three hours later. From our bunks we heard the finish horn in the night, the shouts of congratulations as the Kettenberg took its berth near ours. It was true, we didn't count, and I decided then and there that racing multihulls against monohulls was itself no-count. It was our brash presence in this race that induced ANGELITA's crew to drive her to dismasting, so perplexed were they to have this upstart contraption get past. The ill will resulting from that race was added to my heartbreak at seeing such an elegant yacht so indisposed, and I resolved to leave racing to others.

It was not my real interest and I didn't care if my reputation would benefit or not...

The management at Santa Cruz Marine was pleased with the boat but displeased with me, partly because I declined to become a Jehovah's Witness with them and partly because I was not pleased with the boat. I insisted that it needed massive re-design before production, and we had a fearsome falling out.

When later I went back to the drawing board I was armed with one irrefutable fact: Any multihull, given light weight, a deep centerboard and a lofty rig could go to windward at least as well as its monohull counterpart. The last time I saw CARAVEL she was declining rapidly in a Sausalito storage yard but she holds a happy place in my cranial shoebox of shuffled snapshots.

Divided I Stand...

I now resolved to put some form of drop keel in all my boats in the future. Both OFF SOUNDINGS and MANTA had followed the Piver example of omitting the dagger board for reasons of its complication and the seemingly unacceptable interruption that the daggerboard trunk caused in the main cabin. Indeed a big trunk could spoil the layout of any main saloon. However, the cost of omitting the board, in reduced windward performance and maneuverability, was too high for me to pay. All multihulls without deep keels of some kind were contributing to the general reputation of the type; "Those things won't come about and won't go to windward." Piver would never have omitted the centerboard from any of his early designs like FROLIC and NUGGET, and indeed his first NIMBLE, the one he sailed to England in 1961 was equipped with a 'board. Mainly it was pressure from the clientele for greater interior commodiousness that led designers to omit centerboards, and the addition of fins in the floats could not, in my opinion, compensate. I had used float fins in my first two designs and found them to be a reasonable compromise, but after CARAVEL they were not enough, neither for me nor, I believed strongly, for my clients. I saw that truly sharp windward performance and crisp maneuverability was within reach for serious cruising multihulls, and I was determined to address their negative effect on interior accommodations. I also believed that vertically-articulating daggerboards were unacceptable in a cruising boat because of the obvious hazard of serious damage should the dagger strike hard bottom at speed. There was no way to make the trunk strong enough to resist grounding, it could tear out the bottom of the hull, and indeed has done so on many boats so equipped. No, a boat with a vertical daggerboard was no way for me to send neophytes into the big briny. Perhaps it was acceptable in California where the water was almost always deep, but I knew that most cruising destinations are strewn with shoals, rocks and reefs, and so I resolved that any kind of retractable keel must kick up automatically upon striking obstructions.

What was the answer? I designed the BROWN 41, a big trimaran ketch whose cockpit was located dead amidships, right on top of the centerboard trunk. Now there was plenty of room for the great big trunk required to house a great big swing-up centerboard. Indeed the top of the trunk opened into the cockpit sole, thereby providing a huge self-bailer should the cockpit ever take a wave.

The first of these vessels to be completed was built by one Dave Green in Toronto. It was very nicely done. I had the chance to sail in this vessel from New York to Bermuda with Dave and his family. Aside from getting lost and having to follow aircraft contrails to find Bermuda, and struggling with seasickness in the "Gulp Stream," we had a good passage. The boat's fine appearance earned her some exposure in the yachting press, and the fact that another of my boats had made an offshore voyage did worlds for my credibility. But more important was our chance to learn that this vessel's unique central cockpit layout had real advantages. It killed the chance for a house-like main saloon, for the trunk and cockpit occupied that space, but it split the accommodation into two cabins separated by the cockpit. The resulting privacy and quiet now offered by the forward sleeping cabin was very welcome, and the dinette (which normally occupied the very center of the boat, could be moved to the stern where a very pleasant sterncastle could be developed. This "divided cabin" layout was very different but it worked, especially at sea where the off watch could really get some rest without trying to sleep in the kitchen/living room. On deck, the deep, central cockpit well was secure from falling out and unlikely to be swamped by storm waves, and best of all we had our deep, swing-up centerboard! The boat sailed well, climbing to windward and tacking more like a deep-keeled monohull, and the vessel was distinctive, robust and seamanlike.

But it had two real problems. Its cross beams, the usual heavy boxes running laterally through the main hull to mount the floats, were a serious interruption in both cabins of this boat (and indeed in most multihulls of the day). The crew was obliged to duck under – almost crawl under – these obstructions. Consequently the interior was a maze of small compartments with restricted access and lacking in communal space. Everyone could socialize in the large cockpit, but if the weather was inclement there was no real "living room" below.

The position and construction of the cross beams was in large part dictated by the vessels rig and sail plan. To accept the extreme columnar loads delivered to the platform by the masts, these masts were logically stepped on the already massive cross beams. Thus the designer's hands were tied to given spacing requirements for both major components... crossbeams and masts. These problems were yet to be addressed.

The Sea Ray Surfaces...

I remember clearly the night it happened. I'd been working late as usual, trying to finish the plans for builders who had started their projects before their drawings had been completed. It was my belief that construction drawings sold for hard-earned money to amateur builders should contain at least two orthogonal views of every detail in the boat plus perspective views to integrate the entire structure. For a self-taught draftsman this was extremely tedious work, and my clients were often building themselves out of drawings.

One problem was that the basic layout of every boat was different. I longed for some continuity so that one drafting format and one set of instructions would apply, with minor variations, to a whole series of designs all identifiable as the work of one designer. I realized that this identity should be unique, unlike anything offered by the competition, and that the series should be focused on a specific purpose, in my case ocean cruising. The boats all must have a swing centerboard and, I decided, a single mast setting the two headsails of a cutter rig.

I had become dissatisfied with the two-masted ketch and yawl rigs of my existing designs for they were heavy and complex and the after (mizzen) sail seemed to develop little power relative to headsails. The usual single-masted rig, the sloop, carries only one headsail at a time, so adjusting sail area to suit the frequent changes in wind force is done by changing to headsails of different sizes. This was a practice I regarded as dangerous drudgery, the crew clinging to a pitching bow often in waves and dark. For my clientele it was unjustified. The cutter, however, has only one mast but carries two headsails or "jibs" of different sizes which, because they have no mast in front of them to turbulate the wind each develop lots of power. Furthermore two headsails of different size allow sail area to be adjusted easily to suit the wind force without actually changing headsails; both the smaller, inner jib or "staysail" and the outer larger "headsail" could be used together in lighter winds, and either one could be simply lowered as the wind increased. (This was prior to the popularity of roller furling-and-reefing hardware for headsails. This hardware now commonly appears on both headsails in cruising cutters).

But things were piling up in the middle now. With the cockpit on top of the centerboard trunk, both located dead amidships, the cutter's single mast would be located there also. Yes! Step the mast on the centerboard trunk right in the cockpit. Why not! On the other hand, why? What other consequences would attend this arrangement?

Back in my schooner days I learned that the greatest single hazard facing ocean sailors was falling, or being knocked or swept, overboard. Would this mast-in-cockpit rig be a way to minimize this risk? I thought it would be, for the crew would have access to the halyards (for raising and lowering all the sails) and to the gooseneck on the boom for reefing, the mainsail... all without going on deck. Now the boat could be operated even in heavy weather without leaving the safety of the deep and central cockpit... hard for waves to jump in or crew to fall out of. The more I pondered the rightness of this arrangement, the more it became incumbent upon me to do this thing.

But I still had to finish the plans of the earlier boats. This provided time for me to ponder attendant possibilities for a central cockpit cutter. The main structural difference was that the mast was no longer stepped on a cross beam, thus the beam itself could be vastly different. Instead of the usual massive box that had to be ducked under down below, the main strength of the structure could be more like a full-width "diaphragm" bulkhead that spanned all three hulls. And because there was no mast trying to crush it at its centerline, this "main strength bulkhead could be designed with a large hole in the middle for the crew to step through instead of crawling under. This would open up the accommodation dramatically while saving weight as well.

The narrow hulls of most trimarans with the normal saloon cabins amidships featured a cramped dinette on one side with a narrow passage opposite, and there was lots of traffic past the dinette. Even in wide-hulled monohulls the usual saloon table blocks traffic from moving through the cabin, from the cockpit or the galley to the head. In the 41 we had placed the dinette in the very stern where nobody had to get past it on the way to anywhere. I realized that if the afterbody of the new trimaran's main hull were made wider than the 41's then there would be space for a generous dinette in the very stern, more generous than in the 41 and also unobstructed by the cross beam. A small superstructure over this dinette would create an ideal communal space, intimate yet open, for the eye level of those seated there would be at window level. A large window facing straight aft with a sheltering brow could be left open even in rain and flying spray thus reducing the queasiness often caused by dining or navigating in a deep cave far from the view and the air. This was a layout not unlike the great sterncastles of the square-rigged ships of Nelson's time. It was the captain's cabin, the preferred location in the ship. Why would it not work in a trimaran?

And if it did, would the boating public regard it as just another example of the abounding quackeries of the time?

I had loads of work to finish on other designs, but I could not resist the temptation to draw a small boat of this basic configuration, hoping not to make mistakes on something big. The result was a 25-foot pocket cruiser whose wings could be folded for trailering. It had a "double chine" main hull something like the BROWN 41 except for the addition of a small flat plank in the very bottom. She was not as chesty as CARAVEL and the flat bottom greatly simplified the installation of the centerboard trunk. Also the bottom plank could be made relatively thick to give the craft a strong surface on which to rest on a trailer or during purposeful or accidental groundings. The floats also had a single chine but were not nearly as asymmetric as CARAVEL's. I was nonetheless convinced, and remain so, that asymmetric floats in a trimaran definitely pay their way by improving windward performance even beyond what is achieved with a centerboard. The float chines placed plenty of buoyancy down deep where it was needed for initial stability while avoiding the ungainly breadth on deck of the standard V-section floats of the Pivers and others.

Called simply the BROWN 25, this boat's plans sold well from the start. They were inexpensive, and the size of the project was appropriate for the garage-type woodworker. Like in the 41, the 25's cockpit also was located amidships on top of its large centerboard trunk. She had the diaphragm-type main strength bulkheads but her cockpit was too small to accommodate the mast so she was originally rigged as a sloop with the mast stepped on the main bulkhead, a risky compromise which succeeded only because the boat, and the mast loads, were small and light.

The first of these 25-foot vessels to be completed locally was built by one Max Hemminger, a stoic field surveyor who rented shop space in the defunct hide tanneries at Redwood City, California. A large, ramshackle complex of barn-red wooden buildings, this site was taken over by do-it-yourself boatbuilders. Many of the craft constructed there were ferro-cement monohulls but multihulls were well represented by Max and others. Before his boat was finished we made changes to allow it to be rigged as a cutter, giving him a very powerful and handy micro-cruiser.

Sea trials in Max's DHARMA were very encouraging. She sailed like a witch even in big waves, and Max stated his intention to sail her single-handed to Hawaii. Jo Hudson and I admired Max for his hard-core undertaking and we helped him develop the boat for single-handing. For working on the bottom, Jo suggested we trailer DHARMA to a secluded place in Carmel Valley where the branches of a huge oak tree and Jo's heavy duty chain fall could be used to suspend the boat in mid air, free of its trailer. So it was that Max and Jo and I had a little camp fire one night and watched the boat swing and spin like a mobile in the firelight. While looking at her anatomy from this perspective, as her shadow soared in unison through the leafy canopy above, I imagineered a somewhat larger version, went home and sketched out what would become the Searunner 37. But again I had work to finish.

Max was to encounter a real gale in mid passage, but news of his safe arrival in Honolulu brought other aspirants to my door. The first was Jerry des Roches, a very lean and energetic physical therapist who sailed a Piver NUGGET, which he had built himself. His lady friend Patty, (same physique, same energy) was supportive of their having a larger boat for voyaging. I offered them the 34' MANTA but when they learned of my fledgling 37-footer concept, they wanted to start building right now. I protested that the plans were barely started, but they prodded me with money. Jo Anna and I were so broke at the time that there was no refusing so I started to draw yet another new boat, and Jerry began to build yet another from unfinished plans.

About the same time I was approached by the young John Marples, then nearing graduation in engineering from Cal Poly. Six-four, clean cut and articulate, John was a keen dinghy sailor and had become interested in multihulls for cruising. Again I offered him the 34, but he was hesitant, so I told him of the 37 and he, like Jerry, jumped in.

Soon, here came my old friend Mark Hassall. Having recovered from the shipwreck of his OFF SOUNDINGS and come ahead financially by building giant fiberglass slides for amusement parks, he and Bonnie were ready for a new boat. All at once we had three 37's under construction, and I knew that Mark Hassall was going to build faster than I could draw.

I also knew that this frantic level of activity was being experienced by all the other multihull designers. Some of them, like Dick Newick in the Caribbean, Lock Crowther in Australia, Derek Kelsall in England and several newcomers in France were all moving strongly into designs for ocean racing. It was still the mid 1960s, but multihulls were moving pretty fast!

The Vanishing Skipper...

What explained this activity? Of course the enticement of corporate-sponsored ocean racing had a lot to do with it. The sponsors had three hulls and big sails on which to post their billboard messages and the winning sailors became superstars especially in France. Some exquisite multihull yachts were being produced with private funding, and the pure race boats were astronomically expensive yet they were often used for only one or two races and then dumped on the market for peanuts.

Like many of my clients I was not enamored with this aspect of multihulling but instead I was feeling a compelling urge for Jo Anna and me to build our own cruising boat and "bug out" with our boys. I had always promised that we would take a big boat ride one day. Jo Anna was supportive and the kids were growing into it. Largely because of hours spent in our little JESTER dinghy, Steve and Russ were becoming mighty little mariners at an early age.

Furthermore, I found the late sixties were not just frantic, they were threatening. The rebellious chants of the Beatles, Baez and Dylan and the hit musical HAIR typified the many formative influences on popular culture, which still reverberate today. We dragged our kids through the anti-war demonstrations in Santa Cruz and San Francisco, my boats gained a following among physicists at the Berkeley Radiation Laboratory and the grinding national news confirmed that things were getting tense for Tricky Dick. But it was mostly the lunacy of nuclear proliferation and what Martin Luther King called "the agony of Viet Nam" that catalyzed our impetus to somehow escape.

By 1968 the crack-ups and capsizes in multihull ocean racing were being sensationalized in the yachting press. Nevertheless, many of the designers saw racing as an opportunity for name recognition. Arthur Piver was among them. He had tried before to get a boat to England that was ready to race against the formidable competition in Europe. Finally in 1968 his 38-foot trimaran BIRD was there and entered in the upcoming OSTAR. This race is a single-handed dash – one man, one boat – across the North Atlantic against prevailing winds. But Arthur himself was in California when the race committee announced that all entrants must have made a qualifying run of at least 500 miles single-handed. This was something Art had never done. At the time this qualifier did not have to be sailed in the same vessel entered in the race, so Art borrowed a boat, one of his 25-foot DART class vessels, and planned to sail from the Golden Gate to San Diego, a sufficient distance to qualify. These were waters he knew well and the trip should be easy relative to the North Atlantic. So Arthur Piver cleared the Golden Gate, and he and his borrowed boat were never seen again.

To my mind, this is by far the most momentous multihull event of the sixties, and its repercussions are still being felt. Here was the man who had "ocean tested" his boats by making significant passages in both the Atlantic and Pacific, usually with the help of his Viking-like friend Rich Gurling as crew. He had done little ocean racing but for him to disappear at sea seemed inexplicable, and to this day nobody knows what happened to Arthur Piver. The event was shrouded in mystery and intrigue, with all kinds of rumors circulating to nourish the hope that he was still alive. These did little, however, to relieve the loss of confidence in multihulls that resulted from his disappearance. For me his loss engendered grief for his family and personal guilt; I had always felt some sense of betrayal to him for hanging out my own shingle. Today I realize that we all stand on someone else's shoulders. I certainly stood on his, and he stood on those of many of his clients who helped him bootstrap the trimaran into acceptance in the early days. In inventing the modern trimaran, Piver also benefited greatly from his correspondence with John Moorwood of the Amateur Yacht Research society (Chapter 3).

To me, Arthur Piver's main achievement was his many protégés, all the members of the early barnstorming gang and many others world wide who realized that there was a future for them in either designing, or building and selling multihulls. The fact that "the Skipper" (as he called himself in his own writings) had disappeared was a disaster not only to his family but to all of those who had been stimulated into action by his creativity and drive.

Moving On...

One day in 1968, at about the time I was dealing with this loss, Jo Anna and I were visited at home by a Catholic priest who explained, very considerately, that our house had been bought by the Church and that it would be torn down to make way for a driveway into their cemetery, which bordered our back yard. I was incensed that a perfectly good home, perhaps the most mellow and welcoming abode we had ever enjoyed – and with quiet neighbors behind – was to be razed for this purpose. But it was time to leave town anyway. It seemed we were always pestered by trimaran tire kickers at dinnertime; my patience with being a horse's mouth was growing thin and the traffic in town getting thick. We pined for the redwoods once again. With the very best of good luck we found a unique home in Big Creek canyon some twenty miles north of Santa Cruz and moved back into the country.

Jo Anna and I had spent our first four years together in Sausalito, the next four in Big Sur, the next four in Santa Cruz, and now we moved to Big Creek for what would be our last four years in California. Such mobility was typical of the time. A great roil of humanity resulting from the postwar westward wave of American culture that crashed upon Pacific shores from the landward side and reflected back upon itself. The same ground swell was being felt world wide, and it was from this context that modern multihulls emerged.

....

Illustrations for this chapter, narrated by the author, are available online at ...

www.OutrigMedia.com/books/atm-volume-one.html

7

JAILBREAK

1972 > 73

Now we return to the brink of that "precipice" where I left us hanging at the end of Chapter 1. Yes, Jo Anna's greed was greater than her fear. Indeed we were all greedy to go. After all, we had been trying to get away as a family for thirteen years, ever since that first fiasco in Baja with our little trimaran JUANA. For me it went back more like sixteen years, since the big schooner JANEEN and the ketch LABRISA. It went back all the way to Wolfgang Kraker von Schwartzenfeld! Then, just to get ready to go we had to survive the sixties, somehow manage to make a living as a renegade with Searunners, hold the family together and build my "baby," SCRIMSHAW.

It was a frantic time, but in no way was it more remarkable than what anyone goes through to focus obsessively on a deviant goal. It seems that in order to arrive, one must buy into the program – house, car, job, family and some kind of stone to roll (like a boat to build) – and then muster the gumption to buy your way out. That's unless perhaps you're willing to go it all alone, and what's the point of that? To me, that's just as nuts as sailing around the world without stopping; you miss out on the world! We chose to pick out a juicy piece of it to really savor, and finally we were not just "able to go" but also ready, so we went.

Routine Traverse?...

Sterling Hayden has called most yacht cruising "a routine traverse." It is true that the popular cruising routes, such as through the Bahamas, the Antilles, the Med and even the South Pacific, have become well trodden with the wakes of yachts and the cultural taint of yachtspeople.

Our junket in SCRIMSHAW was no exception, for we were far from alone on our way from California to Virginia via Panama. On the west coast of Mexico, in particular, we had not only balmy breezes and deep water with no outlying dangers; we also had lots of company from other yachties. It may have been "routine," but it was lots of fun. We did find one place that was relatively "undiscovered" at the time, and we had several unique experiences ashore for we left the boat to travel and live on land for over a year of the three years we were away. So this account is not a ship's log of navigational details, although we had our share of challenges at sea, and it is not a list of ports and people, although we found our favorites of both.

Instead what follows in the next four chapters are "incidents of travel" in Mesoamerica and the Western Caribbean. The real story, however, is about the effect of those incidents on a young family with a too-small sailboat, just enough money and, with the help of someone whose name I can't remember, plenty of time. It is the story of how we bailed out of involvements at home, hit the briny trail, and returned to find ourselves strangers in our own homeland (volume two).

Tight Little Bundle...

We departed from our dear home harbor at Santa Cruz, California, but our actual embarkation occurred late one afternoon from a thick bed of kelp on the Big Sur coast. It was September 1972, in the seasonal lull between the rousing summertime northwesters and the gales of November. We had learned our lesson well in JUANA, and were not about to go again into the wrong ocean at the wrong time. The sea was so calm that we could have landed on Point Sur, so we anchored overnight in the lee of Pfeifer Point. This jagged promontory is right at the heart of the South Coast, a stretch with no harbors where the mountains literally tumble into the sea. Here we had a restful night, and were visited next morning by Jo Hudson and friend Dean Taylor who both swam out from the beach despite the numbing water. They suggested we stop again behind the jagged rocks just offshore from Jo's place, fifteen miles south at Dolan Creek.

This we did despite the risk of exposing our new boat to the prospect of an early demise, but the Pacific was so pacific that we managed to get ashore by scrambling up the rocks at the top of a surge and dragging the dinghy behind us. We then ascended the 1,200 vertical feet to Jo's abode. This was done with the help of his Jeep and the three-mile trail along the cliffs and through the canyons.

From his aerie the whole Pacific stretches wide open to the horizon some sixty miles out. Earth's curvature is clearly visible from here, and arching over all is the thin membrane of atmospheric gas, filtering the sunlight with its hues of blue, pale overhead to azure straight out.

We looked down on SCRIMSHAW, a tight little bundle of plywood and glue bobbing on the boundary between land, water and air, all three seen in extreme. Our floating home was clinging to the feet of the Santa Lucia range where it steps into the sea, a coast where we had lived ashore, sailed along before and were now departing from.

While gulping snacks and drinks on the mountain, all of us were anxious for the lonely boat, its anchor clinging to the bottom in a place where, should it come dislodged, would surely lead to shipwreck. I mumbled to Jo Anna, "That's a powerful little tool we've got down there, but we can't leave it overnight. Remember Todos Santos and Strong eyes?"

"How could I forget," she said. "Let's go use that implement of ours," So we hurried back down the mountain. With hugs and send-offs from our closest friends we scrambled into SCRIMSHANKER, as our dinghy was called, and made it back aboard at dusk. After a meal and other preparations for our first night at sea, we paused to gaze at the cliffs in skylight. They obscured one whole quadrant of the universe but the rest of the heavenly hemisphere shone black and all aglitter. We upped the anchor and sailed away.

Minimum Security...

And ended up in prison. After stopping in the open rodestead at San Simion to visit the Hearst Castle, we entered Morro Bay, which became our favorite California harbor. The place is dominated by a huge monolith, an old volcanic hummock, much like Point Sur, but here there is a tight harbor behind the rock. (Incidentally, there is a small, natural harbor of refuge behind Point Sur, too. It is forbidden to the sailor by the Federal Government, probably off limits because of the heavy-duty underwater mumbo-jumbo that the Navy sends and receives from here. But if you were ever being swept ashore by overwhelming winds and seas, it would be better to defy the warning on the chart and tuck in just south of the rock at Point Sur than to suffer the surf on the north side. I don't think the fuzz would mess with you if you really needed refuge, but your anchor might foul on something sinister.)

Tidal currents are severe in the Morro Bay anchorage, which provided son Russell the conditions needed to develop an inventive stunt with the dinghy. Using the centerboard and rudder, but not the mast and sail, he trailed the little SCRIMSHANKER behind SCRIMSHAW crosswise to the current. By hooking the towline around the daggerboard trunk so as to pull sideways from the middle of the dink, he could play the daggerboard against the stream to hotrod the little boat at planning speed. He went zigzagging across the current from one "tack" to another, whooping with glee and jerking our home to port and starboard for hours. Not to be outdone, Steven rigged the bosun's chair to the spinnaker halyard, sat in it with his feet on the outboard end of the boom, and flung himself seaward so as to swing clear around the headstay – gyrating all the way – to return bruised and dizzy back to the end of the boom from its opposite side. When both of these "activities" occurred at once, our boat yawed and rolled and pitched in the quiet anchorage looking rather like a circus act while Jo Anna and I sat in the sterncastle, heads in hands, realizing that this sort of exercise was to be a necessary fixture of the trip. As it turned out, we came to accept that all of us would be required to yield the space, time and tolerance for each to originate and practice his or her own personal pursuit.

We then rounded Point Conception in perfect weather and stopped at Oceanside. There we were contacted by a close friend who we'll call Ken. This young rascal had used one of our 38-foot trimarans to go contrabanding, not unknown among multihullers at that time. He had been apprehended and put away at the Federal Correction Facility at nearby Lompoc. In this "minimum security" prison there was a club of inmates who, with the help of the staff Cultural Director was able to invite speakers to a monthly function. A letter from this Director said that the club wanted me to come and talk about trimarans! I accepted with the proviso that I could bring my wife and young sons, for I wanted us all to see the inside of a real prison. After some negotiation in which I pressed my luck, Tom Freeman and John Marples and their female companions also were invited. They met us at Oceanside and, one clear October night, we all went to jail:

The security of getting in and out is far from minimal. There are two Cyclone fences surrounding the place each twenty feet high, topped with razor wire and separated by a fifty foot-wide span of open ground covered with white-marble gravel and floodlighted. There are guard towers at intervals all around this dry moat. We are met at the Cyclone gate by the Cultural Director. After introductions, a guard opens the gate and I ask him quietly, "Why the white gravel?"

He reluctantly explains, "That's where we shoot. The contrast improves marksmanship."

Once past the guarded gate we are ushered into a long chamber lined with steel benches and with massive doors at each end. Saying, "I'll be right back," the Director leaves by the door we have just entered and locks us in. Like Houdini he soon reappears at the other end to admit us behind the walls.

While we pass through a concrete hallway the Director warns, "Some of these Men haven't seen a woman in years so you ladies are not to leave the podium."

We enter an auditorium where about a hundred men sit in folding chairs neatly arranged in arc rows beginning a respectful distance from the podium. There are chairs and a large screen behind. The audience is silent and totally uniform in appearance; short haircuts, neatly pressed khakis with no insignia or labels, all staring at the women. Tom and John load and aim our projector. Steve and Russ scooch their chairs close to Jo Anna.

After a brief introduction by the Director I begin my practiced presentation. During the initial remarks, intended to inform the Non-boating listeners of the nature of multihulls, I am suddenly aware of a face in the front row. "Ken!" I gasp, dumbstruck by the thought of my friend being among the incarcerated. Compulsively I stride to him, we embrace and the crowd responds with a burst of laughter. As I go back to the dais I see the Director returning to his seat looking very much relieved. The ice was broken.

During the slides the audience participates noisily, urging me on to animate my show. In the Q&A afterward I am bombarded with the most intelligent and pertinent questions ever presented to me before or since:

"What do you mean by 'isotropic' materials?"

"The same strength in all directions, like a piece of metal or plywood. A simple plank of lumber has less than half the strength across the grain than along the board."

"Aren't most boats built out of planks?"

"Traditionally, yes. It's like building a giant basket. But you can't build a multihull out of planks; there's too much twisting stress or global torsion, loads in all directions on our sprawling platforms."

"Oh, I gotcha."

"Mmmm," mumbles the audience.

"What's form stability?"

"That's when you have a single hull that is wide enough to sit upright in the water by itself,"

"How wide is that?"

"About one fourth or fifth as wide as it is long, which is really fat for pushing through the water at speed. That's why single-hulled boats push a wave ahead of them and drag a wave behind. The trouble is, waves that close together just can't go very fast so neither can the boats. They are locked between their own waves."

"Mmmm," goes the audience.

"So, aren't multihulls wide?"

"Not as the water sees them, that's their whole point. The individual hulls are very narrow – at the waterline – by comparison to monohulls."

"How narrow is that?"

"Anywhere from one seventh as wide as they are long for a cruiser – like our boat – up to even something like one-fifteenth as wide as they are long for a racer. But here's the crux; taken alone, any one of those narrow hulls would tip right over in the water by itself – no form stability -- so we have to join two or three of them together wide apart. Now you've got narrow hulls that don't make waves nearly as much. And that is combined with what I call raft stability. In a single-hulled sailboat of course when the wind blows on the sails it tries to tip the hull over. So they put a big chunk of lead on the bottom of the keel, and this ballast more or less doubles the weight of the boat! Whereas multihulls have enough raft stability to really stand up in the wind without hardly leaning over, at roughly half the weight."

A man in back blurts out, "So you've got a combination going!"

Ken shouts over his shoulder, "That's what I've been telling you, man."

"Aaaaah," goes the audience.

"Right," I say, "narrow hull form, light weight and raft stability."

Someone changes the subject: "How can you just sail off to Mexico? Don't they guard the borders and the ports?"

"Yes, we have to get visas, show passports, and get clearance or permission from your last American port and show it in your first Mexican port, or almost any country. It's easy once you get the system down and sometimes it helps to grease a few sweaty palms (laughter). Some yachties bend the rules and just go, no papers at all. They often get away with it, but it's not cool because it sours the officials for everyone else."

"You mean that with a little bit of paperwork you can just blow in to some island and hang out!?"

"Yes. There are time limits, but you can often get an extension. So long as you don't cause any trouble, you spend a little money, or you offer some skill that is needed, yes! Most places the people are glad to see you coming."

"Wooow!" goes the crowd, and the questioner shouts, "I had no idea such an avenue of freedom still exists," (Cheers)...

The group was getting just a little rowdy for the Director's comfort, so he called an end. But I was able to speak briefly with Ken, who said they had impounded his boat but had offered to save it until he got out but he would have to buy it back. It was very hard to leave him in that place.

On our way out, I asked the Director what the future held for most of these inmates, and he said, "The emphasis here is on rehabilitation, and we really try. For a guy like Ken the chance of a normal life is pretty good. He's told me he was just trying to make some cruising money and figures now it would have been easier to earn it digging ditches. But unfortunately, about 85 percent of these people will eventually find their way back into the penal system. (We all gasp or sigh.) Once an individual makes the conscious decision to step beyond the law (he glanced at Steve and Russ who were still escorting their mother closely), he has a hard time getting back."

It was just what I had hoped for.

The So-Cal Scene...

We spent a month in Southern California harbor hopping, visiting friends, cruising the Channel Islands and checking out the local multihull scene. Things were going well on board partly because we all enjoyed the socializing. Steve and Russ were often able to hook up with others their age, and we all found plenty to do. Jo Anna and I expected this situation to change when we entered Mexico, and we wondered how we all would deal with increasing isolation.

There were literally hundreds of multihulls under construction in So-Cal, some in back yards but many in large, hardscrabble compounds like Multihull City near Los Angeles; Rancho Verde near Camarillo; and another at Chula Vista near the Mexican border. The end ties in most of the marinas were choked with multihulls, many of them trimarans. However, catamarans were well represented especially by boats designed and built by the CSK partnership (Chapter 5).

To give credit where it is really due to the other professionally successful Southern California multihull designers of the time, I must take a little space to highlight just four among several:

- Ed Horstman, an aeronautical engineer who designed a popular series of cruising trimarans that very cleverly maximized the multihull's potential for interior spaciousness in a configuration that was shown capable of rounding Cape Horn.

- Hugo Myers, whose catamaran designs rivaled the best in achieving that most difficult compromise between spaciousness and speed.
- Norman Cross, whose designs for both cats and tris I always thought were right down the middle between utility and style.
- Jay Kantola, a commercial artist who designed the first – and arguably still the most – really beautiful and seamanlike cruising trimarans.

As we approached San Diego in SCRIMSHAW, Norman Cross arranged for me to present a slide show at the prestigious San Diego Yacht Club, where he was a member. At their monthly weekday luncheon meeting I faced the largest audience I had ever addressed. I was a bit intimidated by the big-name sailors among them, and did not present well. The house was rather predisposed to monohulls anyway and had no questions to ask, quite a contrast with the prisoners. (Interestingly, in 1988 it was the San Diego Yacht Club that first entered the Americas Cup with a multihull: they won.) We soon embarked for Baja.

The Way South...

Jo Anna and I had not been to Baja since before Steven was born, and it was great to sail again for foreign waters. Our memories of drifting down that desert coast in JUANA, sweltering in calms at exactly the wrong time of year, did not invite repetition. We resolved to push for tropical Mexico, and with the boys in agreement we sailed straight from San Diego for Cape San Lucas, or "Cabo" as it was now called. Being November we had wind and plenty of it, right on our quarter! In about a week of sailing day and night we had one hour of calm, which gave us all the chance to bathe and eat well, and then came the wind again. It was great fun, but this lap was a big joke on me:

The wind-actuated self steering device that I had designed for Searunners, and which had been used by my clients with splendid results on some much longer passages, did not – for some reason I will never understand – work on my own boat. Despite hours of tinkering with and cursing at the contraption, in the end we had to steer the whole trip by hand! A profound disillusion for me, my crew didn't seem to care so long as we were really moving. So the four of us traded the tiller watch-on-watch, day and night, in the old fashioned way. It was almost a week of glorious romping down the waves, and it would become the best sustained downwind slide in our (so far) 38 years of sailing SCRIMSHAW. Except for demanding to be steered by hand, the boat did rather well and so did the crew. In part this was because steering gives everyone something meaningful, even crucial, to do.

Finally we rounded the great Cape San Lucas in a sunrise scene with high russet rocks reaching into pinks and purples in the clouds. But when we sailed into the open bight, Jo Anna and I were jolted by the changes on the beach. Our old friend the cannery was still there, more ramshackle than ever, but the spot where JUANA had survived the hurricane in 1959, spiderwebbed to dead men in the sand, was now occupied by a big white hotel. (Today that hotel and most of the beach are gone to make way for the dredged channel into the sports fishing marina and the flamboyant Cabo resorts.)

While anchored there among a fleet of other yachts, Jo Anna and I had a hankering to return overland to Todos Santos and the Pescadero beach where we had lost JUANA and, with the help of Strong Eyes, found her again. I was half hoping that we could find Strong Eyes himself and thank him properly for the great deed he had done for us years ago. There was now a road and a bus to Todos Santos, so, in the face of great protest from the boys nonetheless we all went off through the desert to find a big piece of Mom and Dad's past.

The boys were not into it, and we now learned the value of consensus in the crew, for traveling with sourpuss kids was no fun. Nevertheless, he old town was much renewed – a paved street included – and we spent the night again in the partly refurbished Hotel California. But there was no one there we knew. We enquired for "Ojos Fuertes," (Strong Eyes) and learned that he had passed away. We went down to Pescadero beach, found it vacant and unchanged, mused on our intense experience there while the boys sulked, and headed back to Cabo.

The Cruising Mode...

For the next four months we practiced consensus. It worked, yet those happy times are rather a blur to me now. I see glimpses of:

- Thanksgiving with the yachties at Puerto Vallarta, mariachis belting out their anthems at Guadalajara, grooving on the palms and papaya at Yelapa, and anchoring by the stern off of many Mexican villages to catch the evening land breeze through the sterncastle window.
- The somber thud of Spanish iron church bells, the laughing bray of burros, the early morning thumping of little diesel-

powered corn mills, the salivating handclaps of fresh tortillas in preparation.

- Steve and Russ making friends with Mexicans their age, Jo Anna and I making friends with Mexicans our age.
- Baking best bread in a stovetop oven, poaching fish in a rolley anchorage, distinctive cuisine at a taco stand, shopping all over town for five items formerly found at one Safeway.
- Snorkeling in warm clear water, sailing in balmy breezes, struggling with huge fish, contending with the paradox of accepting generosity from impoverished people.
- Looking out for other yachts with kids, bearing down on the boys to put aside their sibling rivalry , making out as man and wife when they are ashore, sorting out the wheat from the chaff of family life on board.
- The long run to old Acapulco, the short time with newfound friends, meeting up with old shipmates, seeing other Searunners in quiet coves and raucous ports.

Somewhere along in there the boys started making waterproof matches and selling them to other boats in the anchorages. Russ dipped each matchstick in melted paraffin, which really messed up the galley. Steve drew custom labels with colorful marine scenes for gluing onto every box, which really messed up their cabin. They sold more than they could make, and I'm sure the other yachties thought we were penniless. Russell took to making little model boats, especially of proas, which was the shape of things to come for him, and Steve spent hours with Jo Anna's guitar, also a prophetic move. Soon his plunking even sounded like music.

A fantastic new resort complex was yet to open at Las Hadas (The Fairies) and we were so taken with the Mediterranean/Mother Goose architecture of the place that we asked if we could rent a room. Pleased with the chance to train their staff, the management obliged at a token rate, so Jo Anna and I lolled in luxury ashore while the boys reveled in having the boat to themselves for a few days. In the lovely swimming pool of the hotel Russell began testing his boat models in the seismic waves generated by Steve's cannonballs.

Stopping for an overnight at a quiet anchorage called Tenacatita, we were entertained by a herd of giant manta rays performing their mating ritual underwater somersaults. I found this a good omen because of the similarity of these creatures to our Searunner sail emblem logo. The "flying whale," as it became known, was riding high on lots of mainsails, and perhaps for that reason one of these fabulous creatures arranged to take us for a ride:

The anchorage has been dead still but I awaken from the strange sensation of the boat being under way. Incredulous, I listen to the slightest sound of water flowing past the hull. Lying there I muse on how sensitive we have all become to changes in conditions, but I reject this sensation knowing that when I dozed off we were anchored in a calm harbor. Slowly I ponder that in this little bay there is no discharging river and no tidal current, yet we really are moving slowly through the water! Confused I crawl from our bunk, trying not to wake Jo Anna, and go on deck. The night is clear with a fingernail moon. Rubbing my eyes I see... Nothing. Just flat water. There is no bay, no lights and no... No land!

Checking the anchor I see the rode straining out ahead, cutting a small wake where it pierces the surface of the dead-calm sea. We are being towed – apparently have been being towed for some time – out to sea by what must be a manta ray caught on our anchor line. Unconcerned for us but disturbed for the animal, I remember that rays are members of the shark family and some of them depend, like most sharks, on retaining forward motion through the water in order to respire. They cannot pump their gills like the fishes in order to breathe. Restrained by its collision with an anchor line the beast would pour on the power, possibly even yank an anchor out of the bottom and head for deeper water.

I awaken the boys and explain our situation. They too are concerned for the ray. Quietly we attach one end of a hundred feet of spare line to the boat, the other end to the on-deck end of our anchor rode and toss all the slack overboard at once. Jo Anna comes up and asks, "What's going on?" As SCRIMSHAW slowly comes to a halt she disbelieves our explanation but then is struck by the absence of the continent that was there when we retired. We pull in all the line and the boat length of chain attached to the anchor. There are chunks of flesh and lots of slime at the bitter end, and we are all upset. We have injured – albeit inadvertently – a creature that symbolizes the perceived grace and freedom of our boat and ourselves. Choosing not to return to the anchorage where this affront might be repeated, we get under way, motoring slowly off to the southwest. At dawn, we see the peaks of the Sierra Madre in the sunrise...

At another cozy little cove we joined three other yachts at anchor expecting to socialize with our compatriots. But there was something going on ashore. The boys hit the beach, Steve on the surfboard and Russ via dinghy, and promptly they mingled with several men who were harboring in the shade of a palapa (thatched awning, open sides). Besides a ramshackle rancho in the distance where we later learned there was a bunkhouse, there were no other structures or signs of habitation near the beach. Steve soon returned leaving Russell to surf the dinghy in the mild swash. He reported that a group of about ten men and one woman were preparing for a little fun and that we were invited to join them.

I swam to the beach and met this group of Mexican businessmen from a nearby farming town. They were all shirtless and in swim trunks, said they owned the beachfront and kept it just for such occasions. There were two country people, a man and woman who were caretakers for the place and hosts to the owners. The rancher had shot a deer and had it hanging, smeared with sauce and peppers to ward off the flies, and he was grooming a fire on which to roast the venison. The matron was slapping tortillas and stewing beans, and the men were chipping ice and pouring mescal, the cactus-based elixir one step down from tequila. They had it by the gallon, said there was plenty for their anchored guests and suggested I extend their invitation to the other boats. Russ rowed me around to the other boats where we explained that all were invited ashore; we should all bring something to contribute, and that I had no idea of what would result.

Aside from the outstanding food and drink there was an earnest reaching out from both sides across the culture gulf. Most of the Mexicans spoke some English and most of the yachties spoke a bit of Spanish, and we all sampled one another's food and beverages. We talked of politics and family, traveling and home, work and play.

At dark a mantle lamp was lit, more ice was chipped for drinks, and the Mexican men formed up and began to sing. Their traditional songs were spellbinding, deep with emotion and harmony. Their voices called out to the firmament with startling volume, pleading to be understood. Everything from Moorish chants to Aztec huapangos were casually performed, and we gringos (not a pejorative term in Mexico) were swept away. Until, that is, our hosts asked us to sing for them! We tried. I mean we really tried, but the only things we all knew were bits of things like Old Folks At Home and I've Been Working On The Railroad. These came out weak and pinched. Our hosts were nonplussed and we were chagrinned. I asked if the men were of a practiced group; did they sing professionally? They insisted not, saying that all Mexicans can sing their traditional songs together, and they thought it sad that Yankis could not. In the end it didn't matter for we were all bumping into the non-existent walls of the palapa. It's a good thing no one had to drive home.

Now we were getting far enough south to experience a lot of light airs. Compared to most of the other cruising boats, SCRIMSHAW would glide along on zephyrs, so we resorted to motoring only in real calms whereas most of our company was motoring all the way, at least when their motors would run. In every anchorage where there were other yachts I was impressed with the degree to which these cruisers were suffering equipment breakdowns. This was particularly true of vessels that were highly dependent on their electrical systems. It caused them serious delays while waiting for replacements, and for some of the more unfortunate it seemed to take the fun out of cruising.

At the time SCRIMSHAW had no electrics at all except for the dry cell-powered compass light and the fluorescent tri-color masthead running light, both of which were used only when really needed. In addition our shallow draft often allowed us to anchor much closer to the beach than the monohull fleet; there was better shelter in close – smoother water -- and a shorter run to shore. One afternoon I was napping in the shade of our superstructure when I heard an approaching outboard motor suddenly splutter and die. Sounds of a struggle ensued, with repeated yanks on the starter and answering curses. Then came the sounds of the boat being rowed; again it approached our shallow anchorage. As it came close I looked up sleepily and was greeted by a skipper we had met before. Standing in his inflatable dinghy, which was only semi-inflated, he stared at me disdainfully and spluttered, "You don't understand the problem!"

"Er, what problem?" I replied.

"You just don't understand! And why should you? First of all your dinghy is not a deflatable like this damn thing. You don't need an outboard for it and now mine's conked out. Ever try to row a deflatable?"

"Oh yes, I know what you mean," I said. I also knew that fancy, motorized dinghies are so bulky and heavy that they are usually left afloat at night, tied to the sterns of their mother ships. As such, they are a favorite target for thieves. Because of our wide side decks, SCRIMSHANKER could be easily pulled aboard every night. However, she had to be rowed wherever she went, but at least she was dependable.

"No you don't know what I mean!" the skipper went on. "You can't possibly. Here you've got this boat that sails fast in no wind, anchors in no water and never breaks down. Now our generator is out and the whole boat depends on it. Our frozen stuff is thawing, we can't cook anything or get water to the sinks. We can't even raise the anchor!"

"Gee, that's a nuisance," I said. "How can we help?"

"Do you have an extra can opener? Ours is electric and we can't even open some tuna for lunch!"

We did not have a spare can opener but gave him the one we had. The boys rowed ashore and bought another in the nearby village, the simplest Mexican kind. We still have it on board today.

The Horny Donkey...

At length we arrived at a squalid little Indian village called Huatulco (now a resort) on the western edge of the Gulf of Tehuantepec. This gulf is located on the Pacific side of a narrow, low pass in the isthmus of far-southern Mexico. There are mountain ranges on each side of the pass. High pressure in the Caribbean, pushed south by winter fronts coming all the way from the Canadian breadbasket, squirts through the pass to cause dreadful gales in this gulf; "tehuantepeckers."

There was one other yacht in the anchorage, mercifully with kids in the crew, which had attempted to cross the Gulf and turned back. Using the tiny steps attached to our mast, I climbed to the top with binoculars (something I still do often) and was able to determine that indeed the sea was blown to solid white out there. We decided to wait.

Our visit just happened to coincide with an upcoming Indian festival. For a week we watched the local population grow from its usual 100 souls to something like five thousand. A large beachfront cantina was erected, together with a log stockade, and the Indians kept arriving over the long dirt tracks, which led down from the surrounding territory. Temporary stalls of many traveling merchants popped up behind the beach, a band stand appeared, trucks and animals jammed the vicinity and the rout of little generators was drowned only by the braying of amplified hucksters and the halting downbeat of Juapango music.

There was cold beer at the Cantina, and as visitors we were made welcome. One afternoon while we imbibe with the crew of the other yacht, the ruckus all around was punctuated by the hoots of a horney donkey pleading for a mate. Indeed there was a ready female nearby, and presently the two of them came charging through the cantina, toppling tables and scattering the patrons. Over two days his happened several times until finally the stud was tethered to a bush nearby, his distended lovemuscle dragging the ground and blown with flies. We named the poor beast Tehuantepecker.

For the most part the Indians were a bit remote. Many of them spoke little Spanish and it became clear that this was their holiday, both commercial and religious, so by late in the afternoons we gringos normally retreated to our boats to observe the hectic scene from the anchorage.

By day the beach was crowded with bathers but strangely there was no swimwear; the people simply entered the water in their clothes including the women who wore very full and decorative garments. There was no swimming as such; the people just lounged, swishing their limbs – seemingly entranced – in the gentle surf. At dusk we saw that many holes were being dug in the sand by hand, as deep as human arms could reach, and by nightfall candles and lanterns were placed in the holes. The affect was of portals to an illuminated underworld. Family groups lolled about each radiant excavation apparently praying.

Captivated by this sight I ventured ashore one evening to discern its significance. I was politely told that it was the end of the dry season, the rains would start soon, and the people had come to the seaside to "celebrate the waters" and pray for enough rainfall to nurture their crops. Feeling very much the intruder I returned to the boat.

The next day we went ashore for the final day of the festival. I was not feeling very well, a bit headachy and no appetite at breakfast, but still we wanted to watch the exodus of all those people. Once in the throng we saw a pathetic drunk being released from the stockade. and Jo Anna noticed a mature Indian woman who was wearing the black blouse common among these Indian women. This one was beautifully embroidered with an earthy floral pattern that we agreed was especially attractive. "See if you can find out where to get one," Jo said. She was obviously imagining herself in such a garment, so I mustered my nerve and approached the woman. With hand gestures made to my own torso, not hers, I mimed her embroidery and pointed to her sleeve. Without responding she led the horse to a sizable tree and swung its lead rope around one side. She caught it as it whipped around the other, and magically tossed a bowline knot in the rope faster than I had ever seen it done by a salt sailor. She motioned for me to follow her. Striding out like a cake walker, she led me through the crowded aisles between merchant's stalls in the process of being disassembled for the trip home. I scurried to keep up with her, dodging carts and other scurriers, and realized that I had lost Jo Anna. We came to a stall where the keepers were packing up but where a few such blouses were still on display. My guide abruptly left.

Without Jo Anna's help I picked out one of the blouses, negotiated the price (about three dollars) and returned to find Jo Anna. Back on board later she put it on and we agreed it looked better on an Indian so we squirreled it away. This was the first piece of what would become hundreds in our Central American textile collection. Today when we examine these treasures we recall with pleasure the story behind the acquisition of each one. Like Russell with his dinghy tricks and Steven with his high wire act, "looking for cloth" was destined to be a prevailing theme of our travels for Jo and me.

"Welcome To Guatemala"...

After the festival I climbed the mast again and saw that the white tehuantepecer had melted into blue-black ocean. When discussing with other yachties the tactics for crossing this Gulf, the sage advice was to hug the beach all the way. The worst gales come from the land, and if one can avoid being caught offshore at least there are no huge seas. But after only an hour of motoring in a flat calm with our little four horsepower motor (which gave us only four knots), I bit the bullet of temptation and we headed straight across the Gulf for a landfall in Guatemala. It was risky as hell but we got away with it. After motoring all day and all the next night, a time during which I was feeling a bit ill, sunrise revealed a stunning range of some thirty volcanoes that was Guatemala.

We were relieved but by now I was definitely sick; so fevered and fagged out that it was frightening. I had a blinding headache but otherwise no pain. There was no real doctor within reach and we had no idea what I'd come down with. Mercifully, I was the only one. Steve and Russ took over the boat, I cowered in my bunk and Jo Anna did the navigating.

We had planned to stop in Guatemala anyway. A friend there, one Arturo Herbruger, had once owned a trimaran of my design. When learning of our trip Arturo had urged us to visit him in his home country; "You'll be surprised at how great it is," he had said repeatedly. So I had called him from Acapulco to say that we were coming, and when I questioned him about details he said, "The trouble is there's really no place to land on the Pacific side. (Like Mexico, Guatemala has a coast on both oceans.) You have to clear into the country at a place called Puerto San Jose, which is nothing but a long old iron wharf sticking out through the surf. It's our only railhead on that side, and ships anchor offshore to receive cargo that is carried out to them in lighters from the wharf. You have to anchor near the wharf, and the officials will come out to you to handle your paperwork."

"Then what?" I asked over the weak phone connection.

"You have to continue three miles south and enter the country at an unprotected river mouth. The surf can be challenging." This sounded interesting because at last we would be off the yachting circuit, but it also sounded daunting. "Once inside," Art concluded, "there is a huge jungle lagoon where a little local resort can keep your boat safely while you catch the bus to Guatemala City, about three hours inland. You've got to come inland and up to the high country to see what we're about." With no more information than this, plus Arturo's phone number, it was now critical that we somehow get me ashore.

Our chart showed the unlikely position of the wharf, and when we approached the area we saw a small freighter anchored about two miles offshore. Sailing closer in very light airs we spotted the wharf extending defiantly for what looked like half a mile out to just beyond a raging surf. The chart also showed the continental shelf to be wide in this area, shoaling very gradually in from the ten fathom line about fifty miles offshore. This allows the ocean swell to "feel the bottom" over an extended time and mount up steeply before collapsing near the beach. We anchored in thirty feet of water about a quarter mile off the wharf in the open sea. We set the Guatemalan courtesy flag and our quarantine flag, indicating that we wished to enter the country. Having no two-way radio aboard with which to explain ourselves to the authorities we just waited.

A cute little donkey engine was hauling small railcars of cargo down the wharf and into the long warehouse at its outer end. A lightering barge clanged violently against the old pilings while big bundles of cargo were lowered into it by crane. A small tugboat was returning from the ship. After it deposited its empty barge at the wharf, it came toward us.

As the tug slowly circled SCRIMSHAW we all showed ourselves on deck to reveal our entire family crew. Four uniformed men stared at us silently from the tug. It circled again. Finally one of them commanded in English, "Hey! Bring your papers here."

I was feeble, practically on hands and knees, but I did not want to send Jo Anna or either of the boys aboard that vessel. It was rolling in the swell and the idea of them bringing it close enough to SCRIMSHAW for anyone to transfer was risky. I had no idea of the skill of its operator, there was no question of which vessel might be damaged by poor handling and from the sound of their instructions it seemed they wouldn't care if we were sunk.

The boys offered to swim over, but instead they hung a plastic bag containing our clearance papers from the end of our ten-foot boat hook and motioned for the tug to approach. It came close gingerly in reverse with its low towing bulwark inching toward our stern. As they took the bag I said "Need doctor. Doctor?" and the tug instantly pulled ahead to a safe distance. The men opened the bag, talked rapidly among themselves in Spanish, and one of them called across the water, "Infermo?"

I said "Si, yo soy infermo."

"You come here!" they said.

We put my shoes and wallet and a change of clothes in another bag and again the tug approached in reverse, its batters steel stern heaving menacingly in the swell. With the boys helping me on our boat and the men catching me on theirs, the transfer was made.

Using both languages we conversed on the tug. They understood my predicament. Shouting feebly across the water I explained to my crew that I would be back as soon as possible. "Stay anchored here unless the wind comes up. If you have to put to sea I'll find you at La Union" (which was in El Salvador and the next real port to the south). With this I left my family bobbing on the ocean:

During the short run to the wharf there is much chatter by radio between the tug and the wharf. With the tug alongside one of the lighters I am assisted by willing hands up onto its cargo hatch. The lighter lurches against its lines and bashes into the wharf. I am knocked from my feet but caught by three men who promptly sit me down in a sturdy oak chair that is suspended by a rope harness from above. Two men step onto the rungs of the chair, hold me in it firmly and, at the top of a swell, we are all whisked into the air, hoisted twenty feet to the wharf deck, swung inboard and set softly down beside the grinning operator of a coal-fired, steam-driven, spark throwing derrick engine.

A bit shaken by this debarkation I am led into the warehouse where men in baggy white suits with red sash belts are pushing hand carts holding huge bales of cotton. Feeling unsteady on my feet I am led through narrow aisles between high piles of bulk cargo out onto the open wharf. Three of the uniformed men from the tug escort me down the long, swaying deck of the wharf toward land. I look down upon the hissing surf, out at my boat, and try not to imagine that boat in that surf.

As we arrive at the very inboard end of the wharf there is a gap between it and the land. I now determine that, relative to terra firma the wharf is indeed swaying! The unsteadiness I feel is not the fever or the "rocking dock syndrome" one often experiences when coming ashore from a seagoing boat. The dock is indeed rocking.

In amazement I gape at the relative motion between the steel-faced sides of this two-foot-wide gap and at the clever sliding-and-slewing joints in the railway that tolerate this motion. The whole wharf is swaying at least a hand's breadth in the surf. In a practiced manner, two of my escorts step across the gap; the third man steadies me from behind, the other two reach back for me and as I step over the gap they all say to me in unison, "Welcome to Guatemala."

Don't Move, Don't Think...

Within an hour I was back aboard SCRIMSHAW. Jo Anna was much relieved to see me but Steve and Russ had obviously enjoyed their responsibility for the boat. I reported that Arturo had been contacted by radio through the shipping office in Guatemala City (there was no phone here) and he had instructed us to proceed as planned with entering the river mouth and he would meet us in a few hours at the little jungle resort. He would then take me to a doctor. "Talk about a friend!" said Jo Anna.

But I was suffering the effects of something like the ultimate hangover; weak as a newborn kitten, head like an impacted molar, gut like a poisoned coyote, and even with two pairs of sunglasses I had to hide from the sun.

We motored the three miles south, spotted the river mouth against a background of jungle, and buzzed around outside the surf line trying to decide if and when to run the gamut. We all put on life jackets, dogged the hatches, lashed the dinghy to the cabin top and installed the drop boards. Steve and Russ had done some surfing and so had experience in judging when the larger waves were approaching the break. Our little outboard buzzed away impotently, giving little more than steerageway. We were all very tense:

"Not now," agree the boys. I steer seaward but before the boat is headed out a huge swell looms up, lifting the boat as in a motorcycle hill climb. As the crest passes under the boat, just ready to break, it hisses "Tssst, tsssst," like a whore from an alley. As we drop – almost freefall – down its back, a hollow roar returns overtop its collapsing, rushing-away wall. I gape at the wide span of deep, white spindrift covering the sea where the wave has swept the blue away. We are truly frightened, for if we had been caught sideways under that onslaught SCRIMSHAW might well have tumbled to destruction in the horrendous weight of water. Another big crest looms up but by now we are farther out, safe from its collapse, but a similar expanse of deep froth is left by its passing. A third, smaller wave heaves us upward on its elevator, drops us off its back and breaks inside of us. The big ones are coming through in sets. How much time elapses between sets? I realize we know nothing of the tide. Is it rising or falling? How much? When? We are too far from the beach to learn anything even with binoculars.

We jill around again, now farther from the break as the boys study a seaward surface all agleam in noonday sun. I can't look; how can they see? Jo Anna says, "It doesn't look bad in there now."

"Not yet, Dad," The boys chime out together. Russell adds, "There's another set coming." With no more than a minute between the last of that last set and the first of the next, I decide to head for Honduras, hesitate as the bar looks passable, circle again as another set sweeps by, circle again, realize that heading for Honduras is the safest option despite my condition. But I feel resentment at missing out on Guatemala. My head swims with an explosive ache, my ears ring with the sound of clanging surf, my gut grumbles as if from starvation but I can't imagine eating. The glare of sun on sea drives my eyelids into a tight wince. It would take only a day and a night to get to La Union where there might be a doctor. On the other hand, if we could only get past the break line during a lull, we could get in here. Russell calls from the stern, "Big set coming!" Like a floating elevator gone berserk we climb up and drop over three steep greenies in succession. I want this over with.

On the fourth smaller crest I steer for the river mouth. The outboard is buzzing steadily. I call the boys to the cockpit and bark, "Everybody hang on with both hands." For a long minute we slide through undulating water effervescing air from its previous inversion. We are in the break line and there are no breakers. The boys yell, "We did it!"

Except now I see Jo Anna staring astern, pointing, mouth wide but silent. Behind us – far enough behind us – another steep greenie rears up, curls and cascades down its own face with a freight train roar. The break is over but the roar continues as a broad bank of froth maybe five feet high announces its approach with an ascending growl, quickly overtakes us and spins the boat instantly sideways to its onslaught. We accelerate to match its speed as deep drifts bury our decks. I think the water is so full of air that it won't float the boat.

We are borne along like this, sideways and heeling sharply shoreward, engulfed in the din, for a long, long way. The ride is fearfully thrilling. We can handle this.

Suddenly I realize I have forgotten all together about the river mouth. As the long, sideways ride subsides I focus landward to see that we have missed the entrance and are almost on the beach. At once the boat grounds with a jolt. Current swirls about us in all directions, in and out from the swash but also laterally, along the beach. SCRIMSHAW rolls drunkenly.

I am totally confused, can think of nothing to extricate us from this desperate position. We will live but I can see our home stuck here for hours, maybe days, eventually pounding to bits in a rising tide and surf. We all hang on to the lurching boat. Nobody says anything.

Now I realize the long-shore current is pouring past our grounded boat. The tide is rising and water is rushing toward the river mouth. It piles up our stern, threatens the little outboard that is miraculously still buzzing away. Surely it had been inundated in froth, another dying installment of which now sweeps in from the surf line.

We are afloat! With both the motor and the current nudging us forward we are soon flushed, whirling like a Dervish, into the river.

Suddenly all is calm. Jo Anna and I hug. Jungle closes in. I am ready to get off of the world. Enormously relieved I decide to run the boat ashore on a marshy bank. "Why are we stopping?" the boys protest.

"To open up and check her out," I say. "And besides, we've got to figure out where we're going."

All at once there is motion in the brush and five fatigue-clad soldiers spring from the undergrowth and leap aboard brandishing combat rifles. (This is not made up.) They look well trained and mean. We are dumbstruck.

Orders are barked. Two men hold us at gunpoint while the others dive below and start rifling through the boat. They rapidly communicate. One man is inspecting the contents of our cereal boxes, smiling. Another is opening a float hatch and says weakly, "Nada." A third points his rifle skyward. The leader asks his men, "Una familia, no mas?"

"No mas," his men reply.

The leader asks to see our passports. Jo Anna shows them opened to the pages containing our brand new visas for Guatemala together with the vessel clearance we have just received at the wharf. Everyone relaxes except me; I melt...

The soldiers, who had apparently been on a routine training foray when we sailed into their hands, guided us through the shallow channels of a gorgeous jungle waterway to the little Guatemalan resort called Likin (Lee-keen). On the way I mused about how we could have gotten through all that with a keelboat. We wouldn't have, I concluded. A monohull would be either pounding to pieces on the outer bar or lying on its side against the beach in the surf, still outside the mouth. If, that is, its skipper had attempted entering in the first place, which he probably wouldn't have unless there was something pressing like illness aboard. Again the wisdom of cruising in a beachable boat had revealed itself to us.

Arturo was at the resort. He took one look at my yellow eyes and said, "You've got hepatitis." Jo Anna looked and swooned with remorse. Arturo whisked me off to a doctor in the nearest big town (Esquintla) who asked me to urinate in a white enameled pan. He swished the coffee-colored pee around and pontificated in Spanish that my urine color was typical of one with hepatitis. Performing no other testing he offered his treatment; in English he said, "Go to your room, don't move, don't think, six weeks."

On our way back to Likin I bemoaned to Arturo the prospect of six weeks on my back. "That means it will be too late to continue south before the storm season so we'll be stuck here for several months."

Arturo said, "We can do better than that. When the locals come down with hepatitis they don't even quit work, they just drink coconut water. It goes through you faster than beer and it'll clear out your liver in a couple of weeks. You won't feel up to snuff for a couple of months but you'll be able to move around, You are stuck in Guatemala anyway, but I don't think you'll be sorry for it."

By nightfall Jo Anna and I were ensconced on cots under a ceiling fan in a thatched hut at the resort. Feeling dumb for eating raw rock oysters purchased from the street vendors in Acapulco, I was nonetheless enormously relieved to have the boat tied snugly to a dock with the boys aboard and all of us safe from that surf. Our friend Arturo had literally saved what had been an otherwise hard day.

The next morning shortly after daylight, an Indian deposited ten half-ripe, artfully husked coconuts at our doorstep. By Arturo's arrangement this happened every morning for the next two weeks. I guzzled the delicious juice until sick of it, pissing like a fire hose but feeling better by the hour. Arturo came to visit twice, the second time taking us back to his home in Guatemala City. From there we visited the nearby town of Antigua, a Moorish-Spanish enclave perched delightfully between two volcanoes. We instantly imagined ourselves residing there, found a nifty place for rent, bought an old panel truck and returned to the boat to gather everything from on board that could be used for shore side living.

The resort's management suggested we move the boat to the canal that was crossed by a small bridge thereby controlling access to the resort. An armed guard was always on duty at the bridge. For a dollar a week it was arranged with the guards to keep an eye on the boat. "Don't worry Jim," said Arturo, "If anyone touches that boat they're as good as dead." For the next seven months we lived magically in a magic land. It was no routine traverse.

....

Illustrations for this chapter, narrated by the author, are available online at ...
www.OutrigMedia.com/books/atm-volume-one.html

8

DOUBLE BIND

1973

The man straightens and stares at me, and slowly aims his index finger right between my eyes. When it is certain that he has my attention he says, "Let me tell you something young man. If you try to keep to a whirlwind schedule like that, you're going to ruin your trip for yourselves."

After a pause he lowers his finger but says nothing until I reply defensively, "How do you mean?"

"Cruising to a schedule, other than the one enforced by seasonal weather, is the stuff of greenhorns. If you keep going like that you'll be nothing more than a tourist. You'll miss out on much of what cruising really means." ...

I met this man in an anchorage somewhere in southern Mexico before we crossed the Gulf of Tehuantepec, and I'm ashamed to say I don't remember his name. I've never forgotten what he said, and while we were settling in Guatemala I thought of them often. He was a senior seaman who had cruised with his wife and kids for years, and now that his children were grown and had boats of their own he and his wife were still traveling in their old wooden ketch. When he asked me of our plans, where we'd come from and where we were going I said we were planning to be in New England in about a year to get our boys back in school. It was this time constraint that he had reacted to by imploring me with his finger and his advice. I asked him just what it is that we would miss out on:

"That feeling of being a traveler instead of a tourist, of knowing that when things go wrong you can handle them yourself. It's the confidence that comes from discovering that there is a place for you in the world wherever you are, of knowing you can go anywhere and make out all right. But you can't get that by constantly rushing through the world on a schedule."

"Why not, exactly?"

"Because you have to cut lose from the usual false sense of security that depends on always having a pretty good idea of what's going to happen next. You have to let the trip itself set the schedule. In a wider sense, it comes down to letting whatever happens on the trip tell you where and when to move and go, or just to stop and truly be wherever you are without regard to the time it takes."

"But our kids. We have taken our kids out of school."

"We traveled with our kids for years, and believe me they are not uneducated. Yes, there is a lot of information they don't have in their heads but they know where to get it if they want. And they have something most kids – most adults – never get. It's that feeling of belonging almost anywhere in the world. And that, right there, is probably the most valid thing parents can give to their offspring. It's the confidence that comes from being a true traveler. After all, that's what all of us are doing anyway, just traveling through. So hear me now! To get that kind of confidence – to have that view of the world as being essentially livable wherever there are people living, and to give all that to your kids, you've got to forget about the time it takes. Next to belonging, time is unimportant."...

So here we were in the mountains of Guatemala, literally forced into letting what had happened on the trip, and the seasonal aspects of sailing, determine our course and schedule. Despite my illness, this was to be the most fortunate happenstance of the whole endeavor because without being forced to stop I don't think we would have. I wished then, and do now, that I could remember that man's name. Oh true traveler, if you are reading this, thank you!

Between Fire and Water...

Guatemala is like a twist in the continental chain. The mountains that start in Canada and course down through the Rockies and the Sierra Madre have a break at Tehuantepec and then re-emerge in Northern Guatemala as the range called the Cuchumatanes. These are jumbled, rounded peaks with steep valleys and strange outcroppings all covered with lush forests. Cliffs seem to overhang like breakers ready to plummet into clouds, and one is reminded of the kind of surreal beauty seen in those classic Japanese landscape paintings. I came to call this country tropical alpine.

Then, right in the middle of the Guatemalan isthmus, the mountain chain takes a hard turn to the left and dives into the Atlantic to emerge again later as some of the Caribbean Islands. It is in that hard left turn that a combination of tectonic collisions and upwelling magma cause this country to be home for some thirty volcanoes. You don't hear about them much because they tend to frighten off the tourists, but in truth this is a very active wrinkle in the Planet's crust. Eruptions and earth quakes are relatively frequent and have played a major role in the country's history.

When these volcanoes erupt they don't often spew molten rock as do the volcanoes in Hawaii. Instead they spew ash, such as when Vesuvius smothered Pompeii. Some of this ash takes to the air, of course, but much of it cascades down the mountain slopes as a fast-moving dam-burst of super heated, gas-emitting, self-lubricating, gravelly dust. It has buried villages, choked rivers and blocked valleys. It has also fed civilizations, for in time this ash makes extremely fertile soil. In modern times most ash has been airborne, sifting down to fertilize the country's great plantations of coffee, corn and cotton. So this unique, unstable and sometimes lethal geology has been an agricultural blessing in disguise.

The city center of Antigua, Guatemala is composed of only eight oblong blocks surrounding a central plaza and the main cathedral. It was the first Spanish seat in the new world and capitol of a one-time integrated Central America. It was from here that orders were given to mount the Cabrillo Expedition to explore California and establish the Spanish mission system. Construction of the city started in the late sixteen hundreds and the place was really built for permanence. It displayed the very best of Moorish/Spanish architecture with massive stone columns, arches, vaults, walls and courtyards. Almost every block was adorned with a considerable cathedral or church. The streets were paved with jumbo cobbles and the official buildings on the square were glories to behold. In a leap of faith, this compact metropolis was situated between two conical volcanoes, one named Fuego (fire) and the other Agua (water). These monsters are well named, for Fuego was the more active, sometimes shooting sparks and ash, and Agua had a magnificent lake in its crater. Aside from an occasional dusting from Fuego, Antigua did not suffer from eruptions. But in the 1770's this city, was largely destroyed by a series of severe earthquakes. One of these unceremoniously dumped the contents of Agua's lake onto the town causing further ruin.

Paradoxically, a great part of the city's charm today is created by the remains of the old cathedrals, which have been largely left as they toppled and are venerated as remnants of history. For example, when we were there the main market plaza was staged in a cathedral so ruined. Temporary merchant's stalls were set up against huge jumbled fragments of stone archways and columns giving a surreal time warp atmosphere to shopping. Our late, great friend Tom Freeman visited us there, and Tom and I enjoyed browsing in this marketplace together. Tom and I were both six-three, so most of the local Maya-descendant Indians crowding the scene came up to our navels. I was a skinny, blonde geek with glasses and Tom a heavy, dark dude with a pronounced silver streak through the middle of his thick, black hair (caused by his pesky psoriasis). We were so imposing to the populace that they were reluctant to make eye contact until we bent down, smiled broadly and said right into their faces, "Buenos dias!" Then they would light up and answer briskly "Buenos dias muy senores!" And several others nearby would do the same, laughing and waving to others to come and see. When buying something, like a hand-carved Spanish cedar toilet seat (still used in SCRIMSHAW), we and they would all make a great display of the sale amidst shared joviality. (Sadly, the town has since built a "proper" market complex.)

In A Foreign Land...

Besides Guatemala's geography and history we were soon surprised by her people. There are three basic groups; the first two are called Latino and Ladino. The Latinos have descended almost purely from the Spanish and other European stock including a liberal smattering of gringos. For example our friend Arturo is of German/Spanish parentage. The Ladinos are a large group that combine European (mostly Spanish) with local Indian heritage. The third group is pure Indian. Called Indigenos, these people comprised, when we were there, about eighty five percent of the total population (now reduced by civil war and the burgeoning Ladinos to less than fifty percent). This pure Indian population descends directly from the ancient Maya inhabitants of the region.

The Ancient Maya were Stone Age but sophisticated, having achieved high levels of agricultural development, astronomy, architecture and art by about 1,000 AD. However by the time the Spanish arrived in the sixteen hundreds the Mayan city states had declined from agricultural collapse into warfare. The great Mayan centers had been abandoned and the survivors had fled to the mountains where they still survive despite the usual cataclismic onslaught of the modern world upon isolated cultures. We saw that it was the same old story: All the machine-tillable land had been usurped by latinos for export crops like sugar and cotton. The Indians had been driven higher and higher up the slopes of the volcanoes to scratch out their corn plots on land so steep that in some cases the tops of the corn stocks of one row were tied up to the bases of the row next highest. And still the Indians survived in many highland villages and some large towns.

After personalizing our rented house in Antigua by building some furniture for the place, our first tentative step into city life was to hire a maid. This was something we had never done before, and the notion of having another individual in the house was much resisted at first, but we were advised that the community not only needed but expected outsiders to offer this employment. We quickly came to respect and admire Olga. Shopping for food would have been much more difficult and expensive without her, and she became our first real cross-cultural adventure.

Two Tongues, Two Lives...

Speaking with Olga was a challenge at first. Having flunked Spanish One twice in college my lingua was very limited and the Guatemalan idiom was different from that of Cuba where I had learned some Spanish years earlier. However, we were told of a school in town that specialized in teaching Spanish to Peace Corps volunteers. The school was actually an offshoot of a much larger language project; an attempt to bring into print the many Indian dialects of the country so that the separate tribes could communicate with one another in writing and preserve their culture. This Projecto Linguistico Francisco Morroquin had made great strides in unifying the Indians in their defense against cultural annihilation, and it also provided employment for many young women who had become well educated as school teachers but for whom there were no job opportunities in the very limited national school system. We four Browns enrolled in this language school.

It was intense! The normal venue was one instructor to one student, seven hours per day, six days per week. The instructors spoke no English with the students; none. Actual classes ran for five days, but all Peace Corps students lived in-home with a local family so that immersion in the language was total for them.

We cheated. We lived at home and Jo Anna and I divided our days with a single instructor, but Steve and Russ went all day, and Steven, who took a second six-weeks term, eventually moved in with a local family. The lessons were often exhausting but our progress – especially the boy's – was impressive. Jo Anna had difficulty conversing but soon found that she could go to market with Olga, read the newspaper and understand much street talk. My strength was in blab so together we could definitely get by. The boys, who socialized with the locals all day and through many evenings, picked up Spanish quickly and Steven is still quite fluent.

By half way through the course we all became well acquainted with our instructors and with their colleagues, and we traded off. As I saw it, every morning I would show up an a small room of colonial charm to sit for hours and just talk with a beautiful young woman who considered herself to be my absolute master. She grilled me with verb conjugations, piled on the vocabulary and dragged me through every step with wrote repetition until I began to fade, and then we would just talk. About anything. When I stumbled, she helped, and in a flash it was time for lunch. Sometimes we lunched together at our place, and then she would take Jo Anna for the afternoon while I concerned myself with writing about boats. These were wonderful days.

Soon we were absorbed in the social activities of everyone involved at the school. For my fortieth birthday, certainly the best ever, I arrived at the house to be greeted by six lovely young women, all of whom I had talked with for hours, lined up on our balcony singing Las Mananitas to me in glorious harmony. The party was on!

This language engagement did more to give us that "feeling of belonging in the world" than sailing thousands of miles. But of course, we realized, we wouldn't be here without our shallow-draft boat! All at once we felt like we could go anywhere and make it. Hey, it was happening! This was what we came for.

Story Cloth...

On the day we moved in to our place in Antigua, Steven and Russell took off to case out the town. This was their usual role in any new anchorage, and they often led the way for us to newfound friends. Such was the case on that first day in Antigua when Steven returned from his tour to say that there was a gringo couple nearby who had a shop where they sold Indian clothes. They wanted to meet us. My first thought was that they were hoping to sell us some cloth, which at first they did. But, as we were to learn from Jim and Alice Bell, there was a lot more to it than mere cloth. As our friendship with these people developed over the next few months they freely informed us of the scope and depth of this unique and exciting art form.

Funny thing; aside from that Mexican blouse we acquired at Juatulco, Jo Anna and I had never before been interested in hand made textiles or indeed in collectables of any kind. Now, using their shop inventory and their personal collection to exemplify, the Bells explained that in many cases the people of a given Guatemalan village wore what amounts to a highly stylized uniform. This sometimes outlandish garb identifies the wearer as from that village, and each village population is a clan, often with its own language. The garments are mostly hand made by the wearer or the wearer's spouse, and the styling, colors and patterns are all unique to that village. The growing of the cotton and raising of the sheep, the spinning into thread and yarn, the dying, weaving, embroidering and stitching into garments is sometimes all done by the wearer and his or her extended family. We had already noticed that these people were making a big thing of their clothing, and many of the individual garments were not just beautiful, they were fascinating. For example, Jim and Alice showed us how the patterns in a woman's blouse or huipil (wee-peel) shows to the informed observer details of her standing in the family and community. Often these huipiles are heavy and warm to protect the women against the mountain climate, and include open side pleats to permit breast feeding with a minimum of inconvenience. Mothers carry their infants slung on their backs in colorful wraps tied in front. Long wrap-around skirts sometimes have strands of metallic thread woven in to flash in the light as the women walk. This is high fashion in every day garb, not just dressy things for special occasions. We wanted some for ourselves!

The Bells gave us a crash course in what to look for, explaining in detail why some specimens are better than others and where, in the jumbled highlands of this exotic country, we could go to find them. Now our panel truck, a 1956 Chevrolet that had been completely rebuilt and which we bought for about five hundred dollars, became a part of our lives. Equipped with the truck and our newfound language, and with our adequate income from plans sales at home, we hit the road for the highlands on many cloth-seeking expeditions. We had no idea why, or what we were going to do with this stuff; we just had to have some. Now it is apparent that this quest gave us a real reason to reach across a wide culture gulf to exchange courtesies with a highly unusual people in a surprising setting.

That, in fact, was the prevailing ambience of Guatemala; surprise! Around every curve on the precipitous mountain roads, in every household of these meek yet personable Indians, under every shed roof jammed with hand looms, and in every pile of blankets or shirts or trousers or yardage we came to expect that we would find something quite unexpected.

The weavers use two basic devices, hip strap looms and foot looms. The primitive hip strap loom consists of nothing but a few sticks and a wide strap. Yarn is warped onto two principal sticks to create the lengthwise threads of the piece. One end of the warping is attached to a peg high on the wall and the other end to both ends of the strap. The weaver, usually a woman, steps into the loop in the strap and kneels on the ground with the strap placed low around her hips and buttocks. She then leans back to tension the warp. In this position she now inserts the weft (crosswise threads) by leading them over and under the threads of the warp. Using dyed yarn of various colors she creates the elaborate patterns distinctive of the garments of her village. The size of fabrics created by this method are usually limited to the width of the weaver's hips and the length of her upward reach from her waist to her fingertips. Nevertheless, most of the highly detailed, truly artistic and individualistic pieces come from hip strap looms. It was this method that Russell enjoyed learning, and we have a piece he made now hanging in our bathroom, sticks and all.

The foot looms are hand-hewn wooden machines as wide as a piano and as long as a car. They seem crude and clumsy but are actually quite scientific. Usually operated by men, foot pedals manipulate the warp while the weft shuttle is thrown by hand. These looms are used to produce wider and longer items like blankets and yardage. Neither of these methods uses electricity except perhaps for a single bare light bulb hanging from overhead.

Observing the weavers at work was sometimes unreal. We saw cotton yarn being wound into large coils or hoops. Working in a kind of trance, the Indians then bind the hoops at intervals determined by experience. When the coils are immersed in dye the bindings exclude coloration at those intervals. When this tie-dye yarn, colored intermittently, is unwound from its hoop and woven into cloth various patterns appear. One pattern seen in women's wrap-around skirts reveals, when closely scrutinized, many ghostly, striking, skull-like figures. When I questioned one weaver about how this is achieved he answered reverently, "There is no 'how' in this cloth. We just weave it and then see the faces of our fathers."

A big part of buying cloth – in addition to knowing good stuff – was in negotiating the price. In general, prices were very low considering the time and materials invested in the pieces, and we were reluctant to drive a bargain. Our friends the Bells disabused us of our shyness; "Bargaining is how you gain the respect of the seller," insisted Jim, "and it's how you come to understand the value of the piece in the seller's mind."

"They know what it's worth to them," added Alice, "and they expect you to find out the hard way." We learned that bargaining also opened ongoing relationships with key sellers. Very often we would want several things from a given weaver or merchant. By asking the price of the items individually but showing no further interest until the climax deal, we could then gather up those several items and offer a figure somewhat less than the total of the original asking prices. Volume definitely lowered the total and the seller now suspected we were collectors and therefore potential repeat customers. They would save special things for us, even make things to order, and at times our repeat visits to these contacts resulted in jovial friendships.

On the Carpet...

A tour of the mountain towns can be scheduled to coincide with weekly market days in specific towns and with the yearly religious festivals held on separate dates in almost every town. Market days attract private producers of all kinds of goods from wheat and avocadoes to sandals and toilet seats.

Market day also brings the weavers and textile merchants down from the highest hamlets to sell their wares or exchange for needed items. Much of the internal economy of the country was then based on direct marketing, producer to consumer hand-to- hand. Often there was no money involved. The advantage of this system was soon obvious to us; anyone willing and able to work could make a decent living without supporting the banks, the middlemen and the mass merchandisers. The market scenes were very active and colorful, and we enjoyed participating.

Getting there was half the fun. Guiding our little truck along the rocky roads, around switchback curves and under sculpted outcroppings, we would occasionally come upon a breathtaking vista of broad valleys and silver streams, the greenery speckled with drying clothes spread upon the gorse and herdsmen running their stock as the cuffs of their trousers, each brightly embroidered by their wives, flashed in shafts of sunlight beaming through cottonball clouds. Creeping around curves confined by steep banks reaching way up on one side and way down on the other, we sometimes encountered older Indian pedestrians who, upon sighting our strange truck, would dive over the bank in stark fear of strangers. The more remote the village the more reticent the people at least at first. We learned that this prejudice descended from the days of Spanish conquest when any Indian who got in the way, or who showed the slightest outgoingness or intelligence was summarily decapitated. A fixed smile from us together with a few words in our limited Spanish (theirs was often more limited than ours) usually broke the ice.

One sure way to break the ice was to goof up the language. I'll never forget the look on the Indian woman's face when Jo Anna asked her if she had any eggs for sale. Translating from the English she naturally said, "Tiene juevos?" The woman blushed; she and her companions began to snicker and soon to double up with laughter. Once composed she answered, "Si senora, hay juevos." (Yes madam, there are eggs." Only later did we learn that Jo Anna had asked the woman, in the idiom of that Spanish, "Do you have testicles?" The proper way to ask would have been, "Hay juevos?" (Are there eggs? Not, "Do you have...")

One day high in the Cuchumatanes, as we approached the remote hamlet of Todos Santos we encountered on the road a group of six Indian boys who were clearly not spooked by our oncoming. Garbed in the highly stylized, hand made uniforms of their village they beamed and waved and jostled one another, inviting us to stop. I asked if they wanted a ride into the village, now visible on a nearby ridge. After some discussion among them they piled into the back of our truck with Steven and Russell. Surprised to find their contemporaries, the Indian boys were all a-chatter but there was little mutual understanding. On the ride they exclaimed at every bump and curve, and I soon realized that this was their first experience in a motorized vehicle. Arriving at the town they disgorged in a tumble. I grabbed my camera and asked them if I might take their picture. They eagerly lined up and for the first time I noticed that one of them was not Indian. Dressed in "western" clothes and behaving very stiffly, this boy joined in the group photo with his boisterous companions but was obviously out of place. As it was discovered, he was the son of evangelistic missionaries stationed in the town, and the poor kid was trying hard to fit his square self into a round hole. Today this is one of my favorite photos for it illustrates the true chasm that exists between such disparate cultures even for youth.

On another trip through a glowering valley at dusk, miles from nowhere, we picked up a young Indian couple who were walking. On the ride we talked with difficulty but came to understand that they were on the way to an evangelistic revival meeting. They were walking because the usual traffic, and their families, disapproved of their attendance. He was a bracero de maiz (corn worker) and she was not yet a mother and they were seeking some alternative to the dictates of the usual church... Which was, "Prometer a dios mio" (To Promise my god) to procreate with as much abundance as is humanly possible. This couple was caught in a painful conflict between two doctrines only one of which undertakes to look after more than the spiritual needs of its followers. In these remote communities the evangelicos were making strides against the catolicos on the grounds of birth control alone. But with their revival meetings they were going up against real theatre, for the established religious festivals of Guatemala are bizarre almost beyond description. Still, I'll try:

In the high enclave of Patzun there is a yearly shindig they call Corpus Cristi. For this occasion the citizen's work for days decorating the streets – that is, the pavement itself – with block-long carpets of dyed sawdust and flower blossoms. The patterns are fragile, elaborate and unique to a each block. Often they are created by using an array of wooden templates that are filled with various colors of sawdust, carefully lifted, moved and refilled to repeat the patterns and cover the cobbles with blazing color from curb to curb.

These carpets begin in front of the town's cathedral and follow a prescribed route for a grand procession on festival day. At the appointed hour, with the streets jammed on both sides by the populace, the cathedral doors opened to emit first the priest, usually a white-haired old man in white robes and heavy trinkets who, with back hunched and head bowed, strikes a jarring contrast to the locals all heads up, black-haired and adorned in rich colors. As the priest takes his first strides onto the carpet, thereby commencing its destruction, he is followed by gangs of Indians toting crosses, floats, effigies, mobile sarcophagi and other macabre trappings, all the paraphernalia of a complex religion that descends from both the ancient Roman and the ancient Mayan. Many men swing incense burners to fill the air with sweeping strokes of odiferous smoke. Bells and tambourines compete for attention. Poorly practiced bands play unabashedly, often two or three at once too close together as if purposely to create a blaring discord, and the parade sometimes continues for hours with everyone in town falling in to trample the carpets into slushy ruts of dull fodder. During and after the parade the whole town is strafed with fireworks.

Low Tech Pyrotechnics...

They come in two principal sizes, tiny strings like Chinese rat-ta-tat-tats that never fail to startle, and home made mortars whose concussions jolt one's rib cage. Both types are often heard day and night in Guatemala regardless of festival dates, but celebrations of any kind bring them out in force. The hand made mortars, especially, are worthy of description:

The mortar launchers are three-foot lengths of four-inch diameter steel pipe with one end welded to a flat plate to aim the muzzle straight up. The bombs are in two parts, twin soft ball-sized charges of home made gunpowder wrapped in corn husks and joined by a foot-long fuse of powder-filled twisted husk. One bomb has a separate fuse which is lit as it is dropped into the launcher, with the second bomb dropped in immediately on top of the first. The first bomb explodes with a muffled whomp that shakes the ground and propels the top missile, sputtering its fuse, several hundred feet up. At the very top of its climb the missile explodes with a blast that echoes from the volcanoes all around. This reverberating sonic bombardment goes on almost continually throughout festival days and nights; even market days. Such a celebratory cacophony and vivacious display reaches its peak during Samana Santa (Easter Week) when all the schools and civic organizations perform wonders of both martial and reverent theatrics in the streets. This occasion in Antigua is famous throughout the country, attracting great crowds to the wondrous little city.

Procreation Problem...

For us there was also the big city, Guatemala City, where Arturo and his family occasionally invited us to visit them in their colonial home. These visits exposed us to the graciousness and generosity often extended to visitors by the local oligarchy, and exemplified how vastly disparate are the lives of the Latinos from those of the Ladinos and Indigenos.

After Antigua was wracked by earthquakes in the 1770's the nation's capital was moved to a more geologically stable location. The plane now occupied by the swelling metropolis of Guatemala City is, however, surrounded by steep ravines, which limit its geographic growth. As the burgeoning Ladino population outstrips the rural environment the people are forced either up the slopes of the volcanoes or out into the lowland jungles (where they must practice slash-and-burn agriculture in order to temporarily sustain themselves. As a last resort they flock into the cities in search of work.

This component, having no where else to live, creates huge rag-tag barrios on the sides of the City's ravines which creates an extremely unstable situation physically, culturally, economically and politically. All of this proceeds while the predominant church continues to require all its parishioners to "promise to my God" to procreate as abundantly as is humanly possible."

Of course this predicament is not unique to Guatemala but it was shockingly apparent to us in 1973. As in Mexico to the north, the basic political issue is land reform. The country people ask only for enough land to sustain themselves, but their mushrooming demographics makes this impossible without taking back land once usurped by outsiders who do not eat their crops but instead sell them for money. (Again, all the machine-tillable land is owned or controlled by Latinos who use it mainly for growing crops for export.)

Of course this situation is not limited to Mesoamerica, and my brief construction of the problem is necessarily simplistic. What I want to say is this; the beauty and romance – the peaches and cream – of our lives in Antigua and our travels in the highlands had its obligatory balance in the brutal reality of the big cities where rebel activity threatened civic stability. We were disturbed by the armed soldiers in the banks and on many street corners. These guys looked absolutely goon-like and lethal, but because of them business as usual went on relatively free from the rebels robbing the banks to sustain themselves and their operations.

Even in the highlands there was rebel activity. Arturo had a small coffee plantation high in the mountains. The idyllic setting was reached by a long, steep and barely passable road over which Arturo carried supplies, his pay role – and sometimes us – in his truck. At every major turn along this road he made radio contact with his foreman at the farm. If by chance he did not report from an established waypoint, the foreman was to assume immediately that we had been ambushed, the pay role robbed, and perhaps we taken hostage. Upon this assumption the farm workers would be organized to hunt down and shoot it out with the robbers, their motivating prize being the pay role itself. Again this was business as usual.

Don't Stop!...

In our time in Guatemala we never witnessed any such violence. Except when carrying Art's pay role we felt totally secure out in the country. Shopping, dining and recreating in the city was interesting and fun. The restaurants were great, the movies current and the history captivating. We could buy good food and other supplies unavailable in Antigua. The quality was excellent and the prices right but accessibility difficult. To find five items required going to six or seven places; the streets were confusing and the traffic sometimes maddening. It required a different kind of driving. "Whatever happens don't stop!" Arturo would implore, and start again to tell the story of the doctor whose car struck a child who had run playfully out into the road. The doctor stopped to administer first aid to the child, and the child's father decapitated the doctor with his machete. "So, if there's no cross traffic, don't stop at traffic lights or stop signs, or you'll get hit from behind. And if you have an accident and can keep going, drive to the nearest police or army station and report the trouble.... No, you don't need to get a license, and for God's sake if you hit a pedestrian, don't stop!" It was enough to make one cautious but honking tailgaters, on winding two-lane roads with patchy pavement and no shoulders, often made it impossible to go slow.

Legal Euphoria...

At Arturo's farm we learned all about the process of producing coffee, an experience that has forever changed our appreciation of the stuff. The plants are temperamental, their cultivation is extremely labor intensive, harvesting is drudgery, separating the bean from the fruit is tricky and drying the beans, for mountain-grown coffee, is problematic in the unsettled weather of the higher elevations.

When it comes to brewing the beverage itself, we learned that real freshness of the beans and roasting just before brewing makes an enormous difference in the drink. It matters every bit as much as with fresh fish prepared while it still quivers in the pan; there is simply no comparison with the usual refrigerated fare or with pre-roasted and pre-ground, even vacuum packed coffee.

When arriving home from Arturo's finca with a supply of his green-but-sun-dried beans, we would follow the procedure shown to us by him. We would bear in mind his warning that caffeine, in this concentration, should qualify as a controlled substance.

Indications...
Prescribed for treating morning lassitude, premature dimwittedness and loss of manhood. In higher doses imparts temporary vivacity and legal euphoria.

Procedure...
To brew this beverage at home use the filter/funnel method set to drain into a large stainless steel vacuum bottle (you can bring the one from your boat). The paper filter will retain most of the bitter, burned oil from dark-roasted beans

Roast the green, sun-dried beans in a cast iron frying pan, just enough beans for one pot of coffee at a time. Start them at room temperature in a cold pan on highest heat. Stir and shake continuously until they are glossy black and almost ready to burst into flame.

(**Note:** This process is intended to fill up the house with smoke and a heady aroma strong enough to make your eyes water, your nose drip and your mouth salivate. It's all intrinsic preparation for partaking of the beverage. Have pot holders and a large-enough lid handy to suffocate the flames if necessary.) For best results this operation is performed in a house that has a Spanish tile roof that is exposed inside to allow the smoke to escape through the tiles at an amicable rate; otherwise open the doors and turn on a fan. Also acceptable is to roast on board a boat with hatches open and a fire extinguisher handy.)

Use freshly collected rain water; it really enhances absorption and gives a "clean" taste to this otherwise earthy beverage.

Grind the hot, glossy, almost black beans in a hand-crank corn mill that is clamped securely to a sturdy counter or table.

Drinking this coffee black is not recommended. Mixing it with almost-boiled-over fresh whole cow's or goat's milk is. Do not take with alcohol except clear Mayan guaro, which translates literally as "filth" but it's clean, straight cane alcohol).

The Preparation Ritual...

While roasting the beans, heat the water in a whistling kettle.

While heating the water, start heating the milk slowly in an open saucepan or metal pitcher.

While shaking and stirring the beans in the smoking fry pan (an oven mitt is useful), try not to let the milk boil over; it comes up suddenly and makes a real mess.

Set up the thermos and funnel/filter while shaking the beans and watching the milk.

The beans are ready! Turn out the big burner. Check the milk.

Dump the smoking beans into a cereal bowl.

Leave the fry pan on the stove or it may burn the counter top. Check the milk.

Dump the still-smoking beans into the grinder. Grind them back into the bowl just as the kettle whistles. Turn out the water's burner. How's the milk?

Before putting the hot grounds into the filter, pour just enough boiling water into the funnel to scald the paper filter to remove its taste and pre-heat the thermos; dump the thermos and replace the funnel/filter.

Dump the still-hot ground beans into the filter.

Dribble just a jigger of boiling water over the grounds and allow to soak for seven and one half seconds. Notice the reaction; the grounds begin to fizz.

Dump a big dollop of boiling water on the grounds and stand back! Contact with copious hot water causes the grounds to erupt like opening a warm and shaken bottle of beer, and this eruption is the surest indication of truly fresh beans. Absence of such erupting froth (never seen in the usual retail-packaged coffee) indicates lack of freshness, so unless you get your coffee from some source like Arturo, don't even bother to try this at home. As the hissing froth overflows the funnel it will cast an ethereal spell.

Listen to the milk. When it begins to hiss around the sides of its container it is ready to start climbing into that delicious froth.

Continue pouring water in the center of the funnel – not around the sides. Keep the funnel almost full and do not wash the grounds down from the sides of the filter. Keep pouring steadily until the thermos is almost full. (Note: Try to time the milk so that it is just beginning to rise to a boil as you're ready to remove the funnel from the thermos.)

Use whatever water is left in the kettle to pre-heat the mugs for about ten seconds.

Ach! The milk! Oh well, you caught it almost in time. Pour some into every cup... Wait! First pour out the pre-heating water, then pour in the milk. You'll get it right next pot.

Dispense the coffee into the pre-heated, pre-milked cups. Sugar to taste (at least a little is suggested). Turbinado (granulated but unbleached) sugar is preferred.

Consume!

Side effects...

Freshly roasted, ground and brewed, highland-grown Guatemalan coffee is not for everyone. Ask your doctor about the fitness of your heart, liver and kidneys. Avoid business or political negotiations, domestic issues and appointments with your psychiatrist. Avoid operating machinery unless you can sit or stand still for at least thirty seconds. Side effects are generally moderate to severe and include DT's, diarrhea, insomnia, dyslexia, hyperactivity, verbosity, ecstatic attention deficit disorder, arrhythmia and consequential pregnancy followed quickly by phantom visions and loss of manhood. The latter can be temporarily relieved by brewing another pot.

Family Travel...

While cruising in Mexico we had noticed a kindly deference extended to us by the locals whenever it was obvious that we were traveling as a family unit. It helped to have passports all bearing our family name and the boys seemed to be readily accepted by the local kids. We were never robbed or accosted in any way.

This deference was reinforced in Guatemala when we became residents in Antigua. We all made friends quickly especially among the teachers and administrators at the school. There were lots of gringos in town, many of them students at the school, but as a family we were something different. Partly because we were at least trying to speak Spanish, this deference extended to the local merchants and trades people, and was clearly evident from the Indians who often spoke limited Spanish themselves.

Because the nights were often chilly at Antigua's mile-high elevation, we had a charcoal brazier for heat, and we made friends with the charcoal man who regularly delivered real pit-made charcoal in big net bags. We were visited weekly by a regal, ancient Indian woman who came to collect our disposable glass jars and bottles which she then sold in the marketplace for sustenance. She was an extremely regal person, always offering to pay for the discards we saved for her alone.

I was always tempted to ask her if I might take her picture but restrained myself knowing that she was of an age where this indignity might cause her real distress. One sunny morning it was just too tempting. I went inside to watch her as she sorted bottles. She sat on the sidewalk in a shaft of light, sorting bottles and I assumed that from up on our balcony, looking out through two separated doorways, with a telephoto lens I could grab a snap without any possibility of her knowing. Shame to say, I did that, and at the moment of the shutter's click – which she could not possibly have heard over the noise in the street – she jumped like she had been stuck with a hat pin. She whirled around on her haunches, holding up her arms in defense in all directions while never looking at me, stood, stepped quickly into our patio, peered out obviously confused, grabbed her basket without taking our bottles and fled. We never saw her again. I was – am still – tempted to burn the slide, but to me she is too beautiful. I have kept it to exemplify unexplained phenomena, and to illustrate how easily a well-intended traveler can pratfall into the chasm that yawns so menacingly between disparate cultures.

Apparently we did not so offend most of our local contacts. The town's auto garage was run by a seasoned mechanic named Jesus who was pleased to work on our truck all day, any day, for twelve dollars plus parts; we had the smoothest looking smoothest running panel truck in the country. Once when he was filling her with gas we watched an American hippie couple passing innocently down the street, their long hair, flowing garments and the smell of patchouli oil following them. There were lots of hippies in Guatemala then, many of them living very frugally almost in competition with the locals, usually offering little to the system. Jesus explained this situation with tolerance and, as the tank came full, said, "Pero Jaime, ahhh! Tu no es heepee." It was the kindest thing he could have said to me. Little did he know that I had been so progressively disposed during the moral revolution of the sixties at home.

Our overland treks in Guatemala included visits to many of the ancient Mayan ruins, there were indeed many to visit. Suffice to say that we learned a lot about the ancients of the region. But for now our focus was on cloth, and we searched for it everywhere we went.

In the process we came to know the country's cuisine, not nearly so distinctive as that of Mexico but often inviting nonetheless. Superior to Mexico's were Guatemala's black beans, and I mean black! As black and shiny as dark-roasted coffee beans these legumes are so very appetizing as to have earned the title, "Guatemalan caviar." Stewed and sometimes re-fried, served with steamed rice, a generous plop of sour cream and just a morsel or three of chicken, pork or fish and a side of Guatemala's toasty-fat corn tortillas, this meal rivals the best of what is found in a fine Mexican taco stand or road house.

Of course we also had the chance to sample Guatemala's back-road, non-tourist accommodations. Provided mainly for traveling merchants, these pensiones were usually comfortable and clean if crude. Adobe walls, thatched roofs, dirt floors, hewn furniture, short but wide cot-like beds, hand-woven blankets, thunder jugs and fireplaces were all encountered. A common dining pavilion, usually enclosed, with friendly staff was patronized by individuals who all greeted one another table-by-table with the sincere "Buen provecho." Conversation between tables was expected, and the food was wholesome if basic and without variety; for sure black beans at every meal.

In all this travel we were constantly on watch for unusual textiles; we found lots and agonized over pieces we saw being worn by the Indians and not for sale. In the remote hamlet of Nebaj (Nay-bach) I was admiring a woven belt worn by a young woman who promptly took it off and handed it to me. Warm and thick with intricate patterns both sides, three inches wide and about eight feet long with hunky tassels at both ends, it was a masterful example of the weaving from this area. With great reservation I motioned "how much?" The woman became disturbed, chattered with her companions, they chattered back, she reached for the belt and hastily fled while wrapping it around herself. It was so fine a thing that I am glad she did not want to part with it.

Nevertheless our collection was now amounting to something over two hundred pounds, far too much to carry on the boat. What were we going to do with this stuff?

By now I was recovering to the point where I could tolerate a little exercise and heat, so Arturo encouraged us to travel down to the Caribbean coast. "There's a waterway there that you guys have to see. It's a system of rivers and lakes that comes way up into the country, and when you see it you're going to want to bring your boat around through Panama so you can come back to another kind of Guatemala." So it was that the Rio Dulce (Sweet River) entered our lives.

Because of Arturo we discovered this region overland from Antigua, and it would be almost a year before we sailed SCRIMSHAW into the maw of its entry gorge. For now let's just say that we knew it was there, had seen it, and that set the rest of our trip into motion.

Back in Antigua we received word from friend Mark Hassall. Mark and his wife Bonnie and Mark's 13 year-old son David had left California two years before we had, sailing west in their 37-foot Searunner trimaran. Having crossed the Pacific and Indian Oceans, rounded the Cape of Good Hope and come up the South Atlantic on their three-year world cruise, they were now at Barbados wondering where to go next.

Mark and I had corresponded by audio tape on our respective voyages, so I returned Mark's installment received in Antigua with a description of the Rio Dulce, suggesting that they might like to see the place and that we would be along soon enough.

On receipt of my reply, Mark and crew crossed the Caribbean on a fast run and arrived in the Rio Dulce before we had moved back aboard SCRIM SHAW; she was still waiting for us on the Pacific side. They were every bit as captivated by the Rio Dulce as we had been and decided to stay until we came around through the Canal. With this destination as our new focus we stored our textiles with the Bells, left the truck with friends knowing we would want it later, moved back aboard SCRIMSHAW and sailed for Panama.

Not so fast here. First we had to get back out into the Ocean! All the time we had been in Antigua I had nightmares about shooting the bar at Likin to get SCRIMSHAW free of the land again. The thought of those waves struck terror in the hearts of us all, so it was with a sense of self-sacrifice that my crew and I made ready for the attempt.

Flushing Out...

The greens and browns of wetland jungle are, in bright sunlight, richly contrasted with the black water of the shallow Likin canals and the cobalt of the distant sea. SCRIM SHAW tells me she is ready for the bar but I want another opinion. To our surprise we find a large ocean shrimping vessel, with a Japanese name, tied to a jungle wall just inside the mouth. Its crew is working on their net. Realizing that this powerful vessel must have shot the same bar we did to get inside, I motor SCRIMSHAW alongside and ask permission in Spanish to come aboard.

A crewman answers, "Entra te!" and I am met by the Guatemalan captain. I explain that I am intending to put to sea and ask his advice on how best, and when best relative to the tide, to manage the bar.

He explains that they use these canals for shelter often and he knows when not to attempt crossing the bar. He motions for me to follow him as he climbs the steel rungs welded to the vessel's massive net boom. From above the tree tops he peers over the dunes and says, "Vaya pronto!" (Go right now!)

Impatient with my lingering questions, he tells me only to stay in the middle for the maximum ebb tide current. He points to where this current is clearly knocking down the waves on the outer bar. "Mejor ahorita," he insists, (best right now). We go.

Again there is no wind so our sails are useless. Our little outboard buzzes away, and as we approach the strong current in the mouth, SCRIMSHAW slews helplessly in the roils. Leaving Jo Anna on the helm – all of us are again in life jackets and the hatches are closed – I jump to the stern to steer the motor in a feeble attempt to keep us heading seaward. To accomplish this steering I must kneel on the sterndeck and reach over the transom down two feet to the top of the motor. I can see our puny wake and know that we are in swash, but I can't see what's coming.

Now the boat is bucking in small breakers. The mouth flashes past on both sides. I leave the motor to kneel erect for a glance over the cabin and see Steve and Russ pointing ahead and shouting to Jo Anna. I come to my feet and now see that we are heading straight for those same looming breakers from eight months ago, but just... There! Is a place where the strongest ebb is pushing through the crests like a mountain highway cutting over a pass. I drop back to the motor and correct course in that direction just as the bow heaves skyward into the first big wave. Up and up we are heaved and I am nearly pitched out over the motor. To catch myself I straight arm the top of the motor and notice that my hand is briefly under water! The motor's buzz is instantly muffled, the crest crashes past and the motor comes up running!

We drop sickeningly down the back of that wave right onto that mountain highway, so the next wave is not as steep, nor the next, and all at once we are at sea... at sea, on a calm and sunny day. The boys are whooping. Jo Anna and I are in the cockpit embracing, and now our blessed little motor sputters and dies. We are all dumbfounded but relieved to be safe beyond the breakers. Cat's paws drift from off the land and as we turn to hoisting sail we look back to see the twisted continental chain, the surreal jumble of Guatemala's thirty volcanoes sharp against the sky. I am eternally grateful for having come down with hepatitis.

....

Illustrations for this chapter, narrated by the author, are available online at ...
www.OutrigMedia.com/books/atm-volume-one.html

9

CAN I STEER?

1973

Between Mexico and Panama there are five independent nations – all quite different in character – that are known collectively as Central America. They are Guatemala, Honduras, El Salvador, Nicaragua and Costa Rica. El Salvador is the smallest, has a coast only on the Pacific side of the isthmus, and is the most industrialized. Honduras is the largest, poorest and least developed. Nicaragua was, back in the early seventies, still ruled by the recalcitrant Somoza dictatorship; as traveling sailors we were advised to avoid it. Furthermore El Salvador, then had no Pacific port for non-commercial shipping, so in SCRIMSHAW we visited – besides Guatemala – only Honduras and Costa Rica.

Just southeast of Guatemala is a large inland sea called the Gulf of Fonseca. Its narrow entrance is almost blocked by and island, it has shores on three of the countries, and the inner Gulf is studded with islands. This extensive gulf is dominated by a huge volcano whose top half was, in early history, blown off by a cataclysmic eruption.

We entered this Gulf and stopped at the entrance island where we found only one family living -caretakers of almost desperate means but very welcoming and of generous disposition. The daughters of this clan were all clad in threadbare garments but insisted on giving us much of their produce. Jo Anna responded by giving them what of her clothing she could spare. The patriarch of the family, also in rags, was among the most gracious of men and his boys were lively and welcoming of our boys. We never saw the mother. After only two days we left these people reluctantly, feeling that if we were to stay longer, a deep personal involvement could develop, one with unsustainable responsibilities, and we might never be able to leave. We had felt this sense of growing love and obligation in some of the Guatemalan villages, too. The sensation was rich but disquieting. One wished for an additional lifetime to spend among the people of each such encounter.

Inconspicuous Consumption...
We then entered the Honduran harbor of La Union, probably the most squalid and depressing port on our entire trip. It was here, however, that we met two unforgettable characters who began to educate us in matters of relative wealth. One such character was a middle-aged gentleman, scrawny and tottering in his rags, who undertook to serve as our tourist guide, leading us around the demoralizing town to the various offices for clearing ourselves and SCRIMSHAW into the country. Don Geraldo (Sir Gerald) was obviously well educated. He spoke complete English, so complete in fact that every sentence was repeated several times but with a different structure:

"Welcome to Honduras; Honduras welcomes you; you are welcome to my Honduras. Please follow me to the customs office; the customs office is this way please; come this way to the customs office. So you have come from California I see; so I see California is from where you have come; Ah, so California, I see, is where you come from. Here is my young friend Richard, he too is going to Panama; Richard here is my young friend and Panama is where he too is going; my young friend Richard here is also going to Panama."

It was Ricardo to whom we gave money. A robust polite youth of about twenty, blonde yet Latin, he spoke some English, had done shipboard work, and now attached himself to us only upon our invitation. This was a typically difficult shopping expedition, walking with our burdens to a different shop or two for each item on the list, all of it done in the dank and glaring heat of the breezeless harbor front. Don Geraldo soon retired into some unknown shade; despite his education and vitality there was nothing for him to do here. Ricardo stood by. He was good-natured, interested in our trip, had knowledge of seafaring, was reticent to speak of himself, and helpful with lugging our plunder. He assisted affably in directing our efforts to acquire produce and clean drinking water. After three trips to the boat in our little rowing dinghy, hauling ice, water jugs and groceries we left him on the quay with the understanding that our boat was too small to take him to Panama. It was there, he had explained, that he hoped to contact a previous employer and find badly needed work aboard a tug. His recent job aboard the cross-Gulf ferry to Nicaragua had ended when the Somoza government had ceased to profit from the rampant smuggling created by tariffs WHICH WERE imposed to create smuggling. After visiting SCRIMSHAW Ricardo could see that there was no chance with us for passage to Panama but he expressed his hope to see us again the next day. Or perhaps, after what would be for him a long cross-border adventure hitching rides and living very close to the bone, we would see him in Panama.

That evening a hard, hot wind blew dust across the anchorage. SCRIMSHAW bounced in the chop near a small vacant ferryboat also tugging at its mooring. As we huddled in our microcosm of home, secure and relatively rich amidst our own accouterments, our own food and our own people, we were all a little overcome by the contrasts we had seen ashore since leaving Guatemala. The wind increased, the tide fell, the ferryboat stopped moving and soon SCRIMSHAW, too, was aground in the mud. Dinner conversation was subdued and the boys retired to their cabin.

After doing the dishes, I spoke with Jo Anna of our good fortune. Agreeing that there was no way for us to help Honduras we also agreed that we could help Ricardo. The next day we did. He was shocked, saying, "Why you give me all this money!" It was about $150, enough for him to ride the bus for a few days, buy minimal meals and bribe his way through the borders on his way to Panama. He was such a promising young guy that we suspected he just might not blow the cash or give it to his family. It was one of those things, a chance for us to subdue our sense of being so fortunate in a land of unfortunates, and perhaps a chance to offer a leg up to someone who, once on his feet, just might soar. Maybe all we bought was some relief from our feeling of the numbing contrast between our own guarded frugality and the open generosity of so many of our hosts. We wished Ricardo well but neither saw nor heard from him again.

On the nautical charts, the Gulf of Fonseca begs exploration by boat, and in February it might indeed be inviting. But it was now November and we found the heat debilitating. Furthermore the brooding volcano, with its evidential portent for widespread destruction, seemed to combine with the poverty to demoralize the locals and we visitors too. Feeling a bit sad and inadequate we headed out to sea.

We sailed past El Salvador and Nicaragua to alight in the first of several wide bays in far western Costa Rica. The anchorage was just below the border with Nicaragua and was reasonably protected in this season. The vistas ashore were quite wonderful, yet there were no other boats neither cruising or local. With the whole place apparently to ourselves we rested and cleaned up and went exploring ashore. Wide pastures sloped away from a perfect beach toward nearby hills and jungles. There were fences but no cattle and, strangely, no people.

On the beach we discovered small excavations made apparently by coyotes, their cries prevalent at night. Near these diggings we found turtle eggs, apparently more than the coyotes could consume, scattered in the sand. Following the local method we had seen for preserving this delicacy, we tied each of the leathery-shelled, half-filled eggs around their middle with monofilament fish line, squeezing each egg into a Siamese pair of marble-sized orbs. With several joined in a string, we hung them on board in a shady but well ventilated spot and allowed them to dry for several days. Upon peeling off the now crispy shell we found the contents to resemble the best of cheddar cheese. Now we understood why the green sea turtle is so threatened by predation from both animals and humans. This says nothing of its meat, which we never sampled but is also prized by humans in this region.

It was here that we over dosed on lobster. Directly beneath the boat in about fifteen feet of water we found a large tree lying on the bottom, and beneath its branches were dozens of very large warm water crawfish or pincer-less lobsters. We took several and gorged ourselves for four meals in a row; boiled lobster for dinner, left over lobster omelets for the following breakfast, lobster salad for lunch and lobster tacos for dinner. At that point we were completely sated with the rich, heavy flavor and understood, finally, why in colonial times this fine seafood, which was much more prevalent back then, was considered fit only for feeding the slaves.

We later learned that the reason this region was so strangely vacant of inhabitants was that the Somoza family in neighboring Nicaragua had been quietly buying up the Costa Rican ranches near their border, intending to simply extend their national territory into Costa Rica, a country famous for having no military. This move, however, was politically blocked in time.

Proceeding to the southeast we then anchored in another large bay at the rural Costa Rican beach town of Los Cocos. Here there were several cruising yachts in the open roadstead, and we again enjoyed a rather social scene with other yachtspeople. In particular there was a trimaran named TRES REYES (Three Kings) sailed by Dale and Sandy Stennett and their two young sons. David and Mark were more or less contemporaries of, and soon became fast friends with, Steve and Russ. It was great to have the kids engaged with their own friends.

Jo Anna and I were able to commiserate with Dale and Sandy on the challenges of raising teenage boys aboard. We each discovered that we were not alone in trying to subdue the normal sibling rivalries intensified by adolescent brothers living in confined space for extended periods. Aboard both boats there were attempts to home school using correspondence course materials. The Stennetts were succeeding more than were the Browns. With only fifteen months between them, our boys were closer together in age than Mark and David, which seemed also to intensify their rivalry. School time aboard SCRIMSHAW therefore had become a time to mutter insults, throw books and otherwise disrupt the lessons. Because of my miserable recollections of school, I was a poor enforcer of discipline at such times, feeling that academics served mainly to interrupt the real-world experience we were having otherwise, and despite Jo Anna's teaching background she was not able to control her very confined classroom on her own. We had a problem and it was not limited to academics.

Nevertheless our days in Costa Rica tumbled by more or less happily. At the main Pacific port of Puntarenas we arranged to leave the boat under the watchful eyes of neighboring yachties and take off inland. We rode the colonial-era railroad up through the mountains to the Capitol San Jose. Here we enjoyed the best cheeseburgers ever, saw a movie and spent the night. We noticed a distinct contrast between highland Costa Rica and that of Guatemala - no Indians! Costa Rica was much more "westernized," had many more gringos and Europeans, and the locals almost all spoke some English. They were amicable and generally well sheltered and fed but the place lacked Guatemala's exotic foreign-ness and sense of surprise. San Jose was pleasant and comfortable but shy on the cross-cultural adventure that had so engaged us all in Antigua.

To seek a wider exposure we re-boarded the train for the Caribbean coast. Now the route became extremely mountainous, the little smoke-belching, steam hissing locomotive with its train of ancient, open cars groaned its way around switchbacks outrageously tight and steep, giving the impression that the road bed and its burden were both clinging to the cliffs by hope alone. At local stops the train was boarded by merchants selling trinkets and food. A stately woman offered hard-boiled eggs. I ordered one and she asked if I wanted it opened. I nodded and she quickly whacked the egg against her forehead, briskly peeled the shell in two neat halves and threw them past my face out the car window and presented me the egg on a tortilla with salt and red pepper. Thus the treat of forehead –whacked, hard-boiled eggs became popular on SCRIMSHAW.

As we approached the Atlantic side of Costa Rica the route led through miles of bananas, sugar cane, coconuts and cacao, this latter being the source of chocolate. Like all tropical crops cacao requires intense hand labor to cultivate and harvest. Beside the tracks we saw many long low screen racks for drying the cacao pods, these racks were mounted on rails so that they could be pushed by hand into low sheds at night and when rain approached. We found the region extremely wet, hot and unappealing so returned to the Capitol the same day and we've never quite felt the same about chocolate. Unwrapping a candy bar brings visions of hovel-housed people in rags desperate to preserve every last pod for the export market.

Now we understood why the colonials, and even today's Central American elite, confined their living mainly to the higher altitudes. The Caribbean coast was sweltering and wet for us, the Pacific side was relatively dry, almost Mediterranean in climate but still oppressively hot. It was said that in the right atmospheric conditions one could see both oceans from San Jose. Nevertheless, even the Central American governments largely ignore the lowlands of their own countries especially on the Caribbean side. We later learned that an earthquake had devastated long sections of the sea-to-sea rail line and it has not been replaced. So it would seem that these coastal regions represent opportunity and freedom for investors and travelers, but the climate must be accommodated or avoided in all but winter months; as in Guatemala December and January are often the best because the rains of fall have stopped but everything is still green. The Central American highlands can be pleasant year round.

Back on board we concluded that the only way to enjoy the coasts was from a live-aboard boat. There is often a breeze in the anchorage and one can always cool off in the water and move on by the wind. We moved on.

Land And Water...

Crossing into Panama we followed a meandering jungle river to another squalid port called Pedregal. From there we continued by bus way up into highlands of a different kind; instead of lava and ash here was granite and quartz, a lovely region reminiscent of the hard rock mining terrain of Alberta and Montana. Again we were jarred by contrasts; the people were wholesome and outgoing and the territory was somehow not tropical. This was a puzzle piece seemingly from another game. It made us want to know more but there was no place good, like the Rio Dulce, to keep a boat. We realized it would take a year to get to know this area so we opted for more reconnaissance.

Returning to the boat we sailed for the Secas archipelago, small uninhabited islets off the southwestern coast of Panama (this far "south" the isthmus is running almost east and west). The group offers splendid tropical flora and several protected anchorages; these latter are often shared with vessels of the local shrimping fleet, which usually work at night. The bottom was teeming with lush coral and kelp, so snorkeling was tempting, but we were advised to beware of the sharks. The reason for their proliferation was obvious, the shrimpers sometimes discarded their "by catch," everything caught in their bottom trawls that was not shrimp, into the anchorages. This by-catch often was composed of far more fin fish and mollusks than shrimp, for the trawls effectively bull doze the bottom and scoop up every living thing in their path. While the non-shrimp may not be of commercial or export value, it is nonetheless often comestible. It would feed people but was not good for export, so instead it feeds sharks. The one time I did attempt to go spear fishing for dinner I promptly encountered a big blue tip swimming actively, so I scrambled back into the dinghy and we resorted to our old standby, macaroni and cheese.

The next day we were running short of ice so I took a jar of Jo Anna's apricot jam, brought all the way from California, and approached one of the shrimpers offering a trade. Indeed the crew agreed to exchange ice for jam and took my five-gallon bucket down into the hold. I could hear a crewman chipping away down there, and presently he emerged with my bucket showing a great iceberg extending from the top. It was enough ice to double the volume of the pail. Only as the grinning crewman passed it down to me in the dinghy did I realize this "berg" was a solid block of frozen shrimp. There were no other yachts around, so what were we to do with this treasure but eat it. We chipped it down to several five-pound chunks, put it in the ice chest, threw the beer and soda pop in with it, and ate the shrimp as it thawed. Again it was an over dose, and it took years for us to think of shrimp as a delicacy again. Of course, Panama exports most of its shrimp to earn the hard currency needed to pay for oil.

The Secas Islands are uninhabited because they live up to their name – dry – no reliable fresh water. But the shrimpers told us of a seasonal cliffside spring which they had tapped with a gutter of split bamboo to form a falling water bath. We found it and reveled in the endless gush of clean fresh water. Jo Anna, especially, luxuriated in washing her hair, which she could never properly rinse on board with our garden sprayer.

Our Pacific cruise was made along an arid coast in the arid season. Once we were away from California's marinas, where potable water is automatically available on every dock, almost every drop of fresh water for our family of four was laboriously carried in five-gallon jugs via dinghy to the boat. Every pound of it was hoisted aboard and then siphoned into the tank. Because everyone in the crew participated in this operation, our water was then metered out with careful thought given to every stroke of the hand spigot pumps in the galley and head. Water used in cooking such as to boil pasta or steam vegetables was saved for rinsing dishes that had been first washed in sea water. Otherwise dishes and glassware were washed and rinsed in seawater. Bathing was done mostly in the sea with miserly rinses using the garden sprayer to atomize fresh water. Our bucket head used only seawater. We lived largely in our bathing suits but laundry was either taken ashore or rinsed only when fresh water was abundant.

We were sometimes able to collect rain in our cockpit awning. If it rained while sailing we tried to collect it from the sails. Even with all of these measures it was shocking how much water we needed to survive at just a minimal level of consumption. Aboard SCRIMSHAW the four of us could live all day on what it takes to flush one toilet ashore.

Happiness Is...

One day we met a fisherman who had come out from the mainland in his big, diesel-powered sea skiff. This was a serious boat with a big thump-thumping single cylinder engine. He pulled the craft alongside; we all fended him off with our feet. His rail was gnarly and smeared with tar and as we talked I thought what a mess it would make if this boat was allowed to contact SCRIMSHAW's comparatively fragile white topsides. The man was very cordial and asked if we wanted any lobster. When we respectively declined he apparently understood and then asked if we had any spare diesel fuel, explaining it had become very hard to get. In the conversation that followed we became friends with Ernesto and later he would give us one of our most memorable cross-cultural surprises of the trip.

Unfortunately all we had was gasoline. He went on to tell of the fuel crisis (it was late 1973) that had profoundly affected the whole world. We had heard a little news about shortages on our radio receiver but had grown naively disinterested in world events. Ernesto explained there were long gas lines and a slowed economy in the United States, but in Central America he said there was almost total shut down. In Guatemala especially, he said there had been simply no gasoline or diesel fuel in the country for days on end. Now we listened.

Noticing our kerosene running lights he then asked if we had any spare kerosene. He and his wife cooked with kerosene at home but they had now resorted to fire wood because even charcoal, which they sometimes used for cooking, was unavailable. We too used kerosene for cooking but we gave him a gallon from our half-full six-gallon tank (leaving us only about two) and he was very grateful. Again he offered us lobster, insisting that we accept at least one whopper. Reluctantly I asked if instead his fish box might contain a Spanish mackerel, the fin fish of our preference in these waters. He did not, so we gratefully accepted one lobster to acknowledge his gratitude for the kerosene.

After he left I checked our gasoline supply. Fortunately we still had about nine gallons of our twelve-gallon capacity. With our motoring consumption of about one half gallon per hour we had plenty because of the balmy breezes of this season on this coast. Furthermore SCRIMSHAW could glide along for miles on zephyrs that would leave the usual heavy cruising boats of that time essentially becalmed. We were willing to keep sailing slowly even in very light airs, to conserve gasoline, thus we felt relatively unaffected by this crisis.

Over our lobster salad that night (some of us picked the meat out) we discussed the independent nature of our situation on board. From our encounter with the fisherman we could sense the rather extreme extent to which even depressed and undeveloped regions are so totally dependent on convenient, fluid petro power. In both Guatemala City and San Jose, Costa Rica we had seen thousands of smoking vehicles. In each of these we knew that refined petroleum flows easily through a tiny tube to enter their cylinders as a volatile distillate and leave by the tailpipes as noxious vapors. But in the process these motors move sustenance, including water, to millions of people rich and poor alike. This was just one more example, made so abundantly clear by living on a boat, of the enormous quantity of energy and materials consumed by humankind.

Another shocker was our trash. On SCRIMSHAW all biodegradable were discarded into the sea, paper and plastic were compacted under foot and saved for dumping ashore or burying on remote beaches, non-returnable bottles and jars were often broken over the side by whacking them with a winch handle, and cans were punctured at both ends and sunk offshore. Despite all this the stuff seemed to multiply on board like rabbits. Even when shopping required taking your own egg boxes, plastic bags, shopping totes and returnable bottles, it was blatantly clear that food packaging was the main culprit in trash accumulation. It was more than a nuisance; we often had black bags of trash lying in the after wing nets stewing and stinking in the sun. All of this impressed us mightily with the potential consequences of a long-term fuel crisis. Almost everything we needed, except fish but including water, arrived by motor vehicle at the myriad shops from where we obtained it. Furthermore our leavings were hauled away to the nearest unregulated dump – by some conveyance dependent on fossil fuel.

Even SCRIMSHAW herself, we were forced to realize, was intensely consumptive. After all, she was composed of highly refined and processed materials – plywood, fiberglass, resins, paints, synthetic fibers and non-ferrous metals – whose manufacture consumed lots of petrochemicals, heat and electricity, and that says nothing of the three-plus years of my physical work and personal sustenance expended in building her. Despite the fact that we didn't have a car just now, that we were largely removed from the land, that we enjoyed a high degree of self-contained independence and wind-driven mobility, and that we could feed ourselves at least sometimes from the sea, there was still no escaping the heightened realization that this nomadic life of ours still made us greedy creatures of modern consumptiveness. Not to say that this reality took the fun out of cruising, only that cruising made the voraciousness of the human appetite starkly clear.

An even bigger part of what we were learning was the fact that in the cultures where this appetite is seldom satisfied beyond survival nourishment, the people can still be unreasonably welcoming and generous to strangers. This seemed to illustrate our newfound awareness of the innate but illusive balance between the extremes of human behavior, and indeed in all of Earthly life:

The next morning I am lying in our bunk just at daylight. I hear the thump-thump of our friend's engine approaching. I come awake as it comes closer, louder. Finally it slows to an idle and SCRIMSHAW is jolted by the noisy contact of his gnarly rail with our pristine white topsides. Furious I leap into the cockpit in my underwear to see our friend standing in his boat alongside. Grinning, he is holding up a still-wiggling Spanish mackerel. Befuddled by the conflict between my anger and my gratitude, I now notice the T-shirt Ernesto is wearing. It is black with a bright, multicolored day-glow illustration. It is a cartoon tiger tomcat all orange and black stripes, with a boozy, lascivious look on its face. The cat is holding in its paw a stem cocktail glass brimming with a fruity libation. Little spats of effervescence jump from the drink. (Right now I see this image positively radiating as if in black light, like Ernesto's smile.) Incredulous, I carefully re-read the shirt's inscription; Happiness Is A Tight Pussy...

As the boys and Jo Anna slowly emerged into the cockpit my choking laughter was overcome by anger. Not anger at Ernesto, for he clearly had no idea of the idiomatic meaning of his T-shirt and he had no notion of the tarry mar his boat had left on ours, but anger at my fellow yachtsman who probably had given him the shirt. We had the mackerel for breakfast, lunch and dinner. The whole encounter had been a juicy overdose.

A Lively Thrash...

From the Secas Islands we sailed for the Gulf of Panama, a wide bight in the coast that defines the approaches to the Panama Canal. This Gulf is bounded on its western edge by a promontory that is well named, Punta Mala (Bad Point). To sail east around this headland puts the sailor at the mercy of more high pressure from the winter Caribbean that is squeezed by mountains to pour out on the Gulf as "reinforced trades." Worse yet, to get to the Canal it appears that one must beat dead against this prevailing gale and its consequential adverse current. I resolved not to do that. Instead we would hold the port tack all the way across the Gulf, over to its eastern side and thereby overshoot the

Canal. That way we could get under the lee of the mountains over there and work our way up to Balboa without trying to tack against mature waves and strong current. Despite this one-tack tactic we knew that this leg would be our first real upwind trial of the trip. Could the boat take it? Could we?

Because trade winds usually decrease at least a little at night, we timed our run to round Punta Mala just at dusk. Everything we had heard about this leg warned that we were in for a night of it, so we were all cleaned up, rested and fed. The dinghy was lashed down on top of the sterncastle, the surfboard was securely tied in the net and the anchors and chain were taken below. We deep reefed the mainsail, hanked on the staysail, set the running backstays, stowed the Genoa and set the storm staysail on the headstay. In the end it was an almost academic lesson in handling a blow because we knew it was coming!

Sure enough, just beyond the promontory we crossed the wind line between Walden Pond and Victory At Sea. SCRIMSHAW slashed her way across that Gulf like a good horse running in ploughed ground. It was rough, noisy and wet, the hardest pounding we had sustained to date, but we were ready for it and we knew it would be over some time tomorrow. By dawn we could see the mountains of eastern Panama, by lunch we were approaching a tropical Big Sur and by noon we were anchored in Bahia de Piñas (Pineapple Bay).

Talk about lush! The greenery was so, er, green that it looked like... Well, first of all the escarpment was as steep as the face of a calving glacier, and the greenery made the glacier look like it was covered with Astroturf gone inexplicably to plastic jungle. It was almost fake, a stage setting by Cecil B. deMille.

A small and remote sports fishing resort in this bay gave us our first close look at the aquatic version of the great white hunter's African safari. Killing fish for fun was hot stuff here. There was a gallows on the dock with a winch to hang the kill for taking pictures. The fish landed by the "bwanas," mostly big billfish and tuna, were extremely beautiful but nothing surpassed an eighty-pound wahoo, a near record specimen that was hung just as we arrived. The shape of this fish seemed to me the ultimate design for a sub surface predatory "vessel." Russell and I examined this sleek fish, its flanks still quivering with extinguished power, its rainbow colors still pulsing in the sun as its vital excellence drained away. Our séance was interrupted by the local fish butcher who neatly sliced out its anus and incised from there up its belly to its chin and then reached in to deftly eviscerate the creature, flinging the entrails to a mob of belligerent pelicans. We were bothered by the death of this splendid animal, deprived of its life for a photograph with its proud slayer who had chosen not to witness or record its subsequent disassembly into bricks of glistening pale flesh. Fortunately this food was not wasted as it often is in such resorts. A nearby native village, remote as it was for there were no roads to this place, was expanding demographically on the fruits of the fun-time fish killers. Was this, too, what we had come to see? Not really, and such hard truths were wearing us down a bit. While the cruise was going well enough, we were all a bit rattled by this brand of reality; it was time for an interruption, but to have that we must work our way back to the Canal.

Hey Dad, Can I Steer?...

"Those kids are ruining our trip!" I am growling to Jo Anna. The truth of it makes me boil. Again Steven has been tormenting Russell and the scene has turned to altercation.

"What do you expect..." Jo begins to say, but it is too late. I have already jumped into the forward cabin and cornered Steven in his bunk. Barely able to keep my hands from making fists, I slap the boy around. Jo yells, "Don't! Oh don't!" A delicious satisfaction from the blows clashes with the terrible ugliness that I – yes me, myself, I – am perpetrating. My elbow catches the chimney on Steven's reading lamp sending it bursting onto the cabin sole. The crash of breaking glass freezes the action and the cries. The raw kerosene flame is smoking, Steve is cowering in his bunk, and I am panting with agitation. Instantly my anger turns to shame, then slowly to guilt, and later to fear. The fear is of myself...

After that boisterous gale crossing the Gulf of Panama and two days of rest in Pineapple Bay, today we had all been bored from motoring all morning in a flat calm and ghosting along all afternoon on steamy zephyrs. Since leaving Guatemala we had been exposed to some rather dismal truths, some hard evidence of how the world really works for much of humanity. And perhaps we were apprehensive about what was coming next. Jo Anna had been reading aloud about the rigors of transiting the Panama Canal in a small boat, and we were also bracing for our impending immersion into the modern mania of the Canal Zone. After months of relative isolation and freedom, were we ready for what was described as "America's experiment with socialism?" Then there had been the painful altercation of this evening.

It was now December 1973, Steven had turned thirteen years old in October, Russell was going on twelve, and they were both now quietly brooding in their darkened VW Beetle-sized cabin. Steven had a swelling cheek, Russell a sense of his complicity. Jo Anna was counting sheep in the sterncastle, desperate for rest but wakeful from a damaged image of her husband. We were at sea on a pretty night but there was little wind. I'd been sitting in the cockpit for an hour or more, trying to appreciate the serene oceanic setting backed by mountains while sharing it all with guilt.

I pondered the question of whether or not a man-and-wife team really is the ideal solution to the crew problem on a small boat, and concluded only that the plot thickens when two teen-age boys are added to the crew list. In the aftermath of today's altercation, Jo Anna's silence and condemning glances said much to me without words.

In the very last of the sunset's afterglow, a nearly full moon rose over the mountains, and just as I basked in its truth light we were captured by a thick but glowing nighttime haze. I adjusted the cushions in the cockpit for a drifting watch. After a long spell of struggling with my mean grade of grief, I felt a cooling zephyr. It was mountain air, perhaps pushed over the isthmus, or maybe it was just a draft from that thunderhead, way over northward against the mountains.

The zephyr, helped dispel my funk, and with just the prospect of a sailing breeze I shifted to the other cockpit seat and contemplated other things: The quick years of child bearing with Jo Anna, our tumultuous business involvement, the building of our boat and our extrication from California. Here I was heading for the Caribbean again some eighteen years after that long-ago promise to myself. Keeping that promise had not been easy, was not now easy, but I was about to get back to where it all had started. Instead of meeting up with Wolf and Jeannie, this time I was embarked with two game sons, a plucky wife, and a nifty boat. It was working out if in a vastly different way than originally intended. So why was I so up tight, especially with my elder son? The unexpected answer came as if I had slapped myself in the face. I was smarting from anger, rudely awakened from a wet dream to find himself the captain of a family crew. How did this happen? I had not applied for this position, the job was found for me by the strongest force in life, and like most young fathers I was not well qualified to captain such a "vessel."

I had been fortunate enough to hitch up with a woman who was willing to buy into my trip – not so common today – and she made it possible for me to hang on to my youthful quest for this nomadic aimlessness. In my early cruising days it had been all about pals and gals and flying boats and freedom from responsibility. It's a craving, I now suspected, that had lots to do with lust but little to do with family. It was a chronic affliction that I'd been carrying around and passing on to others – even selling plans and instruction manuals for it -- ever since Old Providence Island. Was this valid? Wasn't there a danger that my continued conviction to cruising would infect my sons with the same craze for chasing geese?

Finally a breeze. It was just enough to sail on. I checked the chart, and guessed the position into which we might have drifted. As I sheeted in, causing the winches to emit their ratcheting chatter, Jo Anna called softly from the bunk, "Do you need any help?"

"No," was my answer, and the boat began barely to move. As usual, Jo had offered to help, and as usual, I had rejected her outreach. It was as if I wanted her to know that if the crew abandoned ship, the boat could sail on with just the captain.

The tropical water was alive with bioluminescence, a phenomenon, which by now, I almost worshiped. I often swam at night just to open my eyes underwater and watch the tiny, blinking plankton zoom right up to my eyeballs and then, like celestial clutter almost in the path of a space craft, swerve quickly aside on the currents parting past my head. During this calm, I had watched the glowing tracks of several sub-surface beasts, great and small. Now I saw three faint, perfectly parallel wakes streaming from behind the trimaran. They resembled contrails from a tight formation of three fighters slowly poking through a moonlit sky.

This was going to be nice. Night watches were my only chance to be alone. They were everybody's only chance to be alone, and we all enjoyed them, but this one I intended to hog for myself. To hell with guilt.

A soft rumble of thunder, up against the distant mountains, briefly distracted my recollections of the day. It had been like many other days along the Pacific seaboard, hot, calm, bright and difficult. Now it was cool, dark and easy, and the draft was building into a breeze. It was shifty in direction, but without holes of calm in it. The thunder sounded closer, but not close, and if I could just work the boat offshore I knew there would be wind tomorrow and it would be that same Punta Mala gale, the same reinforced trade that drives so many sailboats off toward Ecuador as they try to cross this gulf. But because of SCRIMSHAW's deep centerboard, she had beaten against it well, arriving on the eastern side of the Gulf much closer to the Canal than most engineless cruising boats can fetch. If it blew hard again tomorrow, as it probably would, we would just strap her down and chip away at the waves again. It was that kind of sailing that let us all know we were contending with the real ocean and it was the kind that the boys actually preferred. Understandably, Jo didn't like the crashing and banging and the flying spray, but Steve and Russ came alive in hard weather, doing everything they could to help Dad drive the boat. For now, I kept the vessel fairly close-hauled against the breeze, and just let her go whichever course she seemed to sail the best, out into the Gulf:

Do I want them to leave? Am I trying to drive them away? Well, sort of, maybe yes. But why? Because I want the boat to myself, that's why. A part of me wants to slide back into the old single days, the brand new days of youth, to keep the original Providence promise. But that's almost funny! When I was single I always wanted somebody like Jo Anna to be traveling with me, someone with whom to share a time like this.

So here I am right now with Jo Anna herself, not just somebody like her, and with everything else in the world to be envious of, including a business in California that keeps pumping us with enough money to travel like this. And all at age forty, fer crissake! Why the Devil am I so strung out?...

At that point I noticed that the breeze had shifted its direction fair -- not so contrary to the course I wished to hold. The boat was moving now, so it was time to keep track of where we were and where we were going. I ducked below to make some notes on the chart. Jo stirred and said, "Sounds like a breeze. Do you need some help?"

"No," said I. "It's nice up there and I'm awake. Come up if you want, but maybe you'd better get some sleep. There'll be wind later I think."

I drew a course for the Perlas Islands, in the approaches to the Panama Canal, and quickly returned to the cockpit. The haze was still brightly lighted by the invisible moon, but I couldn't see ahead very far at all. The danger of collision was minimal because as yet we were well away from the steamer tracks converging on the Canal. Thunder still rumbled in the distance. I resolved to be alert for the slightest temperature drop, which could foretell a squall. I adjusted the cockpit cushions to my liking, and settled down to steer:

Shafts of moon glow loom through scattered hollows in the haze. They highlight patches of sea, some far away, some near. Wavelets assume a colorless, pewter-like glitter under the shafts. All else is black save the piercing red compass light. I am taken by the thought that this kind of sail, right now, is too nice not to share with someone. But who to share it with? If one of the boys were up, he'd probably prefer to have the night to himself rather than divide it with his increasingly unpredictable father. And Jo? She loves nights like this, and we have shared a few, but if she were to come up now, I would suffer further consequences of my earlier performance. And what about the consequences for my crew? My family?!

"Ah, what the hell," I mutter. "The boat wouldn't be here without me, and we're all lucky to be alive." Inhaling the words I whisper, "Eat it up."

There is more muffled, distant thunder, but no drop in temperature, and there is wind now, not just a breeze. What's more it is a damp wind, and it's blowing across the course. That makes the sails really drive the boat, so SCRIMSHAW is beginning to boogie. I quit my dismal introspection and get down to sailing. In case I might have to slack the sheets in a gust I clear them so that they will run out unrestricted. I stow the extra cushions, which might get in the way. I shine a quick blink of the flashlight on the speedo. A long burning after image of the dial clings in my mind's eye; eight knots minus a fraction. As the image slowly dies away I think, what if the wind increases? That big Genoa jib should probably be changed down to the smaller Yankee. But that would involve calling someone on deck help, and I don't want to call anyone up. The ride is smooth – no sea yet – and they're all asleep. They would come if called, any one of them, and without complaint. But this is my scene.

Is that rain? A little, but no temperature drop. I reach below for my slicker, slip it on and quietly close the hatches. I shiver for a second.

I think that Steve is just trying to maintain his own place on the ladder against growing pressure from his younger brother. And all of them, including Jo Anna, are just trying to hold their own against the advent of some goddam Captain Bligh! "What a waste of a good time!" I whine. Then I whisper at the wind, "What gives? I'm supposed to be enjoying myself."

I shine the light into the sails, then check the compass and realize I can slack the sheets more and still hold course. For once the wind direction is shifting favorably and the boat responds to the adjustment by urging up another knot or so. Pulling up my hood against the rain and groping for the flashlight, I read the speedo again. Nine knots plus; the after image echoes in my eyes. "Cripes! Look at her go," I mutter, and then think, this is crazy. I should shorten sail. She's doing fine, but what if the wind keeps increasing? The waves will build and the boat will start jumping. We could have a nasty scene getting that Genoa down. On the other hand, maybe this is just a draft from that distant thunderhead, in which case it will soon pass and we'll need the big Genoa again. I remember that it's Steven's watch next. Do I dare call him out of a sound sleep? To have his bruise remind him of my outburst? And then ask him to steer while I get the big sail down? Steve loves to make the boat really go, and sure as hell if we change down to the Yankee jib the wind will drop and we'll be left lollygagging along under insufficient sail. The boy will sit here and steer and sulk because dad is too chicken to change back to the Genoa. "He'd have every right to sulk," I mumble. Then I think, this is too nice, slicing along like this. Maybe I'll just slack the sheets a little more, give her some head and concentrate.

So I concentrate. I turn on the masthead light to illuminate the upper telltale. I brace myself against the cockpit coaming and hold the Genoa sheet loosely. It is still cleated in its quick-release cleat, but by jerking upward I know it will release in a second to slack away in the event of a heavy gust. Now I do just that, giving the Genoa sheet three more inches of slack. There is no heavy gust but the wind is shifting more fair all the time. Easing sheets means I can continue carrying the Genoa even in a stronger wind. Now I give a like amount of slack to the mainsail. As the boat surges ahead I check around the deck with the flashlight. The anchors are secure, the surfboard and kayak are lashed down, the hatches are dogged and the ventilators closed. The dinghy is snugged on top of the sterncastle, its oars safely stowed in the port float. The centerboard is in its down position. The only thing I can think of to spur the boat harder is to strap the Barber hauls for both sails, which I now do. We are trimmed for maximum thrust, minimum heel.

Still concerned about overpowering the craft, I assume my "full pursuit posture." Devised to insure that a knockdown gust cannot pitch me out of the cockpit, I brace my feet against the far side of the foot well, hook my windward arm around the lower shroud and hold the Genoa sheet in that hand, the tiller in the other. A limp-wristed grasp is all it takes to steer SCRIMSHAW even at speed. These things done, I consider my sailing machine to be delivering full power for the available fuel, and consider myself to be totally plugged in. "This is great," I whisper.

But I am not convinced. Big sails on a small boat, a shifty, rising wind at night, high speed with poor visibility, thunder in the distance, a light rain at times. My present racing tactics are not the way to manage a cruising multihull offshore, and no way to maintain my top spot in the pecking order of a family crew whose other members are all asleep and trusting me to bring them through the night. On the other hand, there has been no temperature drop and no lightning to announce a squall. There is no real seaway yet. There is just this steady, rising wind, which keeps shifting more and more fair, a gradual increase in the power supply with no corresponding increase in Resistance. It's a one-in-a-million night and the boat is loving it. So am I!

There is something else that makes me feel good. It's a sense of achievement. My family is down below sleeping while I drive the boat headlong across the luminescent interface. We are truly in the cruising mode. We've made it. On land or sea we all know now that we can go practically anywhere and make out all right. I feel fatherly in extreme. Except for the bad thing I've got going with my elder son, I think this must be the ultimate interaction between man and world. Even if that man is acting out some latent maladjustment, he is nevertheless going through life! Oh, is he going through it! "Let them sleep," I say, and the words are siphoned from my mouth as if spoken from that old sailor's whistlejug.

I wonder aloud, "Wolfie, where are you?" I even listen for a reply but the wooing sails and gushing wake drown even imaginary voices. But I can see the sails. They are inflated drumhead tight. When the bows yaw to windward, the leading edges of both sails go slightly soft, emitting an inaudible luff. When the bows yaw to loo'ard the trailing edges flutter like little motors, the rout of two Vespas drag racing when the light turns green. Both sails are taking full advantage of the beam wind and I am satisfied that there is no practical way to improve this machine's use of such bountiful power. The wakes are hissing out behind like onions popping in hot fat, each one lighted from beneath by its own underwater headlight shining straight astern. There are just two wakes now instead of three because with this much wind abeam the weather outrigger flies above the waves.

More thunder.

But no lightning.

The speedo tickles ten, the compass reads course, the masthead telltale and the wakes – and the helmsman -- are steady. "Hang on, Sloopy," I speak through the whistlejug. "We're getting someplace now."

So I go along like that, not steering or driving, but wearing my boat. Twice after the rain stops the speedo tickles twelve so I reach for the hatch to open it a crack and call for Steve. But both times the boat settles back to a comfortable ten or eleven, and so I settle back too. I definitely feel the weight of jacking up our family home at the wrong time and place, and I fantasize on what a capsize would mean to us now. It would mean trauma and suffering. It would probably mean rescue, perhaps some time tomorrow, but if no fish boat came along it just might mean protracted suffering in the sea for us all. At least it would not mean sinking, but either way I was asking for it. "Talk about guilt!" I grumble. But I cannot resist this ride! With the sails slacked out like they are, I know it would take a terrible blast of wind combined with a big breaking wave, to bowl the boat over even with full sail set. Nothing in these conditions suggests a breaker or a blast. The glowing haze is even thinning out in patches, revealing cul-de-sacs and alleyways, avenues and boulevards, plazas and now commons of moonlit sea and stars. "There it is?" I whisper aloud, it is the Southern Cross, arguably the most glorious of constellations viewable from Earth.

Okay, so Guilt, fear and thrill, the thrill of exercising my favorite skill, are all having it out within me, and there is no stopping the engagement. "Fair winds! SCRIMSHAW," I say to my boat, "and to all those who sail in you."

Thunder? No. An imaginary voice? No, a voice! It says, "Hey Dad, can I steer?" I am stunned. I think, Dad who? Me?! Steer what? This?! Now?

It sounds like Steven. He has slid the hatch ajar and is peering out, his maturing face marveling at the moon. His simple question hangs; I fail to respond. His face framed in the hatchway forms an exquisite centerpiece for this exotic setting, and I am frozen for an answer to his warm question.

With another step upward in the companionway he emerges from the hatch far enough to turn forward and survey the silver sea. It is being swallowed grossly down the twin maws between our bows. My son is suited up, ready for anything. I see him but I cannot answer him. Conflicts flash in my head; it threatens to burst. A tight cramp has seized my larynx, a searing pain. Fortunately it stifles my initial reaction, which is to say, “Uh, not now, Steve. The steering’s pretty touchy.” Thank God I couldn't say that. Then I desperately want to say, “Ah, I was just getting ready to call you... Help me change down to the Yankee.” Thank God I didn’t say that either. If I had, I could already hear him responding with something like, “Aw Dad, we were just getting going good.” Everything that tried to come out of me would demean Steve. I even wanted to ask about his bruise, but thankfully my voice was throttled by the cramp.

Fighting the spasm in my throat and in my mind, I pull a breath past the constriction and finally decide what to say. At once my larynx relaxes and with enormous relief my words come from deep within the whistlejug, "Okay, you take it." The catharsis is huge. My knees buckle a bit as I change seats. To cover a cry I fake a cough to loo’ard.

"Hey! Great," says Steve, as he wriggles from the hatch.

"I've been holding about two ninety," I say, "but you can steer to make her go.” Steve slides the hatch closed and assumes the full pursuit posture where I have moved away. The boy’s wiriness shows even through his bulky foulies, and his hair springs from beneath his hood to swirl around his face. The hair and the dark both fail to disguise the extent to which he looks like Jo Anna. As he takes the tiller, I am keenly conscious of delivering the helm, the boat and her people into the hands of my firstborn son. In this act, I become his.

“The wind is pretty steady,” I say, “but she’s in a narrow groove. Just keep her in there no matter where the wind wanders. You can stray all you want from the course, just keep us in the groove."

I wedge myself in the downwind seat facing aft. I don’t want to watch Steve or watch the compass; that would express a lack of confidence in him. But I can see the wakes. They will tell me how he is guiding the ship. The twin underwater headlights are shining straight astern. There's a slight hunting in the beams but no sweeping; he's doing fine.

He says, "You're not going below, are you? This is too good to miss!"

My larynx cramps again. Turning to face the noise of the lee bow I mouth without speaking, "My God, he wants to sail with me." Trying to withhold a sob I fake another cough downwind. While my chest shakes and my eyes run I fixate on the lee bow. It is piercing the waves well below their crests. Only after it emerges through their backs do the crests part in a puff of phosphorescent sparks. Thus split they rush down the deck of the outboard hull in swirls of radium. Now I look astern and see the wakes converging away fast on a plain of waving black grain. My boat, with my son at the reins, is plowing under guilt. In a moment I regain control and allow the rain to wash my face and the wind to wipe my nose.

Only then can I turn to him and say, carefully, "If you want, I'll ride shotgun on the Genoa sheet, so you can concentrate, really keep her on the rails even if it gusts."

"Good idea," he says. "Boy, this is great! We keep going like this and we'll cut ourselves a brand new Panama Canal!"

I laugh and it feels wonderful. I pop the Genoa sheet out of its cam cleat, remove one wrap from around the winch, and hold tension on the line. I don't give an inch but I'm ready to give a yard should the wind decide to gust.

Soon I am able to turn to Steve and say, laughing, "You've really got her going, man. Caribbean here we come. Change your ocean, change your luck." Steve chuckles but his lack of further response brings another spasm to my Adam's apple. I have already said too much...

So then we settled-in to share the ship in silence. Neither of us spoke for at least an hour. Even when Jo Anna passed each of us a cup of bullion from the Thermos, we saved our words for her.

Through the night we just sailed along together. Oh, did we ever sail along! It had never been better between us, and thereafter it never again got bad.

....

Illustrations for this chapter, narrated by the author, are available online at ...
www.OutrigMedia.com/books/atm-volume-one.html

10

OUT OF GAS

1973

Isla Coiba lies in the approaches to the Panama Canal, and the region, as at Bahia de Piñas, teems with marine life including an abundance of game fishes and sharks. The maximum-security prison for the nation of Panama is established on this island, and we heard that some of the prisoners, deterred only by the sharks, were allowed to roam free. Furthermore, an American entrepreneur had been given permission to establish a small sportfishing resort here, and the management welcomed visits from traveling yachts. We learned the prisoners had a little time-killing business making a unique type of textile for sale to visitors. We decided to go.

Cortinas is what they called them, curtains of little seashells. Tiny cowrie shells, big as a peanut and all the same size, were heaped by the millions on the Island's beaches, and some of the men gathered them for crafting these cortinas. We were free to wander from the fishing camp into part of the prison compound where the inmates met us cordially, asked for money and cigarettes, and were anxious to sell their artful wares.

The "curtains" were made in all sizes from letter size to as big as a door, and by selecting shells of different color the maker's desired images were portrayed. In nature all the shells are more or less black in color, but as one of the prisoners explained to me in Caribbean English, "You gots to burn black to gets red, bleach black in de sun for weeks, turn and turn to gets gray, an den bleach gray to gets white." With these four shades, black, gray, red (more like faded pink) and white, the inmates produced a great variety of images. A light wooden bar at the top of each curtain was perforated with little holes on intervals of about three eighths of an inch and strings of shells were suspended from the holes on monofilament fishing line. No attempt was made to join the strings crosswise, thus the curtains resembled those coarse screens of big beads and trinkets, used to cover doorways in some ethnic restaurants and homes. But this work was fine because the shells are small. The inmates selected the proper color of shell for the correct position on the string, thereby causing the desired image to be revealed. And when a passing breeze or hand made the strings sway, the image would undulate. Regrettably we purchased only one piece of this art, a two-foot square image of a butterfly, which hangs in our Virginia home and is sometimes explained to the rare visitor interested in our collection.

We were invited to dine with the fishing guests, about ten American men and women, in the screened cookhouse at the bare-bones resort. They were all there for the fishing, which was apparently incredibly good. This was back in 1974, and I suspect by now the same thing has happened there as has happened in Mexico and other popular sportfishing waters: Each fish has been caught and released so many times that the catchers are obliged finally to keep the ones that have been so damaged by their multiple fights that they will not survive another battle. For the large predatory species like marlin, sailfish and wahoo, being hooked and hauled in amounts to a fight almost to the death. Completely exhausted, they would likely die if simply let go, so those intended for release are revived by holding them head-to-current while the boat motors slowly forward to resuscitate the fish. Only when they can swim away weakly on their own are they released to fight to near death again. When they finally succumb many have damaged mouths and gashed skins from being cut by lines. In time the fishkillers move on to yet another underexploited location, maximum security or not.

The Highlight Zone...

With our cortina stowed safely aboard we continued to an anchorage in the Perlas Islands, another little cluster of tropical keys quite close to the Pacific entrance to the Canal. There we met an American couple on their own little monohull, out for a weekend respite from their jobs in the Zone. Margaret managed the Balboa Yacht Club where pleasure boats await their turns to transit the Canal. Bill worked for the Canal Company in Marine Traffic Control, a team that schedules and handles the ships passing from one ocean to another. We became friends with these folks and they paved the way for a great adventure for us. Margaret managed the Balboa Yacht Club, so she fixed us up with what we needed - a mooring, customs, immigration, shopping, and a cold one or three at the yacht club bar. Bill fixed us up with what we needed from the Canal bureaucracy; measurement, an assigned tonnage and the resulting fee for going through. Based on our "tonnage," how much cargo we could carry, it cost us only $53 to change oceans, a ridiculously low price. Furthermore, most of this was a bond that was refunded once we made it through without damaging the Canal facilities. (Of course this was before the Panamanians took over their property again, and they now charge an appropriate fee for yachts to transit their incredible Canal.)

For a week or so we lay to a mooring there at Balboa, watching the huge ships pass close by our mooring as they switched oceans the easy way. Our friends from Costa Rica the Stennets in TRES REYES were there, also waiting to transit, and their young sons had already made friends ashore. Soon we were invited to attend a July 4th cook out at the home of the parents of some of the local youngsters. The father turned out to be the President of the Panama Canal Company. In the ample back yard of their very pleasant home I spoke with this President while he prepared hamburgers for us and a mob of kids, his, ours and many from the neighborhood who were enjoying their pool.

Responding to a few innocent questions from me, the man explained that the Canal was striving to serve the needs of world shipping with a facility that had been largely unchanged since its opening in 1914. Ship traffic and ship size had increased dramatically since the original installation, and there were three main problems. The President explained the first by telling me, "Few people realize it but this installation is holistic. It is actually powered by rainfall. We have a lot of rain here but it is seasonal and irregular year-to –year. The ships are raised and lowered by discharging water from Gatun Lake, the highest water through which the ships pass. As you'll see, much of the Lake is man made by a dam.

So it is shallow except for the dredged ship channel down its middle. Several other, higher dammed lakes in the nearby mountains serve as reservoirs, but the issue is having enough water in a dry year to discharge lockfulls of it into both oceans in the process of raising and lowering the ships."

After serving the first batch of burgers I reminded him of the other problems he had not yet told me about. "Oh yes," he continued, "Then the ships have gotten so big that much of today's new shipping is either designed to barely fit through here or else it is designed to go around Cape Horn instead. The ones that still fit are surrounded by only a thin envelope of water in the lock chambers. Now, to move from one chamber to the next, all the water that the ship displaces has to pass from the forward chamber through that thin envelope into the space left behind, so it becomes very difficult to pull them through without damaging the ship or the lock."

He opened two more beers, turned another batch of burgers and continued, "The design of the present Canal uses five locks. You'll make three steps up here on the Pacific side and two down to the Atlantic. Each step is about sixty feet, and the system works brilliantly, but with all the traffic today, and the huge variety of ship sizes, from yachts like yours to supertankers and aircraft carriers, the mere act of scheduling the traffic gives us real problems, especially at times when water is scarce. And so far, this scheduling cannot be managed by a computer program. It's why you are having to wait, and believe me the big ships don't like it either."

Later in the evening I continued the conversation by asking this man what could be done about the Canal's inadequacy, and he quietly mentioned a proposal to build a new one through Nicaragua where only one lock would be required. "But," he admitted, "There are lots of problems with the idea, both political and physical. To make it fiscally attractive they want to dig the excavations with 'clean' nuclear explosions of the 'shaped charge' type that would lift the earth neatly out of the way and deposit it in an orderly bank alongside." After some discussion of such a prospect he concluded, "Never say never. The fact is that to sustain growth in the world economy, the Panama Canal is long overdue for a replacement or modification of some kind."

While we were waiting our turn to change oceans, our friends Bill and Margaret arranged for us to visit the control tower on the first Balboa lock where Bill worked. A long room with a central table housed a working model of the lock, with little levers that opened the valves in underground aqueducts to drain and fill the chambers and actuate the lock gates. There were ships in the locks at the time, and Bill explained how the water level in one chamber had to be brought to the same level in the one adjoining before opening the gates. He had Steven watch the gauges showing water level, and when they became equal, Steve threw the lever that opened the gates. The model showed the gates opening, and we all looked down on the real thing, saw the real gates open and the donkey locomotives pull the giant ship through into the next chamber.

Underneath the control tower in a bunker-like vault we saw all the mechanical and electrical controls that allowed the controllers to operate the locks, and Bill explained that essentially all of this equipment had operated flawlessly since its installation by General Electric engineers in 1914.

I asked Bill where the electric power came from. He smiled and said only, "You'll see when you approach the locks at the Caribbean end."

World's Greatest Boat Ride...
At Balboa we take aboard our friends Bill and Margaret as line handlers (six persons on each yacht are required to handle lines) and our Panamanian pilot. He is very cleanly dressed in black and white and very mannerly with his complete English. He carries a hand-held VHF radio and a brief case. He smells of aftershave and exudes confidence.

For our first up lockage he directs us to enter the chamber behind a huge oil tanker named the PETRO PAN. She is almost 500 feet long and 100 feet wide, and we can barely see the space between her hull and the towering walls of the lock. We tie alongside a huge seagoing tug, also in the chamber and dwarfed by the tanker, so that as the water rises in the chamber the tug's crew can adjust their lines but we don't have to tend ours at all. It sounds cushy.

So here we are in the first chamber, with our local line handlers and all their local knowledge – they had been through as line handlers many times before – and they tie us beside this giant tugboat and tell us to double our bow line and also the two forward spring lines. I follow these directions, not knowing why because the single lines we have rigged are strong enough to pull SCRIMSHAW apart.

As our chamber fills with churning roils of rainwater and we rise up SIXTY feet with the tug, our pilot speaks earnestly into his walkie-talkie to the captain of the tanker. He says, "When advancing into chamber two, pleas use restrained power for we are tied up right behind your propellers."

The Captain of the tanker responds angrily, "Well why don't they put you somewhere else. We've got to get moving you know!"

Now I get the picture. Besides the six electric donkey engines (small locomotives) set to pull on each side of the ship (right, twelve locomotives pulling on the thing), she is going to use her own engines to help pull water from the front of the ship through that thin envelope. Otherwise the ship is going nowhere.

The tanker is only half loaded (she won't fit through otherwise) so we are staring at the tops of her propeller blades as they begin to flail at the surface, and suddenly SCRIMSHAW is facing a rage of water that is like sailing up Niagara Falls in a barrel. The torrent sweeps the decks with froth; our speedometer is pegged at 25 knots and then drops to zero, its cable broken.

Who knows how fast we are going through the water while tied to a stationary tugboat, but it is surely faster than our thin plywood hulls had ever gone or will ever go again. The lines hold.

In response to pleading from our Pilot, our other lockages are less dramatic but we have another unforeseen circumstance. To keep the six-knot speed required in the Canal I have rented a 25 horsepower outboard motor. It works poorly, its propeller being too close to the surface to avoid sucking air, and worse, it gobbles fuel. We run out of gas in the Panama Canal.

It happens in Gatun Lake. There is a stiff Caribbean trade wind blowing dead against us, we are not allowed to stop or touch the shore (for obvious contrabanding reasons) so I explain to the pilot that we must sail.

"Sail!" he cries. "You can't sail through the Panama Canal! The channel through this lake is narrow and as you can see there are tree stumps sticking up on both sides. If a ship comes the other way you'll have to sail out among the tree stumps."

As Bill and Margaret watch in disbelief, the boys and I drop the centerboard and hoist sail. SCRIMSHAW slides quickly upwind through flat water in a piping breeze. An approaching ship bound for the Pacific gives us blast after blast from its whistle but we Zigzag up the channel tack-on-tack until the last minute, then drop the Genoa and mosey out into the drowned forest in this artificial lake. We miss the stumps narrowly and bump the centerboard but have no trouble avoiding the ship. After it passes we continue a glorious drive to windward, At the Lake's upwind end we tie illegally to a tug dock while Bill, amazed but not pleased with our situation, defies his training and jumps ashore with a gas can and returns an hour later with enough to get us through...

(There were repercussions later, and without the privilege extended to Bill we would have been in deep yogurt. Ah! Friends in high places. Thank you Bill and Margaret, and my sincere apologies to our very professional pilot, Captain Alvarez. I hear that the Canal, now in Panamanian hands, is operating smoothly, thanks no doubt to men like you. I also hear that transiting with yachts is very much more difficult and expensive than it used to be, and I can't blame you folks a bit for clamping down. It was probably quacks like me who exhausted your patience.)

While we waited for Bill to return with gasoline Margaret told us of their life working for The Company and of living in The Zone, the ten mile-wide swath of "American soil" that then bisected the nation of Panama...

"Everything is provided and it all comes from the States," she began. "There's a cargo ship that leaves New Orleans every week and it's loaded with all the trimmings of life in 'Merika.' It's all available at the PX at bargain prices, our medical, auto and life insurance is a steal, our housing is more than adequate, and the retirement benefits should allow us to have a cushy setup almost anywhere in the world except perhaps the States."

"Are you planning to retire soon?" Jo Anna asked. "And where would you go?"

"We love it here in Panama," she said, "outside the Zone. We often travel to the outlying districts. There are really five Panamas, you know, four distinct regions besides the Zone and in some areas the people don't even think of themselves as Panamanian. But there are some gringos here working for the Company who would never consider setting foot outside the Zone. They won't even go downtown Balboa. They're all sucking on the teat and don't want to know about how this place happened."

Margaret went on to explain that this isthmus had been Colombian territory When the French first attempted to dig the Canal. They failed largely because of diseases, so when Teddy Roosevelt decided to try again he wanted a better deal from the Colombians than they considered reasonable. So Teddy fomented a little revolution here. The U. S. Navy got behind it by defending the local secessionists. Colombia couldn't defend its territory against the U S Navy so the place went independent and the United States got a sweet 99-year deal on leasing the Zone. Colombia lost its most valuable possession and ever since a certain faction there has not felt morally reticent when producing drugs for the American market."

Bill arrived with the gasoline and explained that we had missed our lockage with the PETRO PAN and had been re-scheduled.

At the upwind end of Miraflores Lake Bill pointed out the power plant. Tied to a grassy quay was an old ship with fat conductors leading ashore and underground. Its nuclear-powered generator was quietly cranking out the electricity for the whole Canal Zone plus all the nearby portion of the nation of Panama.

When we finally arrived at Miraflores Locks, Our poor pilot received a stern radio reprimand for our being late, but the two steps down into the Caribbean went beautifully. We had evening light on verdant nearby mountains and there was Caribbean music coming from radios nearby. My head was swimming with anticipation for finally arriving, after eighteen years, back in the sea where I had first lived the sailor's life. While we waited in one of the locks I climbed the mast and peered over the lock's gate. In the twilight I could see with binoculars the Caribbean Sea with its fearsome chop driving in against the breakwaters and I knew we were in for some rough sailing. Our circumstances, sailing as a family crew, were far different than I had ever expected as a greenhorn schooner bum, but we were here and this was now!

But we were early. Most yacht traffic in January is coming from the Caribbean heading downwind for the South Pacific. Going the other way, as we were, implied beating against the reinforced trades of the region at that season, so we were advised to wait a while and it would surely let up. The yacht club at Cristobal was little more than a homey drinking establishment, so we took SCRIMSHAW OUTSIDE THE Zone and around to the local Panamanian club to hang out for two weeks. It was a welcome respite because the twin cities of Cristobal-Colon were still safe for visitors back then (we hear they have since become a crime capitol). But we all felt safe and welcome. I was able to catch up on correspondence and the boys and Jo Anna made local friends. For two weeks the wind blew hard enough to rattle the rigging day and night, but one day it was much reduced as advertised. We were ready.

Pure People...

The Caribbean Sea was once a Spanish lake, and the first evidence we saw of this was Porto Belo, an abandoned fortress not far from the Zone that was used to protect from pirates the gold then being extracted from the Incas. It was also used as a stronghold to transfer other goods coming over the isthmus from their trading operations in the Pacific. It is still an impressive bastion although smaller than the one at Cartagena which I had seen much earlier and which we would visit soon.

On the way from the Canal to Cartagena, an old Spanish city on the Caribbean coast of Colombia, we spent about a month among the Cuna people of the San Blas Islands. This archipelago of small islets is scattered along the Darien Coast of the isthmus just east of The Zone. Panama's province of Darien is a region of almost impenetrable jungle, mountains and swamp, and much of the territory is a semi-autonomous sanctuary for these Indians.

The Cuna people are descended directly from the original Amer-Indian strain of northern South America. Most of the descending tribes were decimated by the European Colonists or, if they refused slavery like the Caribs in the Caribbean Islands, were exterminated. But the Cunas, being more out of the way and inhabiting territory not suited to plantation crops like sugar cane, survived the European onslaught and now considered themselves to be the last "pure race" of people on Earth. To retain this purity their chiefs prohibit their women, once having left the Islands, ever to return. The men often leave to work in nearby Panama and can return, but for fear of carrying an externally fathered child, the women cannot.

Yet it was in some ways a matriarchal society. In the villages, which were all located on the outer islets to improve health and escape the creatures of the isthmian jungle, the men behaved very demurely, almost puppy-doggish, when around the women. When we were there in the early seventies the men wore western clothing (mostly tattered walking shorts and plain, ragged shirts.) But as we discovered, when the men went out in boats without women, to fish or to work their cultivations in the mainland jungle, they turned into rather boisterous roustabouts.

The women, on the other hand, were regal and controlling. They wore wrap-around skirts of dark, machine-made and printed cloth brought in from Colombia. The lifeblood of the Islands was circulated by a small fleet of fifty-to-seventy-foot Colombian motor-sailing freight boats called Canoas. These rugged vessels also brought colored cloth, which the Cuna women crafted into the bodice panels of their extremely artful blouses. Called molas, these textile panels are constructed of several layers of different-colored cloth, each layer cut in unique patterns to reveal the next layer and next color below, which is in turn cut to reveal the next and so on in descending widths of cut-outs. All the cut edges are tucked under and hand-stitched down with minute stitches as in "reverse appliqué." The resulting designs are often garish but dramatically "primitive" and earthy. The women were sometimes pleased to sell their work, whether well worn or newly made for sale, and we collected quite a few examples, especially of the older, well used and less garish but more finely detailed versions. Our prized specimens are those that come in pairs for both the front and back of a woman's blouse. In these, the cut-outs from the front panel are arranged in a like pattern for the back but with the colors of course stacked in reverse order to the front thereby creating a unique, color-reversed pair.

The women also wore highly stylized beadwork made as tight gauntlets constricting their forearms and lower calves. Their skirts were belted with wide bands of colored cloth and their heads covered with printed bandannas. The married women painted a dark stripe down the middle of their foreheads, and all this every day get-up was climaxed by a broad ring of solid gold split to hang in the web between their nostrils. For special occasions additional solid gold medallions were worn. Ranging in size between that of poker chips to coasters, they were worn at the ears and sometimes ganged as necklaces. Word had it that there was gold aplenty in the isthmian mountains, all in territory deeded by Panama to the Indians with the mines closely secreted and guarded by them.

At our very first anchorage in these islands, and at almost every succeeding stop, we were soon set upon by fleets of dugout canoes bearing Cuna women (no men) who without invitation promptly boarded our boat and made themselves at home. Their faces, eyes and hair were dark but bright, their expressions reminiscent of the "Eskimo look" typical of tribes supposedly having crossed the Bearing Land Bridge eons ago. Chipper and agile, the women went through our cabins examining every item of our kits with real interest. They were especially taken by advertisements in magazines, and we suspected they were seeking ideas for their mola patterns. I used our Polaroid camera to give them snapshots of themselves, which were highly valued; I soon ran out of film. Nothing of ours was pilfered and we very much enjoyed the wordless exchanges with these lively people, but on occasion it became awkward for us to indicate it was time for them to leave. We once resorted to pulling up the anchor and starting the motor, whereupon our visitors left, but when we re-anchored another flotilla of dugouts soon collected around our SCRIMSHAW.

The men often traveled by dugout over to the mainland isthmus to get fresh water. The "bedroom islands" are located only a few miles offshore and have shallow wells for collecting brackish wash water, but for drinking and cooking the men were obliged to journey up the several fresh rivers that run down from the highlands of the isthmus. Steve, Russ and I joined the men in an expedition of several dugout canoes to gather this water and to get some for SCRIMSHAW. We saw that the Indians carried water in all manner of containers including coconut shells, rusty tin cans (rare here), carved wooden bowls, hollow gourds and tightly-woven grass baskets sealed with sap. In fact, their canoes were filled with anything – even eggshells – that would transport a swallow of water. Our five-gallon plastic jugs, which we could not afford to part with, were held in awe by these people; we were able to offer them only several empty jars and plastic cups.

This was an all-day trip that began with sailing the dugouts about four miles across open water. Here we learned that the boats, which were handsomely carved from solid logs and nicely painted with decorous patterns and colors, really did sail! Their spritsails, made of many scraps of cloth, were extremely simple but quite efficient on these narrow-hulled vessels. Their narrowness made them easy to propel but quite unstable at first experience. That is, their limited "initial" stability made us wonder how they kept them upright under sail. We soon learned, however, that these Stone Age craft had features that would amaze a modern boat designer. First of all they were ballasted but unsinkable! Right, the topsides of their one-piece hulls were carved rather thin to reduce weight and increase internal volume, but the bottoms were left up to three inches thick (for a vessel of about twenty feet long and three feet wide). To discourage marine boring worms the canoes were rarely left lying afloat when idle, but when dragged up on skids and set level they were often allowed to contain a bit of bilge water. This soaked their thick bottoms giving "water ballast." When heeled over by the press of sail some of this wet bottom wood, being very heavy, would be rolled up above the surface of the sea, and some of the dryer, more buoyant topsides would be rolled down on the other side. The effect was to generate righting moment, making the vessels remarkably stable during their "secondary" heeling phase. Furthermore, if completely swamped they still would not sink. If scuttled awash they could be rocked from end-to-end to purge about half of their water out over their ends, then bailed and re-boarded. So it was that in the warm and mostly sheltered waters of the region these craft needed no outriggers for stability and yet were extremely safe.

No leeboards or rudders were used. The boats were steered by a large paddle held over the lee quarter against the hull, deepened and twisted to act as lateral resistance back aft, whereas the forebody of the carved hull was deep and sharp forward, shoaling toward the stern. The sharp, deep, vertical cutwater created lateral resistance forward and this was balanced by the paddle aft to make the canoes surprisingly Weatherly considering the simple sailing rig. Guiding their direction was very easy although we never saw them steered in a real following sea where they would surely tend to broach. When used for fishing outside the Islands and for inter-island transport, the expeditions would sail out in the dawn and return before the afternoon trades became strong thereby avoiding raucous downwind conditions. The fishermen spent their afternoons relaxing and weaving baskets, thus the local weather patterns and indigenous marine architecture had strong influence on cultural patterns, an aspect of boats that has always fascinated me.

Once up the shallow rivers, the deep, sharp forefoot of these boats would stub on obstructions, so when the water shoaled enough to ground the canoes' forebody, the crew simply jumped out to wade alongside and haul the craft stern first, sliding the deeper (now after) end over the cobbles in the gin-clear streambeds. In this way the canoes were worked up to the headwaters where the purity for drinking was best. In all, these simple vessels were really quite sophisticated, matching closely the local waterman to the local water. And to the local land, the small bedroom islands often had little vegetation, were very densely populated and the Indians' huts of wattle-and-thatch were often crammed cheek-by-jowl with barely enough room for a walker to pass between. The isthmian jungle, in contrast, was vast and gloriously dense except where cultivated, and was vacant of human habitation but frequented by the Indians for sustenance. Their boats were the bridge between these two distinct environments, both necessary for survival in this otherwise forbidding territory.

As we returned from the headwaters the Indian men made forays off into the region and reappeared downstream with armloads of cultivated produce; yams, coconuts, cabbage and squash. At one turn in the river the boat in which I rode was bombarded by a man who canonballed down from a huge overhanging tree. His splash, calculated to barely mist my end of the canoe, was decorated by dozens of vermillion sparks. As his geyser subsided the "sparks" became cashew fruits, their bright red husks glowing brilliantly, floating on the surface around the laughing Indian.

Feeling very much together with our Indian companions, the boys and I dragged, paddled and sailed the canoes back to the offshore islet with them. We had come close to understanding why these people chose to remain so isolated and pure. Having mastered their dual environment with their boats, their close-to-the-bone life style was vaguely similar to our own aboard SCRIMSHAW. It was definitely inviting.

Later we mounted a spearfishing expedition with the men and were greatly impressed with their power as free-diving swimmers and their skill with the spear. In fact they were avaricious, taking every type and size of fish (no big ones remained) and they complained that their fish resource was dwindling fast. It was an example of how our "western" accouterments, like swim fins, face masks, snorkels and rubber-powered spear guns, had allowed these noble people to outstrip this aspect of their environment.

For a month we hopped from island to island, one always within sight of another. Outside the reef which connected many of the islands, Steven asked repeatedly if he could sail the runs in our 7'-8" dinghy instead of riding in SCRIMSHAW. Despite Jo Anna's reservations I relented, and we set him out in the open sea in a cockleshell. Conditions were mild but the swell was deep enough to put him almost out of sight at times. We stayed not too close, giving him the chance to experience his bravery to the full, and we all still remember the relief of getting him back aboard.

We were joined in places by cruising friends from Costa Rica, the Rafters of KAJACK and the Kimble's of NELLY BLY. With them we were welcomed ashore in the villages where we prowled for available mola textiles, collecting several of the older, well worn but more detailed and subdued examples. Jack Kimble found one woman with a large rectangular mola depicting a U. S. Dollar bill. It was so faithfully done, including the five-o'clock shadow of minute stitches on George Washington's face, that I had to have it. The gleeful woman accepted my twenty dollar bill, and the piece now hangs in my office to represent "the first dollar" seen framed in so many establishments.

On one occasion we met a graying Indian man who had worked in The Zone and spoke some English. His English name was Charlie Harris, and he invited us to visit an outer islet where there was no village as such but only a campsite where his family occasionally went to tend and harvest coconuts. We took Charlie aboard for the day hop, and he very much enjoyed a rousing beat to windward in SCRIMSHAW. The islet was extremely beautiful; the Caribbean's answer to the South

Pacific, and the lean-to life style there tempted us all to stay forever. I had strong sensations of deja vu in this place, but Charlie wanted us to visit ashore on his home Island. He said that because we were a family and he had become acquainted with us, he thought he could get permission from his chief for us to be ashore at night to attend an upcoming ceremony. For an extra-tribal adult male like myself to be ashore at night was normally forbidden, but in the end Charlie convinced the chief that, with my wife and kids in company, I was not about to inseminate one or more of their women, and Charlie took personal responsibility to see that I returned to SCRIMSHAW at once after the event.

The ceremony itself was a spellbinder. It was held in a meeting house about fifty feet square, its undulating thatched roof supported by internal posts, very artful truss work and myriad lashings. Its sides were wattle with benches of split planks all around and its floor was hard-packed earth; we were soon to learn how it had been packed.

The event began at dusk with people entering the single doorway and taking seats to reverently watch the strange procedure at the room's center. Three men were there surrounding a small cask topped by a platter containing something comestible. Two of them were in their usual ragged walking shorts but one of them, a very husky man, was dressed in a billowing grass skirt with his bare chest bedecked by an outsized and very heavy necklace of polished animal bones and teeth. This man, attended by the other two, was apparently entranced. He made heavy breathing and grunting sounds, and at times jumped ponderously to stamp both feet at once, shaking and banging his necklace on his chest. Very occasionally he partook of a tiny sample from the platter. This went on until dark while a crowd accumulated and several kerosene lanterns were lighted and hung from the truss work overhead.

We four sat together on a bench, and all the benches were filled. The younger Indians stood facing inward in front of those who were seated until we could not see the central goings-on, but we heard the "singing" begin. It was an acapella wailing by a solitary man who joined the husky grunter. With the lungs of a Caruso, the singer started high with slurred enunciations to his atonal blurts. This continued to descend for longer than seemed humanly possible, finally ending each one-breath verse in a trailing gasp of exhaustion. To this repeated performance, gradually the standing Indians began slowly to sway, grasp hands and side step counter-clockwise before us. There were no instruments and no downbeat from the singer, but soon the dancers were in unison. After circulating for a while a shout would cause them all to reverse direction with sharp precision, and gradually – with no change from the singer – their dancing pace increased. This solo wailing, entirely without rhythm, when combined with the slowly accelerating footwork was good theater, a truly different art. But now began the athletic running and stamping. At no change from the singer and no vocal sound from the dancers, a syncopated but tightly synchronized pounding of bare feet made the earth concuss. Maintaining this display the dancers now moved into the center of the room in elaborate patterns which then dissolved into the outer ring again, and a great deal of athleticism was displayed, all while the dancers continued to grasp hands in this flowing circuit of great vitality. This alien but Virginia Reel-type show went on for at least two hours, and the arena air became heavy with the smells of extreme human effort. When it suddenly stopped, there was no applause, no curtain call and nothing like a "That's all folks." It was just over.

Cartagena de los Indios...

Namesake of the ancient Spanish town on the Mediterranean, Cartagena, Colombia remains one of the most fortified cities in the new world. Replacing Porto Belo in the seventeen hundreds as the main Spanish stronghold for accumulating Inca gold, it was an inviting target for Spain's imperialist competitors and especially for pirates. The Spanish had constructed an incredible stronghold here, beginning with protecting the entrance to the harbor. Actually there are two entrances, one each side of an islet set to the eastern side of the mouth. This created Boca Chica and Boca Grande. The Big Mouth was protected by an underwater wall of stone set just deep enough below the surface to tear out the bottom of any ship attempting to enter. The Little Mouth was guarded by a fortified cannonade on the island and another on the mainland. There was also an enormous chain that could be stretched across the narrow channel to close off Boca Chica. I had been here before with Wolf and Jeannie (Chapter 2). The place had been magical then, and sailing in through Boca Chica now, in my own boat with my own family, was quite fulfilling.

The chain was gone but the cannonades were still in evidence, and as we passed inside I told the boys the story of how the pirate Henry Morgan and his followers had stormed the defenses, ramming the chain and hacking at it with axes while suffering a lethal fusillade from both sides. The fact that they failed to enter with their ships was moot, for the attack was a sacrificial, diversionary action to draw attention from Morgan's overland party, which stormed the main fortress from behind. This tactic succeeded in earning Morgan a trove of Inca gold and his reputation as the most ruthless and aggressive renegade of the Spanish Main.

On entering the inner harbor I found the old Club de Pesca, where we had lain in Hoffman's LA EBRISA, unchanged. The stone quay was guarded by the same old satellite fort, its walls and cannons as beautiful as they were threatening, and a disparate collection of yachts tied end-to and anchored out. A block inland stood the towering walls of the fortress, floodlit at night. Nearby was the main gate to old Cartagena, said to be the only walled city in the New World.

SCRIMSHAW was assigned a space along the quay next to KAJACK. With the Rafters we explored the fortress and the town where I was often overtaken by time warp. The old boat landing at the city market was no longer crowded with dugout canoes bringing produce in from up country, and an open sewer no longer ran through the market stalls; cruise ship tourism had demanded an end to that. On the old sand spit east of town a glitzy hotel complex was springing up and suburban squalor had spread far beyond the old walls. Traffic had increased dramatically, most of it smoky and noisy, and the people seemed no longer quite so open and jivey as I recalled. Inside the walls, however, the same colonial charm had been preserved; grand buildings, residential balconies overhanging the narrow streets, and everywhere a sense of history just waiting to repeat itself.

The little fort at Club de Pesca still housed a nice restaurant where we sometimes dined with other yachties, and the boys soon made friends with a scruffy band of local mestizo wags. It was this acquaintance that led to a revealing incident: Steve and Russ had become very tanned by now, lean and wiry with sun-bleached hair – I suppose so had Jo Anna and I – and we all went around in bathing suits much of the time. The boys' trunks were rather stained with fish blood and boat glop. Usually barefoot and dusty, they looked a lot like their local friends. One day when they were all sitting on a wall outside the fort a group of American tourists emerged from the restaurant and filed aboard their waiting bus. A typical tourist matron, straw-hatted and enduring the heat, broke from the line and ran to Russell at the wall. Wordlessly she thrust a dollar bill into his hands and quickly fled. "Wait!" cried Russell in English, "I'm not poor." The woman scurried onto the bus, it pulled away, and the whole gang of kids went off to the smoothie cart for treats all around.

With encouragement from Sean and Pid Rafter on KAJACK, Jo Anna and I planned an overland trip down into northern South America in search of textiles. For the first time Steve and Russ were left aboard the boat alone. Truth be told, we all relished some respite from one another, and we knew that KAJAK's people would keep a close eye on our sons. Steve and Russ had become close with Sean and Pid who were (at that time) childless but willing to sample parenting with rent-a-kids.

Hard Traveling...

One morning Jo Anna and I were visiting aboard a neighboring boat, and as we left there were guests just leaving from an adjacent boat. Jo Anna looked across just as a young woman looked back at her and they both realized they were looking at old friends from California. They each immediately exclaimed the other's name, and the course of the next few weeks was cast in concrete.

Genevieve, Jo Anna's friend from our Big Sur days, was accompanied by Dan, who we did not know but with whom I quickly made a close acquaintance. They were traveling by whatever means, boat, bus and hitch hiking, headed for the upper Amazon for a river trip down to the mouth. It was very pure wayfaring and they invited us to join them for awhile on the condition that we do it at their absolute minimum budget level. As it turned out, the cheapest way to go for the first leg, from Cartagena to Bogota, high in the mountains, was by plane.

In Bogota I had the chance to contact Hans Hoffman, former owner of LA BRISA (Chapter 2), and we enjoyed a brief – and for me emotional – visit with him. I tried to tell him how formative my time in his crew had been, and he responded by telling of his small tourism operation in the remote Amazon Basin. "You should come and spend a couple of years with us on the River, Jaime," he said. "We could use you all in running our operation, and it would be an experience you will never forget." This invitation startled me with its attractiveness and its intrusion on our travel plans. In the end we declined and it has haunted me ever since. Terribly conflicted by this missed opportunity we stuck to our original plan and boarded the bus to Quito, Ecuador. Now the trip turned to gristle.

Some Third World bus rides can be quite comfortable, and these vehicles weren't bad. It was the roads and the driving that was scary; high speed, lots of trucks and no shoulders on steep-and-curvy, rough-and pot-holed mountain roads. We stumbled around Quito for a day or two, dizzy from the 9,000-feet altitude, stayed in a really seedy hotel complete with bed bugs – there was one bathroom to a floor – and we ate a lot of rice and beans. We were puzzled by the toilets; they had regular porcelain bowls but no seats, and the bowl rims were always covered with mud and gravel. Finally we realized that no self-respecting Indian would think of sitting down on these contraptions but instead they first stood on the rims with their sandals and then squatted, thereby keeping their hindquarters clear of public commodes. It was totally reasonable and the squatting position facilitated elimination, but the athletics took a bit of practice, a few epithets and at least one wet foot.

The bus ride south to Otovalo, a weaving center in a fine mountain valley, became challenging. The busses were jam-packed with country folk and washed by loud Andean music. Their stake bed-like roofs were heaped with baggage, live animals, and produce bundled in large net bags. During the runs when there was sometimes standing room only I once found myself clinging for hours to the overhead handrails while my legs became tightly captured in a mass of bouncing, sleeping people. The challenge for me was to not look out the windows. Having lived and worked in the White Mountains and Green mountains of New England, the Wyoming Rockies and California's Sierras, I thought I knew something of mountains, but the Ecuadorian Andes are something else. They seem to run from peaks to valleys with more altitude difference in less horizontal distance than is understandable. Like overfalling waves, the valleys seem literally to undermine the peaks, and yet the roads somehow scratch their way along precipice after precipice. Looking out and down from my standing position made it seem like the bus was literally hanging out over thin air and it was a very long way down. Imagining the earthly forces imposed to raise rock so high, and the atmospheric onslaught over time – such unimaginable time – that cut the glacial trenches and roaring watercourses so deep, almost pushed my mind into rebellion. I wanted to speed it up, see it happening within the blink of my own lifetime, and have it all resolved again into the seabed from where it all had somehow come.

The Indians and their villages here were dour compared to Guatemala's, with the people mostly secreted behind brutish walls. I had the feeling they were often stoned, a means of defending themselves against the thin air and the stupefying vistas. So big was this "countryside" that one was hesitant to look at it because it engendered a troubling insignificance of self.

At one high town where we intended to overnight, Dan and I tried to help the driver's attendant discharge the truckload of baggage from the vehicle's roof. (These busses always have two operators, one to drive and the other to take fares and handle baggage.) Unlike any of the local people Dan and I were tall enough to receive luggage from above without the attendant climbing down with each piece. This gesture of ours earned the attention of a young mestizo couple, who were also getting off at this stop, and as a result the four of us gringos were invited to spend the night at their home. Not knowing what to expect but thinking it might be better than the local hostel, we accepted their kindness. And indeed it was generous of them to feed and somehow bed down four strangers. They would accept no payment but instead subjected us to hours of evangelistic proselytizing. Their performances included lots of mumbo-jumbo, some of it in darkness except for one candle lighting their faces and their props. They sang hymns in Spanish expecting us to participate, and the man recited verse alternating with the woman moaning and quivering. At length they each ascended into frenzied crescendo to climax in tears. We did our best to be polite, finally complaining of traveler's fatigue to draw an end. Dan and I were to retire on a rolled-up rug under insufficient blankets, and Jo Anna and Genevieve took the bed. But before crawling in, Dan and I stepped outside to view the night sky in wonder. It was the most vivid ever, far more brilliant than at sea, and it contained a dramatically intense Southern Cross - the most memorable constellation I have ever seen. I retired understanding why these people were so spaced out and religious; the wheeling constellations and heaving Earth, all in this enormity of time, were just too vast for human consciousness to apprehend. At least they were for me. There was something else happening here, something unknowable, and one could either shun it or fear it. I wanted to receive it and love it, but felt the need to get back to the logic of the sea in order to further contemplate the balance between splendor and travail. The old swing scale was just too loaded here, its beam ready to break.

But we pushed on for Otovalo, Ecuador, a city not unlike Antigua, Guatemala, and had ourselves a fine time seeking unique textiles. I was taken with the Andean rana, their elegant rainproof version of the woolen poncho. In this quest we were directed to a remote highland hut whose floor was deep in hay and its single occupant harnessed into an outsized hip-strap loom that he operated not by kneeling back against the strap but by pushing with outstretched legs against a timber in the ground. He was nearly naked in the cold, thrusting his body against the warp and tamping the weft with such violence, and clearly for so many years, that his body was grotesquely hypertrophied. Huge muscles bulged from his bare feet, calves, thighs, trunk, arms and hands. He spoke no Spanish and had nothing to sell; the elegant rana he was making was already sold. He was obviously destitute, and wanted our food but had no use for our money. I think of him every winter when I rarely wear my rana, which is similar to but not nearly as fine as the one he was making.

At Otovalo we sadly parted with Dan and Genevieve who headed for Manaus in Brazil. Jo Anna and I returned by air to tropical Cartagena loaded down with heavy woolens, bought partly to keep warm in the mountains and partly to treasure for their art. The boys were just fine, a little disappointed that we had returned so soon, and we told them tales of our brief exposure to minimalist travel overland. We espoused that sailing was easier, but were soon to learn that it too could be hard.

Morgan's Head...
Prior to our overland junket to Ecuador I had ordered a new outboard motor for SCRIMSHAW. Our little four horsepower Evinrude had been remarkably faithful but it was definitely gutless for a 6,000 lb. Boat. It would push us at about four knots in a dead calm but otherwise it was next to useless. The new ten horsepower Evinrude, ordered from the dealer in Cartagena, was equipped with three shaft extensions of five inches each, which immersed the propeller enough to prevent its cavitating.

We departed Cartagena for what would become the hardest sailing we've ever done in SCRIMSHAW. We were headed for Old Providence Island, half way up the Caribbean and pretty much against the regions reinforced northeasterly trades. But I wanted to go back to where this eighteen year-long "boat ride" had started. We knew we were in for a slog so again we were well prepared, but we also knew that this would be our longest bash to windward yet.

Late on the second day out we were climbing through the crests as usual, well reefed down to reduce speed for passable comfort. As my watch was nearly over, Jo Anna came up to take the helm. She was sealed in her foulies, for the spray had been relentless. We spoke of the conditions and the course. We knew from our bash across the Gulf of Panama that with the centerboard full down to its six-six draft, SCRIMSHAW close hauled made only about five degrees of leeway even in rowdy waves. Based on that Jo Anna had advanced the course from our noon fix and said it looked like we were indeed able to lay the line for Old Providence Island. That was very good news.

I went forward to drop down through the foredeck hatch for my off-watch below. This was our way of keeping the cabin relatively dry; a wet sailor could go below directly into the head/shower compartment, strip down and rinse off, and take one step into our "dressing room" to don dry duds and with one more step wriggle into a dry bunk. Ah! Pure bliss after a long watch. But on this occasion as I opened the foredeck hatch to duck below the gale entered first, took hold of the dangling end of the toilet paper roll, sucked it out the hatch and instantly reeled off two thousand perforated squares of bum wad almost horizontally, the long white streamer undulating over the waves to loo'ard. While ducking below I laughed so hard that I slammed the hatch on my head.

Late the next afternoon we sighted the peaks of Providencia, looking very different than they had all those years ago. This was evening and we were approaching from the south, whereas back in 1956, it was from the north in the dawn. That was at the beginning of my big deal private boat ride, and Providencia had been the site of that naïve and fateful promise to myself. Was I now approaching the fulfillment of that promise? Was this the end of a long, hard-dying dream from which I was now awaking?

We weren't there yet. During the night we felt the first sense of shelter from the Island, a slight calming of the seas and wind, but the sky was overcast and we could see no lights and no mountains. Fearful of the reefs that guard the island's approaches, I decided to heave-to until daylight. When it came we had drifted far downwind of the peaks and were getting kicked around. Stiff and weary, we made sail again and spent until mid afternoon clawing our way back to shelter. The going was tantalizingly slow, and we realized at what a snail's pace a sailboat makes its way to windward across the wavy wastes. Jo Anna said, "This is ending just in time. I hurt all over." We agreed that fatigue at sea is not just a matter of being tired and uncomfortable; it's more like self-inflicting real pain. When hand steering in a blow, one must stay alert, but after days and nights of hanging on that helm, you really do hurt all over.

Up close the island seemed smaller than I remembered, less green and in fact almost bare of the lushness I recalled, and the few buildings on the waterfront looked new but plain. At least the light was right, high and from behind, for threading our way through the coral-studded shallows. As we passed Morgan's Head, an outcropping of rock on the end of a small islet, we all were taken by its sea-sculpted likeness to the Sphinx but with the face of a bearded renegade.

As we anchored in the little bay I felt like a circumnavigator who had crossed at last his outbound track. For me this had been a long cerebral circuit around my own rather nebulous netherworld. I was back at the beginning.

....

Illustrations for this chapter, narrated by the author, are available online at ...
www.OutrigMedia.com/books/atm-volume-one.html

11

PROMISE KEPT

1974 > 75

Inevitably I would be disappointed with the Island. That first day ashore, to clear in and look for ice, I was met by Ricksy Higgins, the long ago youth who had identified the giant ray that would become both the name and the logo for my Searunner trimaran designs (Chapter 2). He looked worn and smelled of rum. When I remarked about how changed the island was, he said, "Dis islan now belong to de Colombia nation and dey takes what dey wants. De big trees, de lobstas an de good fish, dey mostly gone. An dey all time tells us what we can do, what not we can do. And many our people lef to Honduras and doan come bach."

He led me to the customs and immigration office, where I was confronted with the most brazen rip-off by officials yet. I declined to pay mordida to the Colombian harbormaster, saying I had no cash on me and would return tomorrow. I wanted very much to roam the island with my crew, to snorkel its reefs and meet anew its people, but the place was simply no longer inviting. I discussed my disappointment with Jo Anna and the boys. Over the years they had heard so much from me about this place, and now I was wanting to leave. They didn't see the place as changed, so it was with great reluctance that they agreed to push on for the Rio Dulce, Guatemala.

Before leaving, however, I studied our chart and found the way to the Rio to be littered with unmarked dangers. The only safe route was to sail far northward, hard to windward toward Swan Island, which was well out of our way. So I asked Ricksey Higginsfor advice on how to make the passage around the Hump of Honduras. Ricksey said, "Go see Captain Bull. He be de captain of our trading schooner in de days before de Sponish come, an he de mon can tell you how to pas tru de reefs. He do it for years an years. Dat mon an dat schooner keep dis Islan alive bach den, before de Colombian nation say we belongs do dey. Now dey sends a little freight bo-ut an we hass to buy everyting we needs from it. But mos our peoples kyan't pay de price dey wants, so dey already leaves for Honduras. I goyn leaf too, but Honduras a hard place for us island peoples. You see John Bull, he doan leaf dis Islan never! But he tell you how."

I found The Captain at his little clapboard, shuttered shack. It was brightly painted, perched on posts beneath waving palms on a solitary beach. When I called his name over the rattle of wind in fronds, his upper body slowly appeared behind the open top half of a Dutch door. His white hair and beard accented his round mulatto face, and a bit of paunch had overtaken his otherwise very rugged neck and torso.

"Good morning Captain," I started. "I was told in the village that you could advise me on how to sail through the reefs from here to Guatemala."

He examined me, thought for only a few seconds and said in a basso voice, "You got a chart?"

"Yes sir, but not with me."

"Bring it today, one o'clock." With that he disappeared into the darkened cabin.

I returned with trepidation to find the shutters on his shack (which were hinged at the top to form an awning when propped up) were all open high. Both halves of the door were swung wide, and in answer to my call the Captain sang out "Entah!"

Inside, sunlight bounced from the sandy ground outside and then off the bottom of the shutters to light the single room delightfully. The sound of the surf, the rattle of the fronds the wooing of the breeze through the many see-through cracks in the walls and floor, and the very flavor of the shaded tradewind air made this room almost magically inviting. There was a canvass cot with its neatly knotted mosquito bar hanging above. There was a galley counter with a kerosene stove and bucket, a foot locker, two chairs and a tiny table, all painted carefully in pastel yellows, greens and blues. Essentially there was nothing else inside other than this imposing man.

We sat at the table, which was a little too small for fully spreading out my nautical chart of the Western Caribbean. We let it overhang the edges while he weighted the corners with his own navigation instruments, all meticulously cleaned and polished, I soon suspected, in preparation for my visit. His battered compass box, now gleaming with what smelled like fresh coconut oil, was a six inch mahogany cube containing a non-gimbaled old Plath with a four inch yellowed card and a bubble in the fluid. His one-hand dividers had gleaming bronze handles and freshly sharpened points, and his parallel rule was a fifteen-inch length of bronze propeller shaft, pitted but glowing lake gold. He demonstrated how to align it with the course and then roll it across the chart to the compass rose. If it had to be shifted lengthwise he simply stopped it against his old basswood ruler and slid it endwise against the rule. His prized possession was a museum-grade sling cyclometer, used for measuring relative humidity but rarely used in the tropics because of their usual freedom from fog.

After quietly displaying the tools of his profession, he had asked me, "How fast your boat go full and by?"

"She wants to go seven or eight close reaching in the trades," I said, "but we hold her down to maybe five to keep from getting knocked around. She's only thirty one feet long."

"How you know speed?"

"We have a tafrail log, Captain."

"Good. You go five, not four and half, not five and half, hear?"

"We can go five, Captain."

"Leave here tonight, ten o'clock. Not half past nine, not half past ten, hear?"

"We will leave at ten, Captain."

"Steer norwess a point nort, Not norwess, not nor-nor wess, hear?"

"We can hold a tight course, Captain. All four of us can steer," I said, but I made a mental note to convert his boxing course to degrees magnetic.

"Good." Now he set his ruler on the chart, locating one end on the Island and the other somewhere in what looked to me like open sea but on soundings. He drew a course line in pencil on the chart; it went from the Island toward the northwest but stopped in the middle of nowhere. Then, making eye contact with me at every step, he measured ten nautical miles from the scale on the edge of the chart with his dividers and stepped off the distance up the course line calling not miles but hours; "Twelve o'clock you here, two o'clock you here, four o'clock you here, an six... Das forty miles in eight hours, so you be here!" He looked me in the eye again, held both points of his dividers on the spot, and marked an X on the course line.

"No current?" I asked.

"Not much dis time of year," he said.

"No leeway?" I asked.

"Little current from south, cancel leeway in dis time."

Still holding his dividers on the spot, he pointed with his finger and said, "Look wess. What you see at dawn?" I studied the chart and noticed two specs I had missed before, tiny indications of land. One was marked Bobel Key and the other, just a mile to the north, was called Cock Rock. "When you see dem two you turn wess between and pas tru de reef."

Amazed, I studied the chart's marked soundings carefully and sure enough there was a three-fathom pass eastward but with dangerous shoals, breakers and coral shown everywhere else.

"Is this the way you took your trading schooner?" I asked the Captain.

"Alliss go dat way to roun' Cabo Gracias. Gives a fair wind instead of beatin' all de way up to Swan Islan. We go mos times to Tela in Honduras but you jus keep goyn wess to reach Guatemala."

That long beat up to Swan Islan, to go around these reefs, was what I had wanted to avoid, and here was the way if we could find it. I was pleased and thankful to this man, so we continued to talk for a while. It was clearly what he wanted. He said he had seen our "outrigged craft" in the anchorage the previous day, and was quite respectful of our having come from California via Panama "in dat class of bo-ut," that we were sailing as a family "lookin for life," and that we could "shoot de stars to fien de way." Celestial navigation was something he had never done because, "We jus know de way." He had taken over the operation of the schooner, a sixty-foot island-built gaffer, from his uncle in 1947 after sailing in her crew since his boyhood. I told him I had seen such a schooner at San Andres (a nearby Island) in about 1957, and asked him the name of his ship. "She be de SEARUNNER," he said, and after a brief recovery from the surprise I explained that I had seen his ship back then.

"I was at her re-launching, after a refit," I said. "Hundreds of people literally carried her into the water, some people under water."

"Das de way we do it alaise, some peoples under water holds their breath while dey pushes up on other peoples who pushes up on de bo-ut."

"I remember," I said laughing. "I was under water pushing up on people, then I come up for air and they push up on me."

"Das de way we do it bach den," he said. "All de peoples come to carry her, an dey carries me too 'cause I be on deck!" He laughed heartily. "So den I pays for de party."

"I am proud to have carried you, Captain, and I'll never forget that party."

We both marveled at how our paths had crossed so closely long before, and he was pleased to learn that I had named my trimaran designs after the name of his ship (which was named with their term for the giant cow-nosed ray). The old gent was reluctant for me to leave, and indeed I could have spent days with him. But everything else about my return to Providencia had been disappointing. He understood why but said, "When de Sponish come from Colombia dey put my ship out of business, an now I gots no place to go, nottin to do, so I just live out my time here under de palms." In the silence before I departed we both listened to the wind and surf, and the scratching of the coco fronds on his corrugated roof. In another ocean he would have been an Outrig Person, and had I stayed in the Caribbean I would have been an Inrig Person, and as I walked back to the harbor I found very little difference between us. Both oceans seemed to tolerate us and our disparate vessels, and I felt real kinship with this lonely man. I could not help wondering where I would be living out my own sense of aging uselessness. Would I too be alone? Would I have a brightly painted shack beneath the palms? At a bend in the coastal track I turned for one more glance and saw the Captain waving from his Dutch door. I waved back, choked up, and recovered by resorting to the hippie idiom for expressing strong approval; "Not too shabby," I said to no one, and walked on.

We sailed that night at ten.

Bottom's Coming Up...

"Hey Jim, get your sextant up here quick. I can see Venus and it's dead abeam."

I grunt "Okay" and while tuning the radio to the time ticks I struggle into salt-stiff, clammy swim trunks. At the radio's sound of a minute gong I start the stopwatch and grab our trusty plastic sextant. Sliding back the hatch I see Jo Anna pointing straight to starboard and half way up the sky. Sure enough there's a break in the overcast but the bulging clouds are moving fast so it won't last long. "Stopwatch" I mutter, and hand it to her wrapped in a dishtowel. She wipes her spray-wet hands and grasps the watch, thumb on the button. While I swing the sextant's arc, trying to find the planet in the eyepiece, a wall of cloud, lit by the lume of glaring Venus to show a touch of silver lining, is closing in on our beacon in the heavens. Standing in the after hatch, my feet on the galley counter and my waist wedged firmly in the hatchway, I try to concentrate. The motion of the boat is wicked, Venus whips across the mirror like a comet, the horizon comes near to its next flash, the cloud moves in and the planet is gone.

"Too late," Jo Anna says, "but there may be another hole."

"I almost had it," I say, "and now I've got the angle pretty close, but you'd better let me set the watch again because I didn't take time to write down the hour and minute of the gong."

I go back below to the radio, listen for an even minute, and start the watch and jot down the time on Jo Anna's notepad.

Back in the hatchway, with the sextant held below out of the spray, I search in vane for a hole in the clouds that may again reveal Venus. Jo Anna says, "Sorry to wake you so soon, but I saw that planet big and bright and it was dead abeam of our course so I thought..."

"Good idea," I interrupt.

"If we can get a line on it," she continues, "at least it will tell us if we've strayed right or left of course."

"Yeah," I agree, "and considering our situation that would be a very nice thing to know. But you've never worked a planet sight before, have you?"

"No, but I think I can figure it out with my little book."

"Okay, it's worth a try," I tell her, "The Kindergarten Of Celestial Navigation has gotten us this far."

Quickly I duck below to clean spray from my glasses and, with a pang of inadequacy, admit to myself that it always takes us both to work celestial sights. We are like Jack Sprat who could eat no fat, and his wife who could eat no lean. Jo is no good with the sextant and if I try using the Sight Reduction Tables, scanning down those endless columns of tiny figures, I get seasick. Our whole relationship has been like that, each of us wondering how the other can be so inept at those things where the one of us excels but in other ways is helpless. It is critical now that together we "lick the platter clean."

Bracing there in the hatchway I suspect that both the boys are sleeping soundly despite this rowdy reach that we are riding out. They steered through the boisterous early watches so that Jo and I could get some rest. Now it is at least two hours before first light, and the dawn watch is going to be tense. We will need their sharp eyes for spotting that rock and that key, which we must find in order to pass through the reef.

I notice there are indeed a few scattered holes in the clouds, but none big enough to see a constellation, or enough sky to identify a given star. Venus, on the other hand, is so bright that she is unmistakable, if indeed the clouds will give us a shot at her.

"Another hole," Jo Anna exclaims, and Venus glares at us like a fixed-occulting lighthouse. It is partially occluded by whisps of glowing vapor sweeping by. I grab at the dodging planet in the lens; it zips in and out of view as I try to steady the sextant on the bounding boat. I locate Venus in the split image of the sextant's mirror and desperately twirl the vernier knob, trying to locate the horizon, barely visible as it is at sea at night. What I think is the horizon heaves in and out of view in the double-image view of the sextant's mirror. Like shooting with a pistol at two jumping rabbits in the dark and hoping to hit them both with one shot, this process has required lots of practice, but now it is for real. I must "bring the celestial body down to the horizon" with this little instrument, thereby measuring its actual angle above the horizon, and this at the very second that SCRIMSHAW is lifted atop the highest of the waves. "Hold the course as tight as you can," I grumble to Jo Anna."

"Holding tight," she says. "Wait! There, we're bang on. Wait! Bang on again. Holding steady now..."

Now I sway the sextant slightly to make the planet's image swing as if she was suspended on a pendulum. Not breathing, I twirl the knob slowly to cause the swinging Venus to kiss the horizon. She dips below, I twirl the other way, she bounds above, I twirl back down, SCRIMCHAW rises on a swell, I twirl again, call "ready" to Jo Anna, the boat heaves as the planet kisses the horizon and I bark "Mark." Jo Anna stops the watch with a pounce of her thumb and a shake of her fist, both wrapped in the dishtowel.

I breathe and she asks, "Did that feel like a good one?"

"The best we're going to get in these conditions," I reply. She gives me the helm and ducks below. As I pass her the sextant she asks where I have noted the time. I have forgotten and am obliged to leave the helm to duck below myself to find it on her pad.

We have often found one another making mistakes, and now I marvel that somehow we get through. Will we this time? She has never worked a Planet sight before. Now we really need to know if we are somewhere near the course line that Captain Bull drew just yesterday. If we really are close to his course, and if our taffrail log has done an accurate job of measuring our distance run along that line (which it usually does unless its trailing spinner becomes clogged with weed or is attacked by a shark) then at about six we should see Bobel Key and Cock Rock. If not, we are lost in very dangerous waters.

I leave Jo Anna to her scrutiny of the "Shooting Planets" section of her little book, and return to the helm. The boat has headed up, the Yankee jib is luffing, the red compass light is like a knife in my stomach, and I need my slicker to protect me from the spray. But I do not disturb Jo Anna from her studies. Shivering instead, I wonder why we put ourselves in such predicaments, and realize that I am loving it. It is real, it is urgent, it is now! Together we can do this. We'd damn well better.

The precise angle of Venus' elevation above the horizon, which together we had measured at a certain date, hour, minute and second, was modified by Jo Anna according to several tabulated corrections. She then used this result to enter a maze of logarithmic tables whose mumbo-jumbo combined with her arithmetic eventually yielded up an azimuth and an intercept (direction and distance) from our assumed position. This information could then be plotted on the chart to give us a single line somewhere along which we were located at the precise time we had "observed" Venus through that lucky hole in the clouds.

While she was doing this I tried to plan what we should do if indeed we failed to see the little key and the rock. The safest way out of troubled water is back the way you came in, but that was not where we wanted to go. And even if we sailed out of trouble that way, then what? Beat up to Swan Island? That would be a miserable bash in these conditions but it would be preferred to shipwreck on a remote reef in these seldom-traveled waters. “What am I leading us into?” I asked myself, and for the hundredth time I felt the dread squeeze of responsibility that comes from skippering in a family crew.

Jo Anna emerges from the hatch and erupts with relief; “I don’t believe this!”

“Believe what?” I say.

“But we’ve got to believe it. It’s too close to be an error. Come and check this out.”

She takes the helm while I go below, re-plot her LOP (Line Of Position) and find, as she has, that it lays down dead on top of Captain Bull’s course line. They are so close that there is not a line’s width between them. We are on course!

I stick my head up into the hatchway, congratulate her on a nifty piece of navigation, and read the taffrail log with a flashlight. I plot our distance run on the course line and we have a darn good idea of where we are at four hours forty-four minutes, and it looks like we’ll be in the right place for searching the horizon at sunup.

“Lightning to the northeast,” Jo Anna tells me. I come up and see the flashes, too far off to hear the thunder but it’s probably coming this way. We sail on through the pre-dawn hour and sure enough, first light shows a gruesome line squall spread out all across the east. We’re in for it.

I wake the boys, tell them to suit up and bring their eyes on deck. Soon we are all in the cockpit discussing the situation. “If it will just hold off long enough for us to see these landmarks, we’ll be okay. Here’s the hand bearing compass, Russ. If you see anything that looks like a clump of palms or a breaking rock, get a bearing on it as soon as possible and sing it out. Steve, get the fathometer going and call out any change in depth, okay?” They turn to their tasks.

Our fathometer is the spinning filament tube type, a whirling bulb that flashes on its way around the dial. The length of time between the sonar pulse and the receipt of its eco off the bottom (or off a fish or a thermocline or a blob of weed) determines when the bulb will flash. Reading the dial against the flash gives an approximation of the water’s depth. “About fifty feet,” sings Steve.

"There's the temperature drop," says Jo Anna, and for sure we are feeling the advance warning of the approaching squall. I reef the mainsail deeper, and we douse the Yankee, continuing now under staysail and deep-reefed main. "That's good," she says. "I can still hold the course."

The thunder is quite audible now. The face of the squall is showing big clumps of cloud boiling upward; it looks like the thing is peeling itself back while pouring ahead. There are flashes behind it all along the line. It must be ten miles long, it is down low, coming fast, and we're going to get it for sure.

As it bears down we feel gaps in the wind interspersed with brief back drafts and wafts of fine drizzle. "Now's our last chance to see the key," I shout. "Keep your eyes ahead to port Russ, but Jo, you look all around. Steve, call out any changes in the depth. In a minute we're not going to see anything but rain and flashes." I glance at the taffrail log; it is almost time for us to turn to the west. With this thing coming at us from the east we're going to get pushed westward whether we see any landmarks or not. "Anybody see anything out there?" I call in desperation. There is no response.

A weighty gust socks into our wailing sails, the boat heels alarmingly and leaps ahead. Spray flies, Jo Anna moans, I slack the sheets and shout, "Bear off and hang on." We turn downwind and race ahead of the rain but it soon catches up, coming down in a deluge of drops seemingly as big as peas. I release the main halyard and Russ drags the sail down across the shrouds and lower spreader. We are still racing ahead. I release the staysail halyard and Russell drags the sail down and stuffs it into the anchor well.

Steve shouts, "Hey Dad, the bottom's coming up."

"How deep?"

"Thirty feet."

"Keep calling them out." Steve begins a long recital of shoaling depths. We can see only one or two boat lengths all around us. The sea turns swimming pool green, a sure sign of shallows, and the raindrops hit the surface so hard that apparently they carry a bubble of air down with them several inches. As the bubbles pop up by the millions the sea seems to effervesce. Thunder booms and cracks, the wind screeches in our naked rig, the boat trudges onward dead downwind and we all just huddle against the onslaught. At Steve's cry of twenty feet I holler, "Hang on to the boat. If we crash on the reef, just hang on!" I am thinking that we may get thrown over it into a hole or completely across it. Again I holler, "If we crash and the main hull is taking water, don't panic. She will not sink!" Even if we're half scuttled I am hoping we can anchor on the other side where we'll have some shelter. "Just hang on at all costs!" The last thing we'll need is for someone to get washed overboard.

"Should I get the anchor ready?" shouts Russ. It's a good thought but I shake my head. I don't want him out on the foredeck if we run into breakers.

"Fifteen feet," shouts Steve. "It's bouncing between fifteen and twenty." Obviously the instrument is reading the height of the waves. Now I notice that they are indeed only about five feet high. It is calming down; the rain has flattened the sea. There are no white horses, no breakers in sight.

"Hey Dad," shouts Steve, "the bottom's going down!"

"How deep?" I plead.

"It's bouncing between twenty and twenty five... There's twenty-eight... There's twenty-five to thirty. It's really getting deeper, Dad. Really!"

Great Sweet River...

According to the chart there was no way we could have crossed that reef without passing between Captain Bull's landmarks. The chance that we had run forty miles at night and turned left at the right point – on the money – is extremely unlikely, but as far as we know that's just what happened. We did our best and were very lucky. It was tense as hell; one of those times at sea when things are adding up against you as a cumulative calamity ready to happen. We don't like those moments but we love the fact that so far we have gotten through them. It is the kind of thing that doesn't happen often today; GPS navigation almost insures that the sailor always knows exactly where his vessel is. Do we now use GPS? Absolutely, and we carry two spare units (also today, two spare autopilot units) but we think that something is lost even if it's not us. The challenge of finding the way by deduced reckoning and celestial observations was a fundamental part of cruising back then, and there's no reason why one cannot practice it today. Few of us do, however, and this is just one of many examples of how today's sailing technology, in design, construction, navigation and amenities, has changed – but not necessarily enhanced – the cruising experience. GPS has certainly made seafaring easier, but not necessarily more fulfilling and fun. And – in the hands of those who are otherwise uninitiated – not necessarily safer.

We were proud of our navigation. At least that's how we felt as we ran on around Cabo Gracias Adios, past the Honduras Bay Islands and into the maw of the Rio Dulce.

We entered the country of Guatemala at Livingston, a Caribbean village at the mouth of the Rio. The paperwork was simple and the atmosphere inviting. Just in time for nightfall we entered the gorge, a four-mile section where the river winds through a wonderland of limestone cliffs on both sides, some as high as 500 feet, all festooned with the very most Tarzan-like jungle imaginable. We were much relieved to be out of the ocean so we tied to an overhanging branch in sixty feet of water and spent the night in the gorge. At dawn we were awakened by a frightful din, the sound of a kennel full of barking German Shepherds – actually a band of howler monkeys miffed by our intrusion into their world.

From the gorge the River opens up into an eight mile-long lake with islands, the Golfete, that is surrounded by wide mountain vistas. There are no roads on its banks and only sparse Indian habitations. The lake then narrows at a ferry crossing (now a high bridge) with a hardscrabble frontier town on each side. Beyond there is an old Spanish fort, compact and quite complete, at the entrance to a large lake, Izabal, that extends another twenty miles inland. With one exception we were the only yacht in the whole system (now there are about a thousand).

On our previous overland visit to the Rio we had made friends with Kevin and Louisa Lucas, operators of the Catamaran Hotel. Kevin had arrived years before from Florida in his catamaran motorboat, married locally and established a cluster of bungalows, a thatched dining area and dockside bar, all squeezed onto a tiny island in the Golfete. The only access was by dugout canoe from the ferry landing about two miles upstream. This juicy watering hole is best described by the lyrics of that old Parisian café song, bout the famed Bilbao Room:

It was the greatest,
It was the greatest,
It was the greatest,
Place on earth.

With Louisa's help we were able to rent an old United Fruit Company crew shack that had been moved to a knoll on the water and fitted with minimal amenities as a retreat. There was a kerosene refrigerator that really worked, a thatched palapa for shading the hammocks and the grill, and a floating dock for SCRIMSHAW. The only access was by boat but the place came complete with a nice dugout canoe. We had kept SCRIMSHAW's original four horsepower outboard motor (after replacing it with a ten horsepower at Cartagena) and the little one now performed yeoman service on the dugout, giving the boys mobility to prowl the River and us a means to reach the over-water bar at the Lucas' Hotel just half a mile upstream. Our place also came with an Indian couple, caretakers, who lived in a thatch-and-wattle shack out back. Beto and Irma became our dedicated friends, and after five miscarriages, Irma delivered a living daughter while we were there; they named her Jo Anna.

We retrieved our old panel truck from friends, arranged to park it at one of the brothels at the ferry crossing, and made numerous road trips back into the Guatemala highlands. Ostensibly this was to extend our textile collection but in fact we just loved the territory. Our main attempt, however, was to get to know the Rio and its region. In this endeavor we used SCRIMSHAW to prowl the tributaries until the mast would no longer clear the jungle canapé overhead or until the water became too shallow even for her 29-inch draft. The fact that we could take our ocean cruising trimaran into these jungle creeks, and nuzzle our bows into overhanging orchids, with our sterns in a gurgling spring, pass the night within the jungle sounds, and then watch the finch-sized bright blue butterflies soar around us during breakfast, was all a grand extension of the cruising experience.

Some of these excursions we made in company with Mark and Bonnie Hassall. In the eight months while we were sailing around from the Pacific side, they had acquired from an Indian a small piece of riverfront land on a cove about a half-mile downstream from our rented quarters. Mark had built a rather fanciful half A-frame home where they could dock their 37-foot Searunner with its deck literally an extension of their living room floor. Mark used his boat to ferry building materials, most of it cut in the jungle, and also as a pile driver for setting the piles on which the house was built. In this operation he suspended a cut pile from the spinnaker pole, cranking it as high over its intended position as possible with his headsail winches, and when the moment was right he released the halyard to let the pile spear itself into the river bottom mud. There was an artful suspension bridge, made of spare rigging wire from the boat, which led over to the riverbank. Occasionally when the army ants invaded the house, Mark and Bonnie moved aboard the boat and anchored in the cove while the ants literally cleaned house.

Just a short walk over planks through the jungle brought them to a small Kakchikel Indian village. It was there that Mark hired an Indian man to help build the house. His name was Concepcion or 'Cion, which Mark in his mextex Spanish converted to Chung. During Mark's and Bonnie's fourteen year-long stay in this setting Chung, a wiry little full blood Maya lowlander, became their omnipotent, omniscient sidekick. When his wife died in childbirth, Chung and his little daughter were unable to care for the surviving infant. Bonnie stepped in, the boy was named Markito, and eventually they adopted him and Bonnie saw to his rearing and education in the States. (Markito now works as a freelance computer scientist).

During their time on the Rio Mark built several other fanciful houses for wealthy Guatemalans from the highlands. Up until this point the elite of the country had scarcely acknowledged that the Rio Dulce even existed, much less that it had recreational potential. (This was typical of Central American aristocracy, who normally confined their attentions to the higher elevations and more or less ignored their coasts.) Near the end of this fourteen-year adventure, Mark built his next and last trimaran, a 62-footer that I designed for him to accommodate his woodshop (he wanted to be able to pass an eight-foot board through his table saw in the main saloon, which determined the overall size of the boat). This big vessel was built in the jungle where there were no roads and no electrification. He named her after an incident that occurred on their world cruise in his 37-footer. It seems they were docked at an East African yacht club, taking respite from dealing with the Argulas Current, some of the roughest water in the world where the waves are known to break tankers in half. They had learned that multihulls were previously unknown in this region. A very proper British-colonial yachtsman came stomping down the dock in his suit and spats. Wearing a monocle and a handlebar mustache, he examined Mark's boat and demanded, "From where have you come?"

"Well, we started from California," replied Mark.

"In THAT?!" huffed the colonial. "You, sir, are a goddam liar!" and he stormed away. Mark resolved at the time that if he ever had another boat he would name her THAT. He later completed a nine-year circumnavigation in THAT, the only Guatemalan-flagged vessel ever to circle the world.

Tales Of The Great Sweet River...

When we were on The Rio in 1974, it was Mark and Bonnie's first year there. Both families were installed in comfortable – if minimal – jungle homes. Both of our boats were right at hand, and we were all mercifully stationary for the time being. Each of us could now undertake projects that were not restricted by living aboard and being always on the move. Our faithful trimarans were both asking for attention, so with the help of Beto and Chung both boats were completely sanded and repainted. Mark had a house to build for another cruising couple that had found The Rio and decided to stay.

Steven acquired a dugout canoe, roughly hewn, and spent weeks planing and sanding it to perfection. He then painted it so artfully as to create a dugout yacht. This canoe would later become the personal waterborne conveyance for Bonnie Hassall. Steve also took off overland with friends for his own visit to the highlands.

In this time Russell built the first of his long series of sailing outrigger canoes. Beginning with a small dugout and a cast-off Sunfish sail, he experimented tirelessly to perfect the craft to the point where, at age fourteen, he was able to take off on his own for a five-day trip downstream to Livingston and back. He camped along the way and stayed with the Indians in complete security, a level of freedom and autonomy that would prove infectious for him.

I built some basic furniture for our crewshack, and we made the place homey with items from our textile collection. Our Aladdin mantle lamp from the boat made the evenings wonderfully bright and still for reading, and the daily rainsqualls were wondrous to watch as they approached across the River and the jungle. The all-around windows were screened but without glass, yet they could be covered by roll-down canvass flaps, so we could shelter from the gusts, thunder and tropical downpours with reasonable protection. This was truly a marvelous setting in which to live, and our eight months here were packed with memorable incidents. Two come to mind; one happened underground, the other up in the sky...

Listen To Your Head...

Mark invited me to join him in exploring a cave that Chung had shown him. It was located on one of the islands in the Golfete, and he knew how to find it. "It's just a little limestone cave," he said, "where the Indians used to hide when the Spanish were practicing their selective exterminations. Chung says that any Indian who showed the slightest sign of intelligence or initiative was summarily beheaded, so they would hide in caves. Nowadays they just use this one for meditations, and I think you'll see why."

So Mark and I took the dugout downstream to the island, moored it to a shrub and climbed up the jungle-covered boulders to what first appeared to me as little more than a badger hole. Mark slithered in feet first and bade me to follow. As he disappeared I saw only his flashlight held in both hands extended over his head.

Taking a similar position I gingerly slid downwards, easily keeping myself from falling by spreading my knees and elbows against the sides of the dry, curvatious, slightly crumbly, limestone chimney we were descending. I could hear Mark's slithering and grunting. In muffled words from perhaps twenty feet below me he said, "There's only one way down, you can't go wrong." I saw no light from his flashlight and realized that mine, too, was useless because the passage we were descending was too narrow to shine a light any way but up. I couldn't even bring my elbows down from overhead, but I could feel with my feet the gentle, rumpled twists and turns that we were making and realized it would be possible to inch-worm my way back up. Mark was coughing from the fragments dislodged by my descent that were falling down on him. "A little tight here," he wheezed. Soon my body seemed to block the passage of any sound from him. Feeling with my feet, I didn't like the convolutions of the space below. The passage seemed to have a crook in it, a dogleg that, while open, was nonetheless abrupt. I decided to find out if I could still ascend. Wriggling like an eel, it appeared that indeed I could climb, so I allowed gravity to take me down-and-sideways a little farther. My hips entered the bend and:

Terror! My ribcage throbs and heaves against the stone but instead of yielding the stone seemingly closes in. I writhe with all strength trying to ascend but am almost totally constrained. My pulse booms in my ears loud enough to burst my head and, I hope, burst the confining rock. Squealing, I writhe again, gasp and strain all extensor muscles in my being, scraping skin from all extremities; shoulders, elbows, wrists, ribs, hips, knees and ankles. Seeing spots I am forced to pause and pant, I whack my ribs against the rock for what seems like an eternity.

Logic intrudes. Certainly the limestone is not contracting in upon me. I am alive, have air, and I am not alone. But what if I cannot ascend even with Mark's help. He too is trapped. When we do not return they will find the canoe. Chung will know where we are. He will bring a rope and more strong arms. I try very hard to settle down.

Soon I hear Mark below; "Come on down Jimmy, its open down here." I am unable to reply partly because of my fury with him. The Indians are little people; Mark is average height but very lean and wiry. I am skinny but very long by comparison to them. It is my length that now blocks the passage, my ribs and shoulders unable to follow my pelvis past the bend. I am literally "high centered," my midriff is captured by my hips on one side of the constriction and my ribs on the other. I am properly stuck, properly terrified and profoundly pissed off, at myself and at Mark.

He climbs to where I feel his hands on my feet. We converse with difficulty. He tries to push me up but I am unable to find handholds to assist, and my bony pelvis acts like a barb in the constriction. Slowly we discuss the situation until it is understood by both of us. I have calmed and regained my breath, and am persuaded that the best way up for me is down. At least then Mark could get out and go for help.

Risking asphyxiation I completely exhale, squeezing all air from my lungs to totally collapse my ribcage. Mark pulls, jerks, heaves and hauls on first one leg, then the other, then both. I wriggle my spine on all axes, scrunch my shoulders, and as my midriff slides downward my T-shirt is smeared up over my face, forcing the back of my head to rasp against the rock. Then I am falling into Mark and we both fall, banging our bones while tumbling through a corkscrew chute to land in a pile of gravel.

I recall now that we each gasped and coughed from the dust for a while, investigating our hurts in total darkness. I was silently livid with Mark for reading me into such a predicament. He scurried around in the gravel looking for his flashlight, found it and used it to locate mine, which no longer worked. In the piercing blaze of Mark's I could see that we were in a pouch-like chamber no larger than a microbus. Snatching his light from him while cursing and hurting I examined our confines, feeling into all depressions and shadows until satisfied that the only way out was by the way we had arrived.

Mark said, "Take it easy, Jimmy," over and over while I muttered curses and dabbed with my T-shirt at my many lesions of road rash. Gradually I realized that I had followed Mark of my own accord, that we were in this together, and that we would probably get out. At least Mark could get out and go for help.

"What in hell were you thinking?" I demanded. "You're a wiry little monkey and I'm a gangly giraffe. How did you expect me to get through that hairpin?"

"I wasn't thinking," he admitted, "but we're going to have to use our heads now. The last thing we can deal with is panic, so calm down." Eventually I did.

Part of my calming was caused, I now realized, by the gradual emergence of some strange sounds. "Listen," said Mark, imploringly. "This is why I wanted us to come down here." It was a faint swishing and thumping, and soon I surmised it was my heart, and his, both pulsing away at slightly different rhythms. Of course we became very quiet – as quiet as one can get while still breathing; I was keenly aware that we were both exchanging quarts of air through our lungs every few seconds, a bellows sound that soon became as noisy as a pod of blowing whales. In time I became relaxed enough to hold my breath, and as we listened intently our heartbeats seemed to grow louder and louder, as if someone was very slowly turning up the volume on some kind of sonic life measuring device.

"What's going on?" I almost whispered. "Some acoustical freak?"

"Chung says it's God reminding us that we are alive because of Him. Personally, I think it's because usually we don't like to listen to ourselves."

"Maybe it has something to do with the shape of this chamber," I say. "The hard walls, and the soft gravel, the chimney coming in... I don't know, but the place just feels like a natural amplifier."

"Chung would say that's how God reminds us, but I think you're right. It's more than just the isolation from outside noise."

Now the orchestration was joined by another instrument, a slow, intermittent squishing and sliding without rhythm. It seemed to grind at times, with occasional squeals. It was definitely emanating from within each of us. When a slight shifting sensation in my gut was accompanied by a definite blurt, and was soon followed by what felt like a tiny – but sounded like a thunderous – fart, I exclaimed, "My God, that's our guts working!"

"Yeah," said Mark, "and it's been hours since lunch. But Jimmy, there's more. Try listening to your head."

"My head is speaking to me loud and clear," I insisted, "and it is asking me how in hell I'm going to get out of here."

"Don't worry, this limestone is soft. We can scrape away a few inches of it."

"With what?! Our fingernails?"

"We'll find something. There's a little anchor in the canoe."

"Oh yeah, anchored in a cave, that's me."

When we spoke, even as softly as we could, the hooting in our throats seemed like growls. Each single vibration of the voice box was distinct from the others; each reverberated in our chests as a unit. Humming a sliding scale made each flap of the fleshy reed a distinct note. Even when whispering the noise tended to interrupt, actually suspend, the other sounds made by our vital symphony. So we scrunched down gingerly in the dry gravel, and Mark said again, "Listen to your head."

It took a while, and it wasn't like hearing. It was more like remembering through headphones. I could somehow sense long ago reverberations in my windpipe; they were resounding in my chest and escaping through my mouth but all nonetheless confined within my skull. It was weird, and the first sounds that I sensed were of me, crying...

I am a boy of about eight lying belly down across the flat bottom of an upturned wooden rowboat. I am trying to hug it, to possess it, to become it. Wavelets are lapping on the slate-and-cobble shore of Lake Champlain. The dock is there, its outer end mounted on the rusting iron axel and high wheels of some old piece of farm machinery so that it can be rolled up and down the beach according to the changing summer levels of the Lake. My wails are echoing within the boat, and my father is dragging the landward end of the dock, its outer wheels crunching on the cobbles under water. "Come on now, Jimmy," he is saying. "We have to go home but we'll come back next summer. The boat will still be here."

Apparently I was muttering something that Mark couldn't understand, and I returned to the present sound of him repeating, "What did you hear?" I told him of hearing the emotional end of my first real boating experience as a kid in Vermont. "That old rowboat was my truest friend," I said. "It took me to where I wanted to stay forever."

"That's what I mean," he said. "The same thing happened to me the first time I came down here with Chung. Suddenly I was on the bluff above Oxnard looking out at Anacapa Island. The surf was booming down below and the wind was rushing up the bluff, filling my shorts and shirtsleeves, and I was telling my little friend that we could build a boat and go out to that Island. He didn't think we could. It took me a few years but I did build me a boat and I did get out to Anacapa, as you know."

"And we did go back to Lake Champlain," I said. "Now I realize that's where it all started, summers on the Lake with that old rowboat. That's what really set me on the water."

"And here we are," said Mark, "both of us cruising around in our own boats with our wives and kids. You never know the long term results of what happens to a kid."

"I wonder if our kids will be as committed to boats as we are. In a way, I hope they at least have something else, too (volume two). I hope I have something else, too! Somehow I've got to get out of this cave."

Eventually we disassembled my flashlight. It was made of heavy metal, the type said to be used sometimes by policemen as a club. We took turns scraping at the limestone in the hairpin turn with its threaded ends. While one of us scraped the other huddled in the chamber, covering his face with his T-shirt to avoid breathing the dusty scrapings. In an hour, and after just one unsuccessful try, I was wriggling through. This entailed a fair bit of wincing from my re-aggravated road rash and Mark pushing on my feet, but the dreaded claustrophobia was held at bay. At length, we emerged from our lightless acoustical anomaly into a blinding twilight and a booming rush of extraneous ambient noise.

Flying Low...

"Come on, Horse, let's take a hop to Belize City and pick up a load of New Years booze." (Kevin Lucas always called me "Horse".) It was approaching Holiday time, 1974, and Kevin needed a variety of spirits for his hotel. A former Naval aviator (in fact a Blue Angels instructor), Kevin was a big, round-faced and affable gringo with the pluck to make his way in a culture other than his own. However, his hotel operation suffered financially from the very high duty on imported alcoholic beverages in Guatemala. It was much lower in neighboring Belize.

However, he happened to have a flying pickup truck, a rugged six-passenger single-engine aircraft that he flew to service his hotel and occasionally fly in guests. A tiny jungle airstrip complete with quagmires, cows and buzzards was located just across the River, an easy run via his motor launch from the hotel. Not fully cognizant of the surreptitious nature of his invitation I eagerly agreed to go along for the ride.

We flew first through the gorge of the Rio Dulce – a spectacular ride wherein Kevin stood his plane on edge to clear the canyon walls. Five minutes later we landed at Santo Tomas. This seaport is the embarkation point for the shiploads of bananas, sugar, coffee and cotton exported by Guatemala to Atlantic destinations. Unlike the mile-long iron wharf protruding over raging surf at San Jose on the Pacific side of the country (Chapter 8), Santo Tomas is a protected harbor with a real airport. We landed there briefly to clear out of the country with Customs and Immigration for our short "pleasure" trip to Belize. When we took off, the control tower informed the Belize City airport, about an hour's flight to the north, that we were on our way.

In Belize City Kevin nearly denuded the package store and filled their small truck to capacity with cases of hooch from the world's best distilleries. We packed it into the aircraft to such fullness that the brand names on the cases – Hennessey, Tanqueray, Canadian Club, Jack Daniels, Moët – beamed like advertisements through the cabin windows. The poor little plane used most of the jetliner runway to clear the treetops.

"Okay, Horse," said Kevin as we lumbered up to altitude, "they've told Santo Tomas that we are coming back but the radar of those two airports aren't strong enough to overlap. We'll be out of range from both of them for a little while. When we were half way between I'll drop down low and head for the River. When we get to my strip we'll have to work fast."

"We're going to the River first?" I asked in surprise.

"Sure, Horse. My caretakers will be waiting at the jungle strip to unload, and then we zip over to Santo Tomas to clear in with an empty plane."

"I see," I said, "Is this the way you do it all the time?"

"Never fails," said Kevin, grinning. "It's the only way to profit from my bar. Otherwise the drinks would be just too expensive even for tourist pocketbooks."

"But don't they know you're playing this game?"

"Probably, but the officials like to patronize my bar and their butts are covered unless they happen to catch me red handed."

"Then what would they do?"

"Throw us in jail."

"I see."

At a point about midway between the two airports Kevin chopped the throttle and the plane sank like a brick to treetop level, whereupon the engine roared to take us under the radar to the River. We were flying low over the Peten Jungle where evidence of intense cultivation by the ancient Maya civilization was still visible. Kevin pointed out the linear scars of ancient roads and aqueducts, and the mounds of as yet un-excavated Mayan structures, which dotted the region. While I mused over what might have caused this isolated civilization to have disappeared, we suddenly swooped over the Rio Dulce and Kevin's jungle airstrip...

"Crap!" Kevin yells, as he jerks the controls to veer the plane violently away. As we peer down I see another aircraft, bearing military markings, parked at the end of the runway. A man in uniform is standing by one wing looking up at us.

"Okay Horse," says Kevin, "you haven't got a hair on your ass if you don't jump out of this airplane."

"What do you mean, jump out of this airplane?"

"There's a parachute right behind your seat. I'll drop you right at your place."

"No! Thanks, just the same, but I've never jumped before."

"It's easy, and far safer than a year in a Guatemalan dungeon."

"Why? What's wrong?"

"That's an Army plane down there and they're just waiting for us. Even if we go to Santo Tomas they've got us red handed. So I'm going to try my luck here."

The plane circles, makes a low pass over the strip to drive the cows to the edge, dodges a buzzard and approaches again. We touch down, jump the quagmire at midfield and spin to a stop - just yards from the Army plane. "Get out with me but let me do the talking," says Kevin. "And don't look so guilty."

With our engine at idle I step just close enough to overhear the two men talking loudly in Spanish. Translated, the conversation goes something like this:

"Hi, I'm Kevin Lucas, owner of the hotel across the river."

"How do you do. I'm Corporal Mendez. My Colonel is across the River now visiting your hotel, and I am here to secure the aircraft."

"Very good," says Kevin. "We have come from Belize with a load of whiskey for the Holidays. My men are waiting in the woods to help me unload it."

"Is it contraband?"

"Sure it's contraband," says Kevin. "Would you like to have some?"

"Sure," says the Corporal, smiling broadly.

Kevin turns to the jungle wall, whistles and waves, and four men jump out of the undergrowth and run to the plane. Frantically we pass the cases out to them, and Kevin shouts, "One box for that other airplane there."

Soon we are in the air again, dodging buzzards on our climb out. I look down to see the hotel launch streaming across the River piled high with booze. We check in at Santo Tomas straight faced with no difficulty, and return to the Great Sweet River. The holidays are coming and the Army plane is gone.

Freed From Freedom...

After those eight great months in the Rio Dulce it became clear that our family trip in SCRIMSHAW was headed into its last lap. The boys and I could have stayed in Guatemala happily, but Jo Anna felt it was important to get Steven and Russell back in school. To do this in Guatemala would require leaving The Great Sweet River anyway and moving to a highland city. So, with some consternation the decision was taken to return to the States. Where in the States we had absolutely no idea, and we would soon find that coming home was like landing on another planet.

Preparations for leaving included building a crate for shipping all the textiles we had collected. In this we were greatly assisted by Guatemalan friends in the lumber business. Our 300 pounds of precious cloth, far too much for SCRIMSHAW to carry, was smuggled in a container load of wood to a warehouse in New Jersey for retrieval later. It was easy, and it could have been three hundred pounds of anything. The hard part was saying goodbye to the friends we had made on the River; Beto and Irma, Kevin and Louisa, Mark and Bonnie and the dog and cats we had acquired from the Indians. We made arrangements for the animals to return to the nearby Indian village, but the dog Gaviota (Seagull) howled in grief from the riverbank, as we slid downstream through the gorge and out upon the Caribbean Sea again.

After memorable stops in the Belize Keys, which are strung along the second-largest coral reef in the world, we headed offshore to Glover's Reef, a tiny island said to be the only true atoll in the Atlantic. We had been living ashore for months, and this rousing bash to windward was a good shakedown for the coming Gulf Stream ride to Florida.

As we arrived at Glovers Reef I was a bit seasick from the romp, and as SCRIMSHAW threaded the narrow pass into the small lagoon my vigilance was diminished. Our main hull almost struck a large coral head lurking just beneath the surface. It was such a close call that I remained upset for hours by the prospect of damaging the boat in such an isolated place.

With a sense of foreboding I spent much of that night in the cockpit ruminating on the past eighteen years. It seemed that my previous youthful time here in the Caribbean had been so enticing that I was helplessly ensnared by the promise of the ultimate freedom latent in a cruising boat. I could almost sense Wolf and Jeannie, down below in LA BRISA, snuggled up like a heap of sleeping puppies in their bunk. I could practically hear those fateful words from Jeannie, "I get the feeling we need a boat of our own."

Now I could more than imagine hearing myself – because I was actually muttering again that private promise made all those years ago: "If we don't pull it off together, I'll pull it off alone. I will, dammitall I will."

After a brief rain I must have dozed off, at least into the semi-consciousness of that so-called alpha state, the muddled midland wherein one can sometimes steer the course of his own dreams. I went back again to that time in LA BRISA (Chapter 2) but it was after we left Old Providence Island and sailed down to Colombia. Wolf, Jeannie and I had become embroiled in a sticky immigration problem with Colombian authorities, partly due to our employer scheming to keep us longer than we wished to stay. In effect we could not leave legally except as the crew of the boat in which we came, so our solution was to build a 24-foot "triple cat" out of oil drums and slip away in it for Panama.

Wolf designed the thing to have six drums for each outrigger hull and eight for the central hull, all butt-welded together with the end drums having their ends cut out and pinched together to form welded stems and sterns. These "hulls" were lashed to timber crossbeams and covered with a slatted platform. The mast was a giant bamboo cane. We named the craft ESCAPE, and it was wonderfully whacky. Indeed the whole caper was so nutso that I'm not sure of its veracity today. Even then it had been shuffled to the bottom of my cranial shoebox, but now here it was, emerging from a troubled doze while on anchor watch at an isolated atoll off the coast of Belize:

Since the rudder broke last night Wolf has been trying to steer with the makeshift oar. The tubular hulls of our "trrri-maran" are not leaking, and their butt-welds are holding, but the harebrained vessel yaws and plunges unmanageably and is capable of downwind courses only. Clinging to its slatted platform we have been alternately soaked, chilled and cooked for two days and three nights. We all suffer from sunburn and seawater boils. Jeannie is weak but she still tries to help me with the lashings. So far we have held the boat together but it is still falling apart. Desperate, we pull up on the mounded white sand beach of a palm-crowded islet somewhere off the Darien coast.

Stumbling into the grove we are presently surrounded by nearly naked Indians. The men wear fibrous breech clouts and carry machetes tucked under their arms pointing backwards. The women's bodies are all painted in primitive colorful patterns and they wear fringed belts low around their hips. They all stare at us, apparently displeased by our arrival. Soon we realize that they think we are missionaries. With gestures and very broken Spanish we try to convince them that we are not. Wanting us to prove it, the men proffer two of their breech clouts and insist that Wolf and I strip down to their attire. The ice is broken by the stark contrast between our deep tans and stark pelvic whiteness. After much consternation, Jeannie is suitably belted and painted by the women: she looks like a psychedelic contour mapping of the human female, and she is liking it.

These images blur into many scenes of revelation and exchange with our curious hosts. Days later, after these Chucunaque people have helped us make improvements to our boat, we find that leaving them is an emotional wrench.

Soft thunder brought me into woozy wakefulness, and slowly I recalled that the oil drum caper had been my first exposure to a multihull at sea, and it was nearly the last. I remember thinking at the time that the story deserved to be told fully in a format wherein the reader is expected to willingly suspend his disbelief.

With time the small squall passed, and I went below to wriggle quietly in beside Jo Anna. "Is everything all right," she asked sleepily.

"Anchor's holding," I replied.

Lying there in our tight sterncastle bunk, I tried to sort the fiction from the fact. Or was it the fantasy from the reality, the promise made from the promise kept? My last three years with Jo Anna and the boys had been very, very different from the original imaginings that had sustained me since leaving the Caribbean as a boat bum. Family cruising was not fantasy! It was much more powerful and valid than the goals of youthful wanderlust, yet both versions were equally felt, equally real. My old thirst for pals and gals and sailing ships, had not been sated, and I suspected that it never would be, but what had transpired on this trip was far finer and more authentic than all the imaginings that had fostered my obsessive boyish drive. I wrestled with images of contrast - canyons and volcanoes, isthmuses and oceans, poverty and wealth, water and wind. They all seemed far more diametric out here in the very real.

Fully awake now I felt secure and lucky. I'd been dreaming but it was over. This was all about my shedding of that promise which had kept me bending down but looking up for years. As the burden fell away the freedom latent in our SCRIMSHAW now became the freedom to do with her whatever was not promised. Our trip was far from over yet, but it was no longer encumbered by some nebulous goal. Our craniums were now well crammed with contrasting impressions of reality, and these impressions had yet to help us formulate conclusions, but I felt that was to come. Only one conclusion loomed assured: When we hoisted the main tomorrow, no matter where we were to go or stay, where we ended up or settled down, and no matter how our time among the multihulls might shape our future lives, we will forever feel that we are merely sailing through.

The last thing I recall from that night at Glovers Reef was a sense of being very much alive. There was the presence of my sons nestled in their bunks, the feeling of Jo Anna there beside me, and the sound of SCRIMSHAW, embracing us all while slow-dancing in the anchorage. At least we, I knew, were real.

....

Illustrations for this chapter, narrated by the author, are available online at ...
www.OutrigMedia.com/books/atm-volume-one.html

Breinigsville, PA USA
07 November 2010
248849BV00004B/1/P